# SOFT PRETZELS
## WITH MUSTARD

# DAVID BRENNER

# SOFT PRETZELS WITH MUSTARD

**ARBOR HOUSE** *New York*

*To Mom, Lou, Moby Dick, Bib, Cole Jay,*
*Steve, the ol' gang from Sixtieth Street,*
*everyone mentioned in the book who has been good*
*to me, New York City, Philadelphia,*
*cheesesteak sandwiches, hoagies,*
*ice cream and, of course, soft pretzels with mustard*

# Introduction by Joan Rivers

The way I decide how much I like a book is by how late I'm willing to stay up reading it. I began David Brenner's book early one evening, and during the night I heard Edgar scream, "Please turn out the lights" at least ten times. I finished *Soft Pretzels with Mustard* during breakfast the next day.

This book is very special to me, but I knew David was someone special the day I met him. Sharing a stage with him so many times has reaffirmed that belief. But David is more than a very good friend to Edgar and me. He's Melissa's godfather and a member of our family.

That's why I'm so surprised by this book. It reveals a whole other side of David I didn't know. True, there are countless examples of that wonderfully funny man who can paint a story with delightful comic touches. Yet here is a more personal side of David, unveiling the hurt behind some of the experiences from which he later salvaged humor.

If the world cuffed David in the ears as he was growing up, he set his goals on getting gloves to box his environment. It's this side of David which battled heavy odds to score a first-round knockout.

In this book there's a David Brenner who has the ability to share his great successes as well as to confess his mistakes. On one side there's a King of Practical Jokers; on the other, a man who deeply cares about all of life's other underdogs. There's a boy who spent much of his youth developing plans to escape his poor neighborhood and a successful man who returned to the places of his youth to learn more about himself. And there's the award-winning creator of television documentaries who dared to give up the stature, the money and the medical plan to walk onto a stage and take a chance.

Here is a David Brenner who displays an unusual awareness of life's fragility, and who shows how much he appreciates it through a passage which may shock some readers. This is also a man who writes with a sense of warmth. People who were David's friends at age nine are still his friends today. He is one of those rare men who, in spite of his success, has held onto his old values.

*Soft Pretzels with Mustard* is one of David's favorite things about Philadelphia. One of *my* favorite things about Philadelphia is that it gave us David Brenner, a very funny and very complex man.

After this book I know him even better. And I like him even better.

Joan Rivers

## Introduction by Barry "Beb" Black and Edward "Dee-Dee" Romoff

We first met and became friends with David in kindergarten. He didn't actually become part of "the gang" until two years later, so officially we've only known him since he was seven and a half years old. He was doing his own comedy material back then too, although *some* of what he's doing today is new. Seriously, David was always funny—the best. And it seemed that the worse things got, the funnier he got. He was the soothing salve on the wounds of our tough early days trying to grow up in the streets of South Philadelphia. The three of us were almost inseparable during those days of Saturday afternoon matinees, stick ball, box ball, twenty-five-cent lunches of four vegetables and two rolls (non-government subsidized). But the neighborhood world we knew and loved shrank slowly—so slowly that we didn't notice until it had completely disappeared from our lives, taking with it the thousands of free things we did as kids, the hundreds of faces and voices of the people who lived in the neighborhood, the dozens of friendships and the handful of dreams fostered by some of us, the biggest and best of which were David's. Eventually Dee-Dee, Beb and Brenner were three young boys becoming men, following separate paths in life, but always remaining friends. You don't let a guy like Brenner get away from you. He was—and is—too special to us.

We can remember when the combined assets of the three of us couldn't even buy one of those twenty-five-cent lunches, but

Brenner nonetheless walked around like "Kingy," as his dad called him—always on top of the world in attitude. He pulled us right up there with him, and if he didn't lift us with a joke he did it with the hope we found in his dreams and his unshakeable desire to be "somebody."

David, though, was more than a dreamer, and more than the funniest guy in our crowd—he was generous with the little money he had, often splitting his hoagie sandwich three ways or giving us money to buy our own. He was the last to want to fight but the first to throw a punch if he had to help one of us. He was more popular than the high school quarterback without having to play football. If David was your pal you had yourself the best pal you could ever want. On the other hand, if he was your enemy you had more troubles and worries than you could ever want.

The three of us grew up crazy about movies and movie stars, aspiring someday to see our names flash on the screen, even if only as part of the last names to appear in the smallest print in the closing credits. You can imagine the emotion we felt in 1971, driving into Lake Tahoe, Nevada, and seeing for the first time "David Brenner" in twenty-foot-high letters on the marquee of the Sahara Hotel. At that moment we knew that the 3,000 mile car trip from Philadelphia had been worth it, just to stand in front of the marquee, tying up traffic while our picture was taken with our pal's name booming behind us.

David Brenner today is pretty much the same person he's always been. He still sees things as they are, tells it like it is and continues to see the humor in the foibles of so-called proper social behavior. The only real changes in him are that he's taller and, better yet, what used to be his street corner dreams are now elegant, self-achieved realities. David has done with his life everything he said he would. But you know, way back on Sixtieth Street in the old neighborhood, we always knew he would.

Barry "Beb" Black
Edward "Dee-Dee" Romoff

# FOREWORD

I'm a very lucky guy!

Everyone has parents. Most have a sibling or two. But not everyone, if he or she were given a choice, would choose these same persons to be their family. I would, every time! I have always been wildly in love with my mother, father, sister and brother. As a child I was also surrounded by fantastic aunts and uncles. This is real luck!

A lot of kids grow up with few or no friends—many children are loners, ostracized by their peers. Their childhood memories are either ugly or purposely forgotten. I have had a lifetime bursting with marvelous, everlasting friendships. Again, luck!

Like many people, I grew up in a poor, tough, big city neighborhood. Sunshine rarely shines in such places. However, amid all that was wrong in those dark streets and back alleys, there were stockpiles of laughter and many crucial benefits. That's also lucky!

Then there's getting out of the neighborhood, bucking the odds, beating the system, becoming "somebody." So few do it. So few win. I won. I got out. That's a lot of luck!

There are many lousy jobs in this world. I've had my share of them, beginning at age nine. But, since June 1969, I've spent my working hours making people laugh, feel good, escape momentarily from their problems and I've been payed well to do it. Lucky! Lucky! Lucky!

That is what this book is all about—my family, friends, neighborhood, getting out of the neighborhood and into show business. This is not an autobiography, but rather it is a collection of anecdotes, a collage of events, thoughts and feelings. Some of them are funny, some are not, because that's the way it has really been.

Some of what you read will definitely surprise you. There are aspects of my life I've never told you about. Some of them have never been told to anyone. There will be parts you may not believe. All I can tell you is that everything is true. Oh, I may have changed a name or place here and there, not so much to protect the innocent but to save me from getting my butt kicked in by the guilty. But, other than these minor alterations, this is a collection of truths.

I hope this book is like its title, taken from one of my favorite childhood snacks—soft pretzels with mustard: An original, straight-off-the-streets-of-Philadelphia treat that is different, twisted, salty, spicy, good tasting, easily digested a little piece at a time and filling, but always leaving you wanting more.

# CONTENTS

**INTRODUCTION BY JOAN RIVERS  7**

**INTRODUCTION BY BARRY "BEB" BLACK
AND EDWARD "DEE-DEE" ROMOFF  9**

**FOREWORD  11**

**PART 1:  FAMILY  20**  *  WITH LOVE . . . 21
WORDS OF WISDOM  21  *  DESCRIPTIONS  22  *  THE
RADIO CONTEST  22  *  FOOLING MOM  27  *  A
MOTHER'S EYES  27  *  THE DAY TARZAN CAME TO WEST
PHILLY  28  *  MOBY DICK  33  *  FAMILY ARGUMENTS
35  *  THE BIG, SHINY BRAND NEW NICKLE  35  *
SPECIAL PEOPLE  36  *  THE ONE COMPLETELY HAPPY DAY
41  *  MOM'S COOKING  43  *  GOOD MANNERS  45  *
THE MASTER PLANNER  45  *  THE COLISEUM IN ROME
46  *  BE FRANK!  47  *  TURNING SIXTY-FIVE  47  *
SLEEP, DEATH'S SISTER  48  *  THE PERFECT ANSWER  49
*  THE TURNING POINT  49  *  HOSPITAL CARE  52  *
GRADUATION GIFT  54  *  THE DRAFT  56  *
CALIFORNIA BY CAR  56  *  A SELLER'S MARKET  58  *
TO OWN A ROLLS ROYCE  59  *  THE THERMOS  60  *
LATE AT NIGHT, ALONE  61  *  BRINGING IN THE SHIP  62

**PART 2:  FRIENDS  63**  *  NEXT TO FAMILY—
FRIENDS  65  *  DYING ON THE BEACH  66  *  ALEX AND
HIS COPS AND ROBBERS  70  *  THE HUNTING CAP  72  *
THE TRANSFER  73  *  STRANGE VALUES  *
76  *  THE AUTO MECHANIC  77  *  A DUMB ANSWER  78

*   THE BUZZARD   78   *   EARNING EXTRA MONEY   81   *
BEB COULDN'T MAKE IT   83   *   CUTTING POTS   86   *
TIME FLIES   87   *   JAY SEGAL   91   *   CARRYING IT TOO
FAR   92   *   NOT FUNNY   93   *   THE BIRD FLIES AWAY   93
*   PASSION PITS   96   *   A MORNING QUIP   98   *   THE
GOLD RUSH   99   *   THE BIRTHDAY SUIT   103   *   FIRST
TIME IN L.A.   106   *   WYNN OR LOSE   110   *   FLIGHT 668
122   *   THE LAST TIME   124

## PART 3:   NEIGHBORHOOD   127   *   THE
STREETS WHERE I LIVED   129   *   THE CAFETERIA   130   *
BUMS, GHOSTS AND GROWN-UPS   132   *   A PERFECT
REPLY   134   *   BROOMHOLDERS AND KNISHES   134   *
THE ROOFERS   136   *   MRS. DEAD PIGEON   137   *
HUNKS, HALFIES AND WHOLIES   138   *   ICE CREAM   139   *
THE COLDEST DATE   139   *   THE HARDWARE STORE   143
*   DR. LASKIN   144   *   THE IRVING STREET AUCTION
HOUSE   149   *   SELF-EMPLOYED   151   *   CARRY A BIG
STICK   153   *   THE BALLERINA   154   *   THE
PHOTOGRAPHER   155   *   BENNY'S POOLROOM   157   *
DO UNTO OTHERS   162   *   THE ULTIMATE WEAPON   162
*   BRICKYARD HELEN   164   *   HAIRCUTS   166   *   TOO
FAR TOO SOON   168   *   GOING HOME   168   *   ONLY ONE
TRULY LIKED ME   173

## PART 4:   GETTING OUT   179   *   MY MAIN
GOAL IN LIFE   181   *   EARLY IDEALISM   182   *   ALCOHOL
AND PHILOSOPHY   183   *   NEW YORK, NEW YORK!   184   *
FLYING AWAY   185   *   STEAK   186   *   J.B. VAN SCIVER'S
WINDOW   186   *   CAREER CHOICE   186   *   HOW TO GET
OUT   187   *   THE LAST OFFICER   188   *   SILVERFISH   189
*   EIGHTY CENTS   191   *   PROVING IT   194   *   TOM
SNYDER: ON ASSIGNMENT   195   *   THE BIG GAMBLE   199

## PART 5:   SHOW BUSINESS   203   *   THE
GREATEST SOUND IN THE WORLD   205   *   MY FIRST JOKE
205   *   HOOTENANNIES   206   *   A WEEKEND AT PIPS   208
*   BREAKING THE HABIT   212   *   THE ELECTRIC
HANDKERCHIEFS   215   *   KARATE MOUTH   219   *   AN
AMERICAN COMEDIAN IN CANADA   220   *   THE NIGHT OF
NIGHTS   222   *   THE BOSTON SHUTTLE   225   *   RICHARD
LEWIS   227   *   JIMMIE WALKER   234   *   THE ROAD
MANAGER   236   *   FAST MOVES   242   *   PEANUT BUTTER

249  *  STORIES I'VE LIKED  256  *  MY MOST EMBARRASSING MOMENT ON TV  259  *  THE BRAVEST MAN WHO EVER LIVED  263  *  PERSONAL PERSPECTIVES 265  *  BECAUSE YOU KEEP ASKING  265  *  THE PRIZE 267  *  THE MAN FROM FREDONIA  268  *  MEETING THE STARS  270  *  AND THEN CAME JOAN  274  *  FREDDIE PRINZE  276  *  NO WOMAN BELIEVES IT  277  *  THE FAN 279  *  YOUR FAVORITE JOKE  280  *  AUTOGRAPHS  280 *  FANS I'LL NEVER FORGET—NEVER!  284  *  MY FEATHERED FAMILY  286  *  COMING HOME  286  *  A MAN'S CASTLE  288  *  THE MOUNTAIN  293

**EPILOGUE  295**

# SOFT PRETZELS
## WITH MUSTARD

# FAMILY

# WITH LOVE . . .

MANY FORTUNATE THINGS HAVE taken place in my life but the most
fortunate of all was to have been born and raised in the midst of
four wonderful people—my parents and my older sister and
brother. Whenever times were bad and all other refuges failed,
my family was always my strong and safe high ground. This
knowledge of a guaranteed haven gave me the strength to ven-
ture out a little further, take those extra steps, reach a little
higher, dream a little bigger, achieve a little more. My mother has
always been my best sweetheart; my father has always been my
best pal; my brother Mel (nicknamed Moby Dick after his favorite
childhood book) and my sister Bib (a nickname taken from the
initials of her name, Blanche Irene Brenner, which she hates) are
both much older than I but, despite our age difference, have
always been a brother and sister to me—and dear, dear friends,
too. I love my family deeply. I could ask for no more.

# WORDS OF WISDOM

WHEN I WAS A little boy of around six or seven, my grandfather
said to me, "David, if you ever see a man wearing new shoes,
follow him, for he is a wise man." My grandfather was a man
whom I respected greatly, and I resolved never to forget his
words.

A couple of years passed, and one day while I was standing on a street corner near my house, a middle-aged man with gray streaks in his hair, and wearing a dark suit and tie and brand new, shiny black imported shoes walked by me. I had never seen such beautiful shoes in my whole life! Remembering what my grandfather had told me, I followed him. After about two blocks, he walked into an alley. I followed a safe distance behind. The man stopped. I stopped, pressed tightly against a backyard fence. The man with the magnificent new shoes then urinated into a garbage can. At that moment not only did I realize that not everything my grandfather told me was true, but a cynic was born.

## DESCRIPTIONS

EACH MEMBER OF MY immediate family has a way of describing me:

Mother: "Every boy has some Peck's bad boy in him. David's problem is he has too much in him, but he really is an angel—when he sleeps."

Moby Dick: "My kid brother believes everything in moderation —*especially* moderation."

Bib: "Thank goodness he's not in jail."

Lou: "Kingy is a bad egg that made a good scramble."

## THE RADIO CONTEST

MY FATHER WAS ALWAYS looking for a shortcut to fame and fortune —the horses, the numbers, schemes, scams, even radio show contests. There was one radio show with a contest that had the listeners guess from where they were speaking—for example, inside a bank vault, on a Ferris wheel, in the Oval Office, etc. Each week they gave verbal hints and sound effect clues. People mailed in postcards with their guesses, names and phone numbers. If you were right about the mystery location, your postcard, along with those of the others who guessed correctly, was put into a rotating drum. If your card was then hand selected, you'd win prizes worth a thousand dollars. My father listened to this show religiously and no one was allowed to talk when it was on. He would call out his speculative answers for our approval or disapproval. For about two weeks, he was positive that the location was inside a submarine.

One evening on my way to the bus after work, I passed by a junky electronic shop. In the window was the usual array of broken TVs and radios. This night something caught my eye. It was some kind of microphone, with a sign that read, "Have fun with your friends by suddenly showing up on their radio." I went inside.

It was a crude sort of microphone that could be connected to any radio and, by simply pressing a button, you were able to shut off the radio and have your voice come out of the speaker. It came with full instructions. It cost me my full week's pay of eighteen dollars, but what better use can one get from his money, especially at age fourteen, than to trick his crafty, shrewd father? I installed it when no one was home, hiding the microphone on a shelf above the cellar steps.

On the night of the contest show my father was glued, as usual, to the radio, "shushing" all of us and proclaiming his guess of the submarine. I excused myself and went outside on the porch. I then ran around the corner, up the alley, into the backyard of my house, and wormed through the cellar window I had left ajar. I could hear the radio clearly.

"Here's another clue. Listen closely. 'Clang, clang.' "

"See. What'd I tell you, Stelle. It's a sub."

"All I heard, Lou, was some clanging noise. How's that a submarine?"

"You wouldn't understand. I was in the navy."

"When you were in the navy, Lou, there weren't any submarines."

"Shhhhh. Here comes another clue."

"Maybe it'll be submarine bang bangs."

"Shhhhhhhhhh."

". . . before we tell the answer and pick out a winner, here is the last clue: 'Whatever goes up must come down, but, thank goodness, whatever does go down must come up.' Ready for the big moment, folks?"

"What'd I tell you, Stelle, did you hear that clue?"

I switched on the mike in my hand. I could hear the radio go dead. I held the mike very close to my lips and whispered mysteriously in order to disguise my voice:

"Here it comes, ladies and gentlemen. The answer you've all been waiting for. The words that'll mean big, valuable prizes to some lucky person out there in the Greater Philadelphia and New Jersey areas. The words . . ."

"For Christ sake, cut the bullshit and give the answer!" My father was never long on patience.

"Hold your horses, folks."

"I'll be damn, Stelle. Did you hear that?"

"I'm about to announce the identification of the mystery location. We . . . are . . . inside . . . a . . ."

It was at this point that I imitated static. My father started pounding the radio with his fist. I had to stuff my handkerchief in my mouth to keep from roaring away and giving away my hiding place.

"I don't believe it! Do you, Stelle? I'll be a son of a bitch! I'm going to take this pile of junk and burn it in the gutter!"

"Easy, Lou, you'll have a heart attack."

I ended the static.

". . . and we're there at night but we'll accept any time of day or night."

"Where? Where are we, you bastard?"

"Lou, your language."

". . . yes, that's where we are."

"Shit!"

"Lou!"

"And only thirty-five people guessed that we were in a (STATIC) . . ."

"Static again! I don't believe it! Do you, Stelle?"

"Yes, Lou, I believe it."

"Now, let's pick one of the lucky thirty-five who guessed a submarine."

"Did you hear that, Stelle? A submarine! Great! I knew it!"

"That's wonderful, dear. Now can . . ."

"Shhhhh. They're picking out the winning card."

"The barrel keeps going around and around and around and . . ."

"That's enough 'around' already!"

". . . around and . . . (STATIC) . . ."

"Oh, for crying out loud. Now I'm going to miss the winner's name!"

". . . and around and around and around . . ."

"Thank God they're still going around."

". . . and it stops. My hand is going inside and I'm going to pick out one postcard, one winner. Here I got it. The winner is (STATIC) . . ."

"No! No! No!"

". . . from West Philadelphia. Congratulations, Mr. (STATIC) . . ."

"Too much! Too damn much!"

"Relax, Lou, I'm sure if you won, they'll call you."

"Suppose I'm not home when they do? Or suppose we get this kind of static on the phone? I give up! I'm so unlucky, if it were raining soup, I'd be holding a damn fork!"

". . . now let's all sing a hip, hip, hooray for Mr. Louis Brenner. Hip, hip, hooray!"

My father's scream could be heard in Camden, New Jersey. I could hear him running around the living room, swinging my mother around. I went down the cellar steps, climbed out of the window, hopped over the backyard fence, ran up the alley, down my block and casually walked through the front door.

"I won, Kingy, I won!"

"Won what, Lou?" (My father called me "Kingy" after King David, and I usually called him by his first name because he was not only my father, he was also my best pal—so was my mom but she was my mother—you know what I mean?)

"The submarine!"

"What are we going to do with a submarine in West Philly?"

"No, dopehead, the answer was a submarine. They picked my card. I won!"

"Wow, that's great! Congratulations!"

"Thanks. Here's five dollars for you. Go get yourself a few gallons of ice cream. Buy your mother one, too. We're rich! And everyone stay off the phone so it's clear when they call me to tell me I won!"

"Sure. Thanks for the fiver. See you later."

I treated myself to a double thick black-and-white milkshake and brought home a double decker coffee in a sugar cone for mom. Dad was sitting by the phone when I walked in. Mom had obviously switched the radio to the classical music station in order to calm him down. I gave her the ice cream and, unnoticed, I slipped down the cellar. I picked up the mike and threw the switch, this time using my English accent.

"Attention, please. We have an important announcement. Even though we are not the same station, we wish to announce that station WIP's radio show, 'Where Are We?' has made a dreadful mistake. The answer to this week's contest is not a submarine, as previously announced, but an elevator. I repeat, an elevator. Next week's answer is a submarine, or, rather, would've been a submarine, but now in light of what has just transpired, next week's answer will not be a submarine, as planned. Anyway, the real winner is not Louis Brenner of 5830 Sansom Street in West Philadelphia, but his much disliked brother-in-law, Irving Rosenfeld. We now return to our regular broadcast. Sorry, Lou. Congratulations, Irving."

I clicked the button. The classical music came back on. I hid the microphone and came back upstairs. My mother and father were sitting on the glider on the front porch. They didn't say anything to me when I came out.

"Well, I guess I'll walk up to the corner and see if any of the guys are around. See you later."

"See you, Kingy."

"Bye, darling."

Later that night when I came home, after regaling my friends with the story of the radio contest, I went right up to bed. Mom and dad were already asleep. I could hear him snoring. I washed, got into bed and switched on my little radio as I did every night. Just as I began to drop off and as the latest Ray Charles hit was playing, a heavy Yiddish-accented voice interrupted the broadcast.

"If a certain young *kinder* by the name of Duvid doesn't repay his father the five dollars he borrowed tonight, plus one dollar interest for aggravation, he will be very, very sorry, I promise you. Good night and God bless."

I was hysterical. I swung my head over and lifted the spread so I could see under the bed. There he was—my wonderful father, flat on his back, microphone in hand, with a smile on his face. I paid him back on payday. He dropped the interest charge. I knew he would.

26

# FOOLING MOM

THIS IS A STORY about me which my mother really enjoys telling. I was ten years old and my mom and I were walking down Sixtieth Street on our way home. It was a cold February evening.

"Mom, I've got to talk to some guy I know across the street. Wait here, I'll be right back."

I ran across the street, ducked into a store and rejoined my mother, carrying a heart-shaped, wrapped object. We resumed walking.

"What do you have there, David?"

"Nothing important, mom, just something some guy gave me."

When we walked into our house my mother had to act surprised when she opened the box of one-dollar candy I had carried home to give her for Valentine's Day.

That was me that night—stupid but thoughtful. Mom would not have allowed the word "stupid" had she written this.


# A MOTHER'S EYES

I DON'T HAVE A "hat face." Never did, never will. The moment I put on a hat, any hat, every hat, and I've been trying them on all my life, something happens to my face. I look like a total schmuck! When I was about nineteen years old, a few friends of mine and my date stopped by the house to pick me up. My brother had his baby there, and my date sneaked up behind me and put the child's blue wool hat over my head. Everyone laughed. She turned to my mother. "What do you think of your son now, Mrs. Brenner?" My mother looked at her schmucky-looking son and said, "David always looked good in blue." Ah, a mother's love!

*The greatest compliment I ever heard any woman pay any man was when I was a young teenager. My mother said to me, "If you become just half the man your father is, you'll be twice the man any woman would ever want or need."*

# THE DAY TARZAN CAME TO WEST PHILLY

"DAVID, TARZAN IS COMING to town. How'd you like to see him?"

My sister's words were too good to be true. Tarzan in West Philly. Wait a minute! What the hell would Tarzan be doing in my neighborhood? I could never figure out what we or anyone else was doing there, let alone one of the biggest heroes of my 8½-year-old life. My older brother, Moby Dick, originally got me hooked on Tarzan, getting me to read all the Tarzan books starting with *Tarzan and the Apes* right through *Tarzan and the Golden Lion*. I practically memorized them. As a matter of fact, at the start of homeroom class every day, Mrs. Bishop gave me ten minutes to tell my bored classmates about the latest pages I had read in my current Tarzan book.

"Tarzan, Tarzan, Tarzan, I love you so much—even though you're not Jewish."

Jewish people aren't built that muscular, even though Benny Leonard and Max Baer were great boxing champions. Besides, we of the Hebraic persuasion are not so crazy about animals that we'd spend the best years of our lives among them in an uncontrolled environment. A small dog in the backyard, fine. A herd, group, flock or whatever it is of elephants making ka-ka every few feet, forget it, not Jewish. Tarzan was definitely gentile, a great gentile!

My sister, Bib, explained that my hero was coming to Philadelphia to appear in the annual Water Show held at the Arena, Forty-sixth and Market Streets. The main point to me was that Tarzan was going to be only thirteen blocks from my house! Only thirteen blocks! Never in my wildest dreams did I ever think this would happen. Who would? But it was true! I saw the ad in the *Evening Bulletin*. Tarzan, just as I had seen him in the movies (saw everyone of them, too, even at the risk of getting ringworm from the backs of the dirty seats). It was true! I was going to see Tarzan in person.

For the next two weeks, I skimmed through my Tarzan books, putting to memory all of the Ape talk I could, just in case I got close enough to Tarzan to call out, impressing him so much that he might take me back to the jungle for a short stay. Of course, I'd have to get permission from mom, which I knew I could, but I'd also have to get Mrs. Bishop to let me miss class and that would be the toughie. Man, I could just see me standing with some of the guys, Morty the Bird, Stan the Dancer, Big Mickie, Dee-Dee and Beb:

"Well, I'm off to Africa with my good pal Tarzan. I'll bring you guys something back, maybe a real shrunken head or a tiger tooth. Okay, *Booranga tankta,* (Ape for 'Got to go fast')." Wow, I'd be the King of West Philadelphia.

I thought it never would, but the big night finally came. I was so nervous that I had to go to the bathroom two or three times while trying to get dressed. Good thing I had only one good shirt, one pair of pants and one pair of shoes or I would've never been able to decide what to wear. My mind just wasn't working. We finally left the house. Bib held my sweaty hand as we walked to the trolley barn on Pine Street. Thank God there was a trolley there—no waiting. I had waited long enough. We got on the trolley. I always loved riding trolley cars, the movement, the studied look on the grown-ups' faces, the sound of the brakes screeching on the metal rail, the difference in how much faster everything passed by outside the window where I sat than through the windows across the way, the clanging bell, the money changer on the conductor's belt, the transit ads, the passed-out drunks, the smells, the whole adventure of it. But this time I noticed nothing, enjoyed nothing. I was too anxious to get to the Arena.

At Forty-sixth Street we got off and started walking the endlessly long four blocks to Market Street. I wished there were low hanging vines so I could swing quickly through the air like Tarzan, above the street, right onto the roof of the Arena. Then again, Jews aren't into physical swinging, except on porch gliders and even then it's slowly. After all, Moses didn't swing out of the desert, he walked, nicely. A nice forty-year walk. Could've swung out in a month or two. What a shame we didn't have Tarzan to lead us out of Egypt. Then again, Tarzan's jungle yell would've gotten on people's nerves. Better Moses.

Finally we were there! The Arena. Hundreds of people were jammed outside. Slowly we shuffled along with the crowd, which is one of the worst moments in a kid's life because you're either pressed against hips or rear ends.

Once inside we headed for our seats. We could've taken another trolley. As always, in my family, we had the worst—last balcony, last row. From there, the olympic-sized pool in the center of the Arena's floor looked like a small, blue blotter someone had dropped on a classroom floor.

The lights dimmed, people applauded. I tried to take a deep breath. A spotlight hit the American flag at the far end and we all stood to hear a recording of the National Anthem, which got stuck on "and the rockets red glare." The crowd laughed and then started whistling and yelling, which I found very upsetting, not because of my young patriotism, but I didn't want Tarzan to form a bad impression of West Philly. I kept singing in sync with the stuck record, the one line over and over and over until my sister gave me a shot in the ribs with her elbow.

Someone moved the needle to the last groove, the anthem ended, applause, lights up, a horrendous microphone screech, an announcement of welcome, blah, blah, blah and the show began. Excitedly, breathlessly, I awaited the entrance of Tarzan. I scanned the ceiling for the long vine on which he would swing, let go, somersault through the air, straighten his powerful body and cut through the water like a dagger. What a night!

"What's going on? Who are all these girls? Where's Tarzan?"

"This is part of the water show, David. They dive and swim in perfect synchronization."

"Who gives a damn?"

"Watch your language!"

"How do you do that—look at the letters as they come out?"

"Shhhhh."

"Shit."

"What did you say?"

"Nothing."

It seemed an unnecessary eternity before the stupid-looking girls got out of the pool. Whistles and applause and then the lights went out. Total darkness. People yelled, whistled and cat-called. I just held my breath and peered into the darkness with my jungle-trained eyes. I saw nothing. Absolutely nothing. Suddenly a lion roared. I jumped with delighted fright. Then the all-familiar cry pierced the darkness. Loud applause. A pin spotlight shone onto the ladder of the tallest diving board I'd ever seen. There he was, hanging out, holding onto the ladder with one hand and waving with the other—Tarzan! Of course from where we sat it could have been an elderly man in a business suit, our neighbor Mr. Gerber or a Martian, but I knew in my heart that it was Tarzan of the Apes.

30

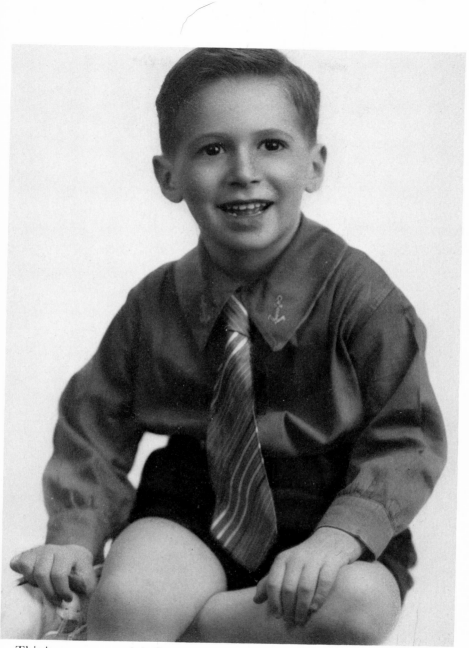

This is me one month before my
fourth birthday. I had just
learned how to tie a necktie and
the art of sitting on one leg. Cute,
huh?

My first photo. That's my mom
squeezing me. I was soooo lovable!

Moby Dick, Bib, Lou, Mom and
the "mistake" on the boardwalk
in Atlantic City. They claim I
made them grumpy.

This is me at age four being held by my brother, Moby Dick, who conned me into thinking he was my father.

This is me at age seven with my dog, Mac, which my "nice" grandmother gave away.

Me at age four with a Charlie McCarthy doll in my left hand and a gun in my right.

By age eight I had already
learned how to sit stupidly.

Standing with my favorite
sweetheart, my mom, who isn't
laughing at my joke (the fur is
fake...shhhhhh).

This is me at age nine looking so happy because my big handsome brother, Moby Dick, is home from the war. Mom is holding me and Lou is "looking cool."

My brother, Moby Dick, who was the Tyrone Power of West Philadelphia. I always wanted to look like him. I never did!

This is the Brenner family celebrating Passover at my Uncle Jay's house. Even on the high holiday, I had trouble being serious (I'm the kid in the center with his thumbs in his ears).

A thirteen-year-old interrupting his homework to feed his dog, Duke, a bone. You'll notice that this was before my nose was broken twice.

Here I am at thirteen terrifying my mother and amusing my brother (in the white shirt) with a made-up story about being lost in a New Jersey creek inside a damaged canoe..

Sometimes my parents got out of hand and had to be disciplined.

Mom and Dad, shown here, were
in love from the day they met
and still are sixty-two years later!

Sixteen years old, suddenly six
feet two inches tall and
wondering about the future.

Isn't it normal for a sixteen-year-old to eat the feather off his mother's favorite hat?

This is not a normal father—but he is the person who made me laugh the most.

"Kingy" is becoming a man. At age seventeen, I'm already taller than Mom and Lou.

At age twenty-one on the beach at Atlantic City with Shelley Lynn, the first of my brother's four children, and Mom. Notice our horrible beach umbrella.

Brother Moby Dick and I (age twenty-one) on the beach at Atlantic City. Now it's not a boy and a man; it's two men!

A recent picture of the same two
guys on the same beach. The
older Brenner is pointing out
Europe to the younger Brenner.

The Brenner kids: Bib, Kingy
and Moby Dick, also known as
Shortest, Tallest and Oldest.

As mentioned in "The Thermos,"
here is my brother and sister
sneaking up on my parents prior
to their first cruise vacation, our
anniversary gift to them.

Moby Dick and I on the coast of beautiful Ireland during our long-awaited and much dreamed about "Brothers' Trip."

Moby Dick trying to pull me down to his size.

How many children are lucky
enough to have parents in their
eighties who earn a living
shooting pool?

Pool hustler, Lou Brenner,
demonstrating his famous nine
ball bank shot.

My father beating my brother at pool. The sucker!

My father beating me at pool. The sucker!

Moby Dick on August 8, 1982, holding his Happy Sixtieth Birthday cake carved in the shape of a whale. Guess who ordered it?

Sherry, my brother's lady, my brother and I enjoying a night out in a New York disco.

This is my favorite cousin, Susan
Diane Kaufman, at age twelve.
She died on an operating table
two years later.

Slowly he made his way up the ladder, rung by rung, pausing every once in a while to wave. My heart was pounding. It was the same kind of climb he had made in *The Golden Lion*, only using a ladder instead of a cliff. He reached the top and stood tall as a giant. I'm only guessing about this because from this distance he could've been sitting. The audience burst into strong applause as he bounced up and down to test the diving board. Then he stood perfectly still and the crowd hushed. I could hear my heartbeat in my ears. In *The Golden Lion*, this is when Tarzan realized, after reaching the top of the cliff, that the native he was pursuing had his friends with him, all of whom had poison dart blowguns. Tarzan had no choice but to chance death and leap from the great cliff into the small lake far below. That's exactly what he now did! I sat transfixed as his body sailed downward, terrifyingly close to the cliff wall, straightening out and slicing into the water like a well-aimed spear. I leaped to my feet and screamed, *"Toolango Bellow mondalado corimba poonga!"* ("Only the bravest of the apes do the bravest of feats!") Several grown-ups told me to shut up and the man seated in front of me called me a "little putz." Not exactly the reaction I would've expected, but I knew Tarzan understood and would appreciate hearing words spoken in his native Ape tongue.

For the next half hour, Tarzan performed several spectacular dives, fast swam from one end of the pool to the other, demonstrated different swimming styles, wrestled a lion to the floor and ended his performance with a blood-curdling yell. A perfect night! My hero—my *koondonga*.

As we made our way down the thousands of steps to the ground floor Bib asked me if I wanted to go backstage and meet Tarzan.

"Of course, but how?"

The "how" would be simple and I should've known, for my sister had an uncanny ability—the combination of a warm personality and a lot of raw guts, that opened a lot of tough doors in life. Within minutes, we were past the guards and backstage. Lots of water pipes, lots of people, lots of talking, but no Tarzan. A few of the girl swimmers came over to me and started with the stupid baby talk, the cheek pinching, the compliments, the head rubbing, all the crap women did in the neighborhood whenever I was with my mother. I hated all of it. Of course, once I hit age thirteen, I would've given even my dog away to get any of it from the girls. Such are the inequities of life.

Finally, the girls left and there were only a few people milling around. I started shuffling my feet, ready to leave, when I saw the door with the white cardboard star nailed on it open and out stepped Tarzan—but he was no longer wearing his loin cloth, he was in a business suit with a tie and shoes. What was he doing wearing this? Disappointment started to creep inside me when I suddenly remembered that once it was necessary for Tarzan to leave the jungle to return to civilization with Jane and Boy, and he did dress in a suit and tie with shoes. My heart started pounding against my little rib cage. God, he was only a few yards away from me. He was . . . I couldn't believe it, but, yes, Tarzan was looking right into my face . . . he . . . he's walking toward me, smiling. My mouth went dry. Sometimes, spit can let you down. My nose started to run as it always did when I got nervous or drank hot soup. As he came within eight or ten feet of me I wanted to raise my arm, fist clenched, and say *Boorunga Powwatung*, but I couldn't move or speak.

Next thing I knew Tarzan put his powerful, massive hands on my shoulders and his voice boomed like a cherry bomb underneath an empty pineapple can.

"And what's your name, son?"

Before I had a chance to answer, not that I could, Tarzan gripped me under the arms and swung me up into the air exactly as he did his son, Boy. Then he swung me behind him and down on his broad shoulders, my legs landing on either side of his head, my testicles crashing against the back of his thick neck. This time I did let out a jungle scream, loud enough to be heard in his tree house back in deepest Africa.

As Tarzan laughingly carried me around, bouncing me up and down on his shoulders, I only wished I had two No. 2 pencils that I could've jammed into his ears. He was saying something, but all I could hear were my loud gulps, and all I could see were the bright little stars that danced in front of my eyes, blurred through tears of pain.

Finally, Tarzan put me down. I clutched my sister's skirt, holding on for dear life, beads of sweat running into my eyes.

"Guess your brother isn't crazy about height." (Her brother isn't about to have his nuts crushed into peanut butter!) "Well, you got some cute boy there."

"He's my little brother, David [who almost became her little sister], who is your biggest fan. He's seen all of your movies several times. Got the Tarzan bug from our older brother." [Who could probably beat the living hell out of you, putz head!]

"Well then, let's give him something to remember this night." [As if I could ever forget the night Tarzan almost turned me into the world's first Jewish eunuch.]

He handed something to my sister, who thanked him, and he rubbed my head again.

"See you around, David."

I wanted to say, "Next time you see me, you'd better be wearing a steel cup between your legs," but I settled for a groan. Tarzan left, thank God, and my sister started walking out with me in tow.

"Why are you walking so funny?"

"I got cramps."

"You want to go into the boy's room?"

"No, thanks. I'll wait 'til we get home."

"You're so pale."

"Cramps always do that to me."

"Here, from Tarzan." She handed me a slip of paper. I read it.

"To my good pal, David. Good luck. Buster Crabbe."

"Who's Buster Crabbe?"

"Tarzan. The man you met."

"If he's Tarzan, why'd he sign Buster whatever? Why didn't he write Tarzan?"

"Because Tarzan is his movie name. Buster Crabbe is his real name. It's his autograph."

"I came here to meet Tarzan," I yelled angrily, "not Buster ballbuster!" I crumpled the dumb piece of paper, threw it into the street and never got another autograph from anyone again. I also never met the *real* Tarzan—but I still have hope.


## MOBY DICK

WHEN I WAS SIX years old, my brother joined the Air Force and was shipped overseas. We wrote each other and he sent me presents. I had his picture in my room, but it wasn't the same as having him share the bed with me, listening to him tell stories, having him carry me on his shoulders into the Atlantic Ocean, going to the movies with him, splitting an extra thick milkshake, playing Monopoly or checkers on the living room floor, or just plain walking down the street with my big, handsome brother, Moby Dick! He was gone a long time, years and years. I missed him an awful lot.

One afternoon, when I was nine years old, as I came out of school to walk home for lunch, I saw my father's old car parked by the curb. He never came to my school. The very first day I enrolled in school, my mother walked me the six city blocks, telling me to memorize the way. That was the last time anyone ever took me to school.

"What are you doing here, Lou?"

"It's raining, so I thought I'd pick you up. Get in."

I got in the car and he took off. Something wasn't right. I had been walking through monsoons to and from school all these years and all of a sudden my father is picking me up.

"You got a lot of work to do this afternoon in school?"

"The usual. Why?"

"Just asking."

Something was really fishy now. My father had never asked me about my schoolwork or anything to do with school. As he once told my mother when she asked him to look at my homework, "Stelle, I didn't like school when I went, so I'm not going to go through it now with Kingy." Another time, when my mother asked him to look at my report card, saying that I got all A's, my father, without glancing up from the newspaper he was reading said, "I expect him to do that." Now, all of a sudden, he's asking me about school? Why would he . . .

"Moby Dick's home!" I screamed.

"Yes. He got in about an hour ago. I talked your mother into letting you stay home this afternoon."

"Great! Step on it, Lou!"

When I got home my mother told me that my brother had gone up to my room to lie down. He had flown all night and couldn't keep his eyes open. I ran up the stairs and then tiptoed into my room. There he was—my big brother! He looked just as I remembered him, maybe he had gotten a little bit older looking in the three years, but he was still the best-looking guy in the neighborhood, and I knew the girls would all be flirting with him again as they used to do. Everything was going to be just like it used to be. I sat on the end of the bed and for three hours watched him sleep. My big brother was home!

## FAMILY ARGUMENTS

IN SECOND GRADE, I made a windmill from thick art paper and colored it with crayon and wrote on the back, "Happy Mother's Day. I love you. Son, David." My mother hung it on the wall over her bed in my grandmother's house where we lived. Mom always said that the windmill was the reason why her bedroom was so cold. One day, when I was eight years old, I had an argument with my mother. It was rare for us to ever exchange words, but I was so angry that I ran upstairs, tore the windmill off the wall, ripped it into little pieces and then flushed it down the toilet. To this day, it hurts me to think of what I did. My mother loved that windmill I had made her so much, and what makes it hurt even more is that I've never been able to remember what the argument was about. It just shows you how stupid fighting over almost anything really is. Give any argument enough time and it will eventually become what it really is—unimportant.

## THE BIG, SHINY, BRAND NEW NICKLE

MY MATERNAL GRANDFATHER, SAM Rosenfeld, who was a clothing designer and a wonderful man, used to play a great joke on me when I was a little boy of four or five. He would open his hand and in his palm were two coins.

"All right, David, do you want the big, shiny, brand new nickle, or the tiny, dirty, old dime?"

Of course I always selected the nickle. But the first time I chose the dime was the last time we played the game.

# SPECIAL PEOPLE

THERE HAD BEEN NINE of them. One died before I was born. His name was Morris. My brother, Mel, is named after him. Only one of them is still alive—my father. They were the Brenners, six boys and three girls born to Molka and Nathan Brenner, a bright, strong, blue-eyed woman from Kovno, Lithuania, and a six-foot-two, white-bearded rabbi from Palestine. After the sixth child was born, they left Palestine. The year was around 1889. Shortly afterwards and until his death, Nathan, my grandfather, was the leading rabbi of Philadelphia. I never knew my grandmother because she died before I was born, but I remember my grandfather, who died when I was four. You don't forget a man that dynamic, no matter how young you are. And you don't forget any of the Brenners, because they were special people.

Esther was the matriarch of the family, the first woman ever to graduate from the Philadelphia School of Pharmacy. Like all of her siblings, she was big hearted and extremely funny. My favorite memory of this remarkable lady was at dinner one night at my house. I was ten years old. As usual, I was ribbing my father. We had a special rapport based on wisecracks. However, this kind of loving jest was new to Aunt Esther. After a particularly good verbal jab at my father, she turned to me and, in the throaty whisper each Brenner inherits at a certain age, said to me, "David, you can say whatever you want to your father, but you'd better be very careful of what you say to my brother." Words and a person you never forget.

Aunt Lena always had a twinkle in her eye and a combination of wisdom and humor in her constant chatter. She could recite verbatim most of the works of Shakespeare, as well as help me with my advanced calculus homework when she was in her sixties! She was the keeper of special dates for the entire family, sending a card for the least auspicious occasion to even the farthest removed tenth cousin, covering the envelope with all kinds of charity seals, a few quips and a kind word for the mailman. My fondest memory of Aunt Lena was the day of my cousin Malcolm's bar mitzvah. The ceremony had ended and everyone was heading downstairs to the basement for refreshments. I watched

Aunt Lena, who was quite up in years, move slowly up the aisle. I walked up to her and we spoke as we continued toward the basement. When we were at the top of the long flight of stairs, I said to her, "Take my arm, Aunt Lena." She looked at me, that familiar Cheshire smile slowly forming on her lips, then took hold of my arm and replied, "If you're afraid of falling down these stairs, David, I'll be glad to help you." And she did.

Belle. Belle was not only a special person in the family, she was one of the most special persons in my life. I loved her very, very dearly and have many cherished memories of her. She is almost a daily thought of mine. I can see her taking off the one expensive hat she owned and giving it to my mother because my mother had admired it when she came to visit. I can still hear her ask me, when I showed up at her apartment in Atlanta while I was in basic training, if I were wearing short pants and if she were old, and, when I answered no to both questions, she asked me why I referred to her as "Aunt," insisting that I call her Belle. That's how she spoke of herself, too. Never "I" did this or that, but "Belle" did this or that. Not for effect, but for fun. I can still hear the words of wisdom she quietly spoke to her husband after he bellowed like an angry bull about something, as he very often did. "Alvin, you can say almost anything you want to say to almost anyone to whom you wish to say it, if you say it with charm, Alvin, charm." My most vivid memory of Belle took place at my Uncle Nisson's house in Germantown. He was the youngest Brenner son. Belle was dying and knew it. She came back to Philadelphia to spend her last days with her family. Everyone was invited to the house for a party in her honor, although we were prewarned of her serious condition and that we would have to see her one at a time in her bedroom. She was much too ill to leave her bed. Every member of the family arrived. Luckily Nisson's house was a large stone mansion and could accommodate all of us. I was standing in the entranceway talking to some of my cousins when I just "felt" the presence of someone. I looked up. Others looked up, too. At the top of the wide staircase stood Belle. She was all made up, wearing a magnificent, floor-length evening gown. She extended her arms like an actress in a 1920s movie and, in her raspy voice, said, "My family. My dear, dear family. Belle welcomes you." Unassisted, she held the balustrade and slowly descended the staircase, ever so gracefully, ever so Belle.

After about half an hour of being her usual charming, gracious, hilariously funny self, Belle slowly climbed the stairs, pausing at the landing. She turned and took a moment to study every member of her family who had gathered in the large entranceway. She smiled warmly and pressed the palm of her hand against her head to smooth her hair.

"Belle must have her little rest now. She thanks each of you for coming. Belle loves you—very much. Good night."

A slight wave and then she disappeared, going up the rest of the stairs to her bedroom where, a few nights later, she would die in her sleep—but never in my heart.

Telli, whose real name was either Michael or Sam, I think, because all the Brenners had nicknames and no one was quite sure which was real and which was nick, was another good character. He, too, was a rabbi. I have lots of good memories of him— bringing me a model ship that was handmade by one of the prisoners in the jail where he acted as chaplain, handing me a couple of foil-wrapped Hershey chocolate kisses, telling me a riotous joke. One afternoon when I was in college, I was on a trolley car heading down South Fourth Street to visit a friend of mine. As the trolley left the corner and started to pick up speed those of us in the last half of the car heard pounding on the back end of the trolley. A fist banging. We all turned to watch the back of this man, very well dressed in a black three-piece suit and black tie and shiny, black-pointed Italian shoes, high kicking alongside the trolley, racing to get up to the front door, trying to get the conductor's attention. The trolley picked up speed and so did the runner. He was actually gaining. Some of us cried out for the conductor to stop and he did. The door hissed open and my sixty-five-year-old Uncle Telli got on. He paid the fare, thanked the conductor and the people in the car, spotted me, smiled, came back and sat next to me. "Late for a funeral service. You'd think time doesn't matter when you die but it does. So, how are you?"

A few years later, when I heard he was dying, I flew in from Chicago, where I was living at the time, to visit him in the hospital. We'd had a fight in the meantime and hadn't been talking to each other for a couple of years. As soon as I walked into his hospital room we spoke like old friends and shared the laughter so familiar between us. When visiting hours were over and I had to leave to catch my plane back to Chicago, I shook his hand and started to leave. At the door I turned and said, "You've been a great uncle, Telli." He smiled and said, "You've been a great nephew." We smiled and I left. Those were our last words to each other.

Nisson was something else. He was the "baby" of the family and maybe the most eccentric. He was so damn funny! Sometimes we'd be on the phone laughing for hours. He'd tell me stories about how he was watching the Late Show, ". . . a wonderful World War Two movie, lots of action, tanks closing in on the surrounded American troops trapped at Bastogne, no hope, when suddenly, over the hill, the cavalry appears and charges down, bugles blowing, flag waving majestically in the wind, swords . . . ! Wait a minute, I say to myself, what the hell is the cavalry doing attacking German tanks? And how the hell did the Indians get into World War Two? Then I realized that I had fallen asleep and woke up in the middle of the "Late Late Show" —Apache Attack." I liked to laugh with him in person even more, so I would frequently visit him at his house. This was fun in itself because a portion of his home was set aside for the Pennsylvania Institute of Criminology, which taught, among other things, the craft of being a detective. Nisson was the founder, owner and sole professor, so there were all kinds of interesting things to look at and play with—lie detectors, a firing range, a display of weapons, dummies used in the reenactment of murders, fingerprinting apparatus, hidden microphones, two-way glass mirrors—lots of fun things. The only problem I had concerning my visits to this lovable madman was a recurring one. I always made a wrong turn somewhere on my way to Nisson's and would drive around aimlessly and angrily until I found his street. One day, after he suggested we finish our telephone call in person, I reminded him of my direction problem. He told me exactly how to get to his house, emphasizing that I must make a left at one little street I always missed. He told me this mysterious street was exactly three traffic lights and one little street from where I turned onto Germantown Avenue and that I should rest assured I wouldn't miss it this time. He guaranteed it! I wasn't as confident as he but I got into my car to begin the forty-minute drive. On Germantown Avenue I began counting traffic signal lights. As I passed the third one I saw a man standing on the curb, his back facing me, his head turned to his right, looking into a shop window, his left arm extended stiffly, his fingers pointing at the little street I always missed. Nisson was a wild man! He died a young man, but anytime he died would have been too soon.

Joe was a good-looking man. He had a pencil-thin moustache, slicked-back black hair and dressed immaculately. Whispered rumors, among us second generation children, was that Joe was a gangster, a former prohibition bootlegger who sold insurance as a front. Who knows? I still don't. Only my father knows and he isn't talking. Whatever Joe really did for a living, he looked, talked and acted like a gangster. He was exciting to be with—a handsome Humphrey Bogart right in your own family. A man of mystery. Who could ask for more? Even when he passed away, Joe left behind a mystery. It seems he leaked out some sketchy information about a secret stash of cash—lots and lots of cash— he had hidden somewhere inside his modest row house. Well, for the rest of her life, his wife redecorated and remodeled that house—this wall came down (carefully) and the room was expanded with the ceiling raised (carefully) and the fake fireplace was replaced (carefully) with a red brick one, facing the new picture-sized window that replaced (carefully) the old ones from outside the house, standing on the lawn which was so beautifully landscaped (carefully) to match the newly landscaped backyard. This was just the living room, mind you. So you can imagine how the rest of the house was redone—very, very carefully. Maybe the story of Joe's stash isn't true or maybe that he even told a story of a stash isn't true. Like I said, my father ain't talking—but we sure keep laughing about it.

Jay Gerson Brenner was the unanimously elected leader of the Brenners. He was the most dynamic with the highest intelligence, a perfect wit, unceasing energy, a generous heart, an uncanny sense of understanding, a captivating personality, and was liked and respected by anyone and everyone who ever met him, friend or foe. He was probably the most popular rabbi in Philadelphia, the first to conduct religious ceremonies in a chapel built inside his home, giving his services for free to anyone serving in any branch of the military, the founder of the first nondenominational house of prayer, a prison chaplain, one of the first Americans to help surviving holocaust Jews escape war-torn Europe and sneak into Palestine, an active fund-raising Zionist and a fun uncle. You could always count on Jay for anything, from solving a family crisis to splitting your side with laughter. Once in the middle of winter, in the wee hours of the night, he came over to our house with a replacement for our heater, which had broken. He was standing on the new heater in the back of an open truck, scarf flying in the wind, looking like a Jewish Washington crossing the Delaware. Who else could've gotten a new heater, had it delivered and installed at such a time—only Jay.

The day before I was leaving for overseas in the Army, I stopped by his house to say good-bye. He came flying into the house (he never walked or ran, he flew), shook my hand and put an arm around my shoulder as he led me upstairs into his library. As he spoke he whipped off his official black rabbi-suit jacket, took off the black silk bowtie, turned it around so the red-and-black plaid pattern showed, put it back on, turned his black vest inside out and put it on with the same plaid pattern as the bowtie, reached in his closet and slipped into a gorgeous black silk smoking jacket. He lit his pipe, walked over to a wall bookcase and turned something, so the books swung around and a small wet bar appeared. He reached in, picked up a bottle of Scotch and two shot glasses and poured each of us a drink. He handed me one, held up his and said, "To your safe return and our next tête-à-tête. L'Chaim!" (A Yiddish word used in toasting whose literal translation is "To Life!")

We drank the toast. I did return safely, but we never had our next tête-à-tête—Jay died while I was in the service, lying on the couch in his library, dressed very much the way he was that day with me, smoking his pipe and reading a book. The family was never the same after Jay's death. I wasn't either. Not everything in life can be replaced, like Special People. I shall miss them dearly all my life.


## THE ONE COMPLETELY HAPPY DAY

"I DON'T EVER REMEMBER having one completely happy day in my life. You know, where from the time you get up until you fall asleep everything goes right, not one bad moment. I'm not saying my life has been terrible. Not at all. All I'm saying is that there

41

was always something, someone or whatever, that would come along and spoil some part of the day. But I know one day that's going to be 100 percent perfect. Guaranteed!"

"What day's that, Brenner?"

"The day I get out of this damn army!!!"

No one knew I was coming home. I wanted to surprise them. For the eighteen months I was overseas, I kept adding or changing some part of the day as I daydreamed about it—the day I would get out of the army and go home, and now my "one completely happy day" was here!

I got off the elevated train in my khaki pants and T-shirt, ran down the familiar iron-tipped stairs that lead to Sixtieth Street. Nothing had changed. Well, almost nothing. I walked to Chestnut Street, turned left to Fifty-ninth, made a right to the 5800 block of Sansom Street where I had lived since age nine.

I stood in front of my house for just a moment, then, two steps at a time, I ran up the front stairs, onto the porch and into the house. The look, the smell, the coolness of the air—everything was as I remembered it. I was home! At last!

"David!"

It was my sister, Bib. We ran toward each other and hugged real tight. She was the most burdened one in the family with my growing up—the eternal babysitter, and I loved her so much, my big sis!

"Why didn't you . . ."

"Because I wanted to surprise you. Where's everyone? Where's mom and dad and Moby? Hello! Anyone home?"

"David, we . . . mother and . . . they'll be here soon. They . . ."

"What's this? Letters to me. That dumb son of a bitch, Caldwell. I told him to hold my mail for a couple of weeks so it wouldn't be returned. Oh, look, a letter from Susan. How is she? Let's see what she wrote. I promised to take her out on a date when I got home. Oh, another picture of her in the back brace, but still pretty."

Susan was my first cousin, the only daughter of my Aunt Gert, my mother's sister. She was also my favorite cousin. I walked her to school every morning, babysat her, played with her, shared her secrets. We wrote to each other the whole two years I was away. The back brace was because she had curvature of the spine.

Tough on a fourteen-year-old girl who's just becoming interested in boys. That's why I had promised to take her out on a date. You could tell she was going to be a real beauty.

"Let's see—'Dear Cousin David. I'm writing this from my hospital room. I'm having . . .'"

"David, don't read the letter!"

"What do you mean, don't . . .'"

"Oh, David. It's Susan. The reason no one is home—everyone is at Aunt Gert's—I just came back to change shoes—the reason is because—Oh, God, David. Susan is dead. Her funeral was today. The doctor operating on her back made a mistake. She was a bleeder. They . . . they didn't test her for it. She . . . she bled to death on the operating table . . . she . . ."

I guess "one completely happy day" just wasn't in the cards.

## MOM'S COOKING

EVERYONE BRAGS ABOUT HIS or her mother's cooking. Not me! My mom was the worst. Still is. She knows it. It never bothered her too much because she hated to cook.

"Human beings were meant to do something better with their hands and minds than stand over a stove and stir a pot!"

So, she used her hands and mind to read a lot, to work with clay and ceramic, to make clothing and lots of other good things. Meanwhile, we just continued to eat tasteless food.

"It may not taste the best but it's all very nutritional!"

Sometimes her combinations were strange. With tuna fish, she always served hot potatoes. When my father asked her why, she simply replied that potatoes were good for you.

She did have a few fairly good dishes. Unfortunately, they were all desserts. Chocolate pudding (so good, I used to wait around for an hour to lick off the wooden cooking spoon), applesauce (which my sister strangely enough ate by spreading it on a slice of rye bread) and ice cream (made inside the ice cube trays).

To make up for her horrendous cooking, she did compensate for it by allowing us to choose what we wanted to eat. So, sometimes, there would be five different meals served. All bland tasting but all different.

She did have pride concerning one aspect of her cooking. She learned to turn the burner lights just high enough so everything would finish simultaneously. A feat of great efficiency!

My mother's inability to cook, or rather her lack of interest in cooking, was consistent from the beginning—the day after her honeymoon. Mom and dad returned from Atlantic City and the new bride wanted to please her new husband, so she baked him an apple pie. It was so hard that my father nailed it to the kitchen wall. Over the years, some of her experiences in the kitchen became legendary. A real beauty was the time she made a chicken for dinner and forgot one small detail—she forgot to clean the chicken. My father to this day insists that we could've shortened World War Two by at least two years if the Air Force would've dropped mom's matzo balls on Germany.

Maybe the best way to describe the family's acceptance of mom's disasters as a normal part of life was the time I put two fake rubber hot dogs on my father's plate. When the one he tried to cut bounced off the table and slid across the floor, he simply picked it up and tried to cut it again. Finally, he got the sharpest steak knife in the kitchen and cut through the hot dog and inserted it into his mouth. To this day, I still believe that if I hadn't laughed so much he would've managed to chew and swallow it.

There was another time he didn't even try to chew the food and swallow it. Mom made liver one night. Now, granted that liver at its best is not exactly the best. It is the Elephant Man of meat. However, no one could destroy the few saving graces liver has faster than mom. My father tried desperately and patiently to cut through it, but all the liver did was rise up on the opposite side from the one he was trying to slice. He put his knife down, stared at my mother, got up from the kitchen table and left the room. I was certain I would never see my father again.

There was a racket in the cellar, things being moved, thrown around, dragged. Then silence. Footsteps coming up the cellar steps. My father reentered the kitchen and sat down. He threw his leg up on the table next to his plate, picked up the slice of liver, placed it against the sole of his shoe and, with a linoleum cutter, trimmed it to the size and shape of his sole. He then took the nails out of his mouth one at a time, and, with a hammer, he nailed the liver to the bottom of his shoe. He then left the room. All night he sat with his legs crossed, so the liver sole would show as he read the newspaper and magazines. Finally my mother looked at him and in her sweetest, softest voice said, "Lou, there are other ways of expressing your dislike for my cooking." What a pair.


# GOOD MANNERS

MY MOTHER TAUGHT ME that a "gentleman" always keeps only one hand on the table when dining. I had a very difficult time remembering that, always leaning on my elbow as I ate. However, I was determined to be gentlemanly and proper, which probably explains why, to this very day, when I eat, I always sit on my left hand.

*Fatherly advice—the Bible says that every man should take a wife, but it doesn't say whose.*


# THE MASTER PLANNER

MY FATHER IS PROBABLY one of the top ten planners in the world. The D-Day Invasion would have been child's play for his organizational mind. The moon shot—a piece of cake. He is Mr. Organization and Mr. Planning. Whenever my parents are closing down their apartment in Atlantic City to spend the winter in their Florida condominium, Lou figures out how many meals they're going to eat right up until departure day, so they don't have one single morsel of food left when it's time to leave. Food should not go to waste.

The last time they were leaving for Florida, I was talking to my father on the phone from New York.

". . . and we just finished our last breakfast and there's not one single speck of food or drink left. It came out perfect!"

"That's great, Lou. You're one of the best planners in the world."

"I'm *the* best planner in the world!"

In the background I could hear my mother's voice. "Tell David what we had for breakfast."

"So, now, we're just waiting for the car to take us . . . ."

"Lou, tell your son about the delicious breakfast you served me."

"Stelle, don't be a horse's tomato. I'm on the phone. Anyway, Kingy, the plane leaves . . ."

"Lou, or should I say, chef? Tell David about the breakfast."

"Stelle, Kingy is not interested in what we had for breakfast. He . . ."

"I am interested. What did you have?"

"Kingy, there's not a morsel of food going to waste in this house and that's all that's import—"

"Lou, tell David . . ."

"All right, for crying out loud! We had hot dogs, baked beans, creamed corn and minestrone soup. Now, you happy, Stelle?"

I could hear my mother's hysterical little girl's laughter in the background.

"Your mother's going senile, Kingy. We may have to put her in a home. We . . ."

"Only if you prepare my meals, Lou."

"I'd like to catch the guy who says get married."

They're a great team.


# THE COLOSSEUM IN ROME

FROM THE TIME I was a child and throughout my teens, whenever my brother thought I was a bit out of line during a family discussion or in one of my conversations with him, he would always say the same damn line to me:

"I have stood in the Colosseum in Rome!"

This was his clever way of saying, "Look, you're younger than I am and have been nowhere; I'm older and have been around. Therefore, I know more."

Once when I was on leave in the army and went to Rome, I bought a picture postcard of the Colosseum, stood in the center of the monument itself and wrote my brother a one-sentence message.

"Now, I, too, have stood in the Colosseum in Rome!"

He got the point and we've been two *men* ever since.

*I once overheard my mother tell our neighbors, "My son, David, walks so proud." I'm still not certain why that made me feel so good, but it did.*

# BE FRANK!

WE'VE BECOME MORE OPEN as a family over the past ten years or so, but when I was a teenager we all had a very closed attitude about expressing our feelings. No one, with rare exceptions, expressed what he or she really felt about something. We rarely hurt each other, and would go to extremes at times to protect the other person's feelings. Still, I felt each of us should say exactly what was on his or her mind and I decided to do something about it. One night after work, I spoke to my family. Rather, I made a speech, a dissertation, to be more accurate, on being open and honest, saying what we felt, telling the unadulterated truth—being frank! No one said a word. I didn't let them. I spoke nonstop. My mother, father, sister and brother just sat in the living room and listened to the "baby" of the family tell them how we should act and talk to each other. For twenty minutes I babbled away and then I stopped. There was a pause. Everyone was seated in chairs and I was perched in the center of the living room, standing proudly upon my two honest feet. Finally, my father spoke.

"Let me see if I got this straight, Kingy. From now on, you want each of us to be frank. Is that it?"

"Yes, that's exactly it!"

"Okay, Kingy, I'll be frank—I think you have a big mouth!"

With that said, my father put the cigar back into his mouth and turned back to his evening paper. The others laughed and followed his lead, and that was the last "frank" discussion in my family for many years to come.


# TURNING SIXTY-FIVE

BECAUSE I WAS AN accident child, I was pretty young when my father turned sixty-five. I started to tease him on his birthday.

"So can you still see me, Lou? Should I get closer? You're not saying anything. Oh, sorry, I forgot—I'll yell from now on. Do you remember who I am? Would you like me to wheel you around the block a few times? Should I read the small print of the newspaper for you? God, even your feet are sixty-five years old. How about that. You're walking on sixty-five-year-old feet. So, what was General Grant really like . . ."

I guess my tirade lasted a good twenty minutes. My father just sat in his chair, newspaper folded on his lap, smoking his cigar and listening. The rest of the family was laughing. I was hot and knew it and kept rolling, line after line. Finally, I finished. I looked at my father. He just looked at me. Then he spoke—not a twenty-minute series of put-downs, not even two minutes—one sentence, one stinking sentence.

"Well, Kingy, at least I know that I made it!"

He went back to reading his paper and I was depressed the rest of the day, worrying if I, too, would be lucky enough to live as long as he.

I'm making progress so far.

*One of my father's best pieces of advice to me was "Never do when you're young what you're going to* have *to do when you're old." Follow this and you won't miss out on very much in life.*


## SLEEP, DEATH'S SISTER

WHEN I WAS EIGHT years old, I figured out that by cutting my sleep down to four hours maximum a night, I would be awake an extra 28 hours a week, times fifty-two weeks, would make it 1,456 hours in a year, which at a 20-hour day, would mean I'd be alive 72½ days each year more than the person who had slept 8 hours a night. If I lived to be 50, that would mean 30,450 days or 8.34 years longer than the man who had slept 8 hours per night. Such a man would have to live to be 58 and ¾ years old to equal my 50 years. Since you can't control how long you're going to live, but you can control how many hours you're awake, I slowly trained myself to function on a maximum of four hours sleep, which I've been doing for years—extra years of life! I'm now 107 years old—and feeling fine . . . a little sleepy, but fine.

*Whenever my father went upstairs to bed, he always said the same thing loud enough for all to hear. He would flop down onto the bed, sigh content-edly and call out, "God bless the man who invented the bed!" Isn't he right?*

# THE PERFECT ANSWER

FOR EIGHT YEARS, MY parents lived at 14 North Street in Ventnor City, New Jersey. It was a ground floor duplex apartment. The landlady lived above them. They never got along too well with her, and when the duplex next door at 10 North Street became available, which was owned by their best friends who lived in the downstairs duplex, my parents seized the opportunity and moved. All their neighbors and friends kept asking my father why he went to all the trouble just to move into an identical apartment next door. He didn't want to bad-mouth his former landlady, who was still his neighbor, but the questions were driving him nuts until he thought of the perfect answer:

"Lou, how come you went to all the trouble to move into an identical apartment right next door?"

"I wanted to be closer to the beach."

Perfect!!


# THE TURNING POINT

"TO WHAT DO YOU attribute your success?" An often asked question. The *truthful* answer is not easy to tell.

She was my maternal grandmother. Her name was Fanny Rosenfeld and I was told that she had once been a beautiful and a wonderful person. It is still hard for me to believe. She was the meanest person I've ever met to this very day.

When I was seven and a half years old, my grandfather, Sam Rosenfeld, died. He was a terrific guy. I really loved him dearly. Shortly after his death, we moved out of my uncle Jay's house in South Philadelphia and into my grandmother's in the West End. It was a move that was supposed to benefit both families: she would not be alone and we would live in a house we couldn't afford by ourselves. It turned out to be a horror!

My grandmother was money crazy to the point of insanity! We had separate shelves in the refrigerator and she would mark her opened bottles of liquids so she could see if any of us were drinking hers. If she thought we were, she would scream at my mother to give her three cents, or whatever. When you walked out of a room, she'd turn off the lights to save money. The house was almost totally dark all the time. It sounds funny but it wasn't, especially to a young and sensitive mind.

As time passed, the situation worsened. One day she just gave my pet dog away. She said it cost too much to feed it. To keep her from gloating over my sorrow and hurt I told her I didn't care about the dog anyway. Then I went into the back alley and cried. She used to sneak quietly through the door which separated her bedroom and mine, tiptoe up behind me and laugh hysterically, scaring the daylights out of me. She would then tell me the devil lived in my dresser mirror and would come out in the middle of the night and pull me into it forever. I told her I wasn't afraid of the devil, but I began sleeping with a knife under my pillow.

One day I was sitting on the living room sofa as my grandmother and mother were arguing. My mother is a very soft-spoken, regal lady and has never raised her voice or used foul language. She has always been a wonderfully gentle human being. She was defending herself quietly, asking my grandmother not to make a scene in front of me. This only made my grandmother scream louder and include me in her vicious tirade. As much as I tried to hold back my emotions, I couldn't and began crying. My mother looked at me and screamed. She ran over to me, picked me up in her arms and ran from the house. I had begun to cry, and, from the shock, I had hemorrhaged my tear ducts, so I was crying blood. The blood had filled my eyes and was streaming down my cheeks, soaking my polo shirt. My mother ran the entire three blocks to get me to our doctor, who told me to lie still and all would be fine. He was right, almost. It's true that the bleeding stopped, but the wound had just begun. I swore as I lay there that I would never cry again as long as I lived and I haven't!

The war in the house worsened, affecting all of us. We didn't have any money. We had no credit to borrow any money. We couldn't move. We were stuck in hell.

A year and a half went by. My grandmother's madness worsened almost daily. She and my father had terrible fights. My father was a man with a sometimes uncontrollable temper. I was sure that one day he would beat her or kill her. I am certain that only his high morality kept him from doing so.

One day we received a letter from an attorney informing us

that grandmother had started proceedings to evict us from her house and he advised us to vacate as soon as possible for the sake of my grandmother's health. We had no way to battle the forces. My grandmother did offer us five hundred dollars to use as a down payment on a house. We didn't have any belongings, so there would be no moving expenses.

That's exactly what came to be. We packed my father's old car and drove ten blocks away to Sansom Street where we had bought a small, run-down house. We had no furniture, no beds, no refrigerator—nothing!

We arrived at night. My sister had walking pneumonia and was wrapped up in a blanket in the backseat. It was a cold November night. I stood on the sidewalk with my mother. She wrapped her fake fur coat around me. I put my hand around her waist. My father was pounding on the front door of the house we were supposed to move into. Pounding, pounding, pounding!

I had only seen such anger from him earlier that day. Before leaving my grandmother's house, he asked me to go down to the cellar with him. My grandmother's prize possession was a large collection of rare and valuable brass pots and pans she had brought from Europe. They were worth a lot of money but never saw the light of day. They remained stored in several barrels in the cellar.

My father took out a pot and placed it on top of the workbench. "Kingy, hold that spike nail against the bottom of the pot. I want you to remember what we are going to do now for the rest of your life. It is the only way I can get even for the horrible things that have happened to us and a *man* should always get even! Remember that, Kingy—always get even!"

We proceeded to hammer holes, many holes, into each and every pot and pan in the collection. Neither of us spoke. I held the nail and he swung the hammer. We were covered with sweat by the time we finished with the last pot. My father threw the hammer across the length of the cellar and we went upstairs. I threw the nail the same way and joined him.

Now he was angry again. The reason we couldn't get into our new house was because the old owners decided they wanted more money and had changed the locks. Finally, either they or their lawyer showed up—I'm not sure who it was. All I know is that someone eventually came and everything was settled and we moved in and slept on the floor in our new house.

51

But while we were standing outside and my sister was coughing in the car and my father was pounding his fists raw on the door, I asked my mother why such things were happening to us. After all, we were good people.

She answered softly, "Sometimes being good isn't enough in this world. Sometimes you need money."

Not taking my eyes off my father, I said, "Someday, mom, I'm going to have a lot of money! This is never going to happen to us again!"

It never has. It never will. And I've found that that's the best way of "getting even!"

I never saw my grandmother after that day. She died when I was fourteen years old. I remember the day clearly because when a friend said, "I heard your grandmother died," I answered, "Do you want to play stickball?" She left all her money and jewelry to my mother's two brothers and sister. I don't know who got her brass pots and pans and I doubt that she learned anything from it, but she taught me a real good lesson in how to hate, didn't she?


## HOSPITAL CARE

WHEN I WAS FIFTEEN years old, my father was operated on. He was sent to a hospital in the Kensington section of North Philadelphia, quite a distance from my house and even further from where I worked.

At the time I was the manager of the Kiddie Land section of Woodside Amusement Park in Fairmount Park. I also operated many of the adult rides as well. I left for work at eight in the morning and didn't get back home until about three in the morning, no days off. This made it tough for me to visit my father in the hospital, but I just had to see him, of course.

One night after work, I took the bus, the elevated line, the subway and the trolley car to Kensington. I got to the hospital at about four in the morning. The nurse told me I had to come back during visiting hours. I explained my situation and asked her to break the rules long enough for me to "just look at my father." She said okay. I followed the signs to the room number she had written on a slip of paper along with her note of permission to visit.

I turned into the hall leading to my father's room when I saw him. My father. He wasn't *in* the room. He was in the hall right *outside* of it. In the hall! With the bright lights shining right on him. We couldn't even afford the damn ward! I was about to turn and leave when I heard my father call out in a weak voice.

"Kingy, is that you?"

"Yeah, Lou."

"Come closer. I can't sit up yet."

I walked over to him. He looked pale and drawn. He winced in pain but was too proud to call out.

"Nice room, huh, Kingy. Lots of space. Private, you notice."

Always joking his way out of the pain and humiliation that poverty had inflicted on us.

"Only trouble . . . I keep forgetting how to . . . turn off the damn light."

I laughed. Not because it was funny. It was funny, but I laughed because he expected me to, wanted me to.

"How you feeling, Lou?"

"Like a turkey the night before Thanksgiving."

"Anything I can get you?"

"Yeah, Kingy . . . a roommate. If you can find such a putz."

I laughed but noticed that his pain was getting worse. I knew my father didn't want me to see him hurting. He was such a proud man.

"I'd better go before mom gives me hell for coming in so late."

"How's she doing, your mother?"

"She's the best!"

"Yes. How's work?"

"It's still shit."

"All work is . . . okay, Kingy, thanks for . . . stopping by . . . try to stay longer next time, and . . . open the window before you leave . . . it's way down at the . . . other end of . . . the room."

I laughed.

"See you later, Lou."

"How much later?"

I laughed and left. It wasn't until the elevated train pulled into my stop an hour later that I noticed I had been standing all the way home, standing in an empty car.

I swore that night that if anyone in my family ever needed medical care again, I was going to be rich enough to see that they got the best! Years later, when my father had a heart attack, I did just that. I paid for the best. Then, when my father had another operation, again I paid for the best. What injustice that our health care is controlled by how much money we have!

After his last operation, as he lay in his hospital bed he overheard some doctors talking in the hall outside his room. They were advising some young doctor that all he had to do was ask the other patient in my father's room (my father wanted a roommate so he wouldn't be lonely) how he was doing, examine him briefly and then the doctor could put in and get paid by Medicaid. Following this conversation, the doctors entered my father's room. My father called out to his roommate, "Oh, Mr. Grantz, I want you to meet some doctors. This is Dr. Bullshit, Dr. Full of Shit, Dr. Big Shit and this is Dr. Just Plain Shit. Now let me tell you doctors something. I heard what you said out there and it's because of people like you that the poor are paying too much for their medical care. Well, you're not going to get one more goddamn dime from me! Now get the hell out of here!"

After they left my father got dressed, after only a couple days of recovery, walked out of the hospital and took the bus home. He was eighty-two years old at the time. One helluva man, my old man!

## GRADUATION GIFT

WHEN I GRADUATED HIGH school, some of my fellow classmates got some pretty "neat" graduation gifts. The few rich kids in my school got brand new cars or new wardrobes while others received at least a few new suits. The girls got the same. Quite a few of the kids got college tuition. You could say that some cleaned up.

During the ceremony, I was literally drunk and teachers screamed at me for being disruptive. What's disruptive about interrupting some stupid speech by the principal about the "future of the world" being in our hands? It's all a bunch of bullshit anyway. I just wanted to get the hell out of there and get to the parties. I hated school so why shouldn't I have hated the graduation ceremony? I got drunk to celebrate and I was disruptive because I wanted to have a good time. Besides all that, and it is true, I was frustrated about my future because I wasn't going to college and I still didn't know what I wanted to do with my life. I was still living in the slum and was still unable to figure out how the hell to get out of it. I had plenty of reasons to be drunk and disruptive!

After the ceremony, I got out of the stupid cap and gown, told a few teachers to go fuck themselves and walked out. My friend Linsey was with me as we started down the wide steps leading to the pavement where many parents were congratulating their sons and daughters.

I noticed a man walking up the steps toward us. It was my father. I smiled when I saw him. I always smiled when I saw him. The three of us stood on a landing.

"You two have been friends a long time."

"Since first grade."

"It's good to have such friends. I've got your graduation gift, Kingy."

I really hadn't expected a gift. We were pretty poor. Just having my family there was enough. My father reached into his pants pocket, took something out which was in his fist. He extended his hand toward me. I put my hand palm up and he let my present drop into my hand—a nickle!

"Buy a newspaper with that. Read every word of it, page one to the last page. Then turn to the Classified Section and get yourself a job. Get into the world. It's all yours now."

I laughed. A nickle! My father gave me a nickle! I put it into my pocket.

"Thanks a lot, Lou," I smiled. The three of us walked down the stairs to join the rest of my family. The "baby" had finally graduated.

That night, I went to all the parties, drank a lot, danced a lot, smoked a lot, and made out a lot with the girls. In the morning I dragged my body into the house and flopped into bed. I think I spent my graduation gift in a pinball machine in Atlantic City. I don't remember. Who would?

I always thought that was a great joke my father played on me until a couple of years later, as I sat in a foxhole in the army thinking about my family and my life. It was then that I realized that my friends had gotten *only* new cars, *only* clothes, or *only* tuition from their parents. My father had given me *the whole world!* What greater gift? I think the day I realized this was the day I became a man.

*My father told me a bit of old Jewish philosophy—Let your partner put his name on the window of the store; you take an extra 10 percent of the profit.*

## THE DRAFT

WHEN I RECEIVED MY draft notice, I told my family at the dinner table and announced that I would be leaving for basic training camp in three weeks. My mother looked shocked, but before she could speak, my father said, "Well, take care of yourself. Please pass the peas." No one said anything to me about it after that, until I was getting ready to board the train for Ft. Jackson, South Carolina, when my father shook my hand and quietly said, "Write to your mother as often as you can, Kingy." It's great to grow up free!

## CALIFORNIA BY CAR

ON THE SECOND FLOOR of our row house on Sansom Street there was a very small room between my sister's bedroom and the bathroom. We called it the "Little Room" and in it we kept a library of a couple hundred books and various odds and ends. This left room for a very small desk and a very small chair. My father sat there at night either figuring out what horse to bet, what number was going to hit, or planning his motor trip to California.

My father had been a very successful vaudevillian, song/dance man and comedian from the time he was nine years old. When he went into the navy in World War One, he continued as a stage entertainer, only then the audience was sailors. He used the name "Lou Murphy" and was a big hit to all the men stationed in Balboa Park, San Diego, California. He would've continued his career after the war but his father was the chief rabbi of Philadelphia and objected strongly to my father working on Friday night, the Sabbath. Very few entertainment spots closed their doors on Friday night, so my father turned down the Hollywood movie contract he had been offered and never went on the stage again.

All his entertainment was limited to his family and friends. I still believe he is the funniest man in the world.

Anyway, those days in San Diego were the highlights of his life. Never again would he experience the feeling of accomplishment, of being somebody, of being special. Consequently, he related over and over again stories of his days in show business to his children and kept talking about returning to San Diego, driving cross country.

Often my father would call me into the Little Room and, with road maps he had gotten from AAA spread out on the little desk top, he would show me his new route to California because of some road repair or new highway just finished. With a marker pen, he would trace the exact roads he'd travel and where he would stop overnight. It was a thrilling trip that my father and I took all those hundreds of times, a trip affordable only in his mind.

Sometimes, I'd see my father sitting in one of the junker cars he had bought and parked on the street. He'd just be sitting there, moving the wheel in his hand and staring out the windshield. Neighbors would kid him about it and I guess a few of them thought he was a little "off," but I knew he was just driving to San Diego.

Needless to say, he never made that trip—not by car anyway. One night I overheard my mother and father commenting about a wonderful deal a bus company was offering—ninety-nine days around the United States. You could get on and off the bus anywhere, anytime. After they left the room, I ripped the ad out of the paper and set up the trip for them as an anniversary present. This was before my present career, so I had to save pretty hard for it.

Without telling my parents, I arranged for them to be met in both Waco, Texas, where my mother was raised until the age of twelve, and in San Diego by the Chamber of Commerce and the press. I had written the C of C in each town, telling them the meaning of their cities to my parents. Well, it turned out great. Mom was thrilled to be shown all the places she remembered in Waco and they put a picture in the newspaper of her standing in front of her old house, which ironically was scheduled to be razed for a highway in a couple of weeks.

In San Diego, they were given a tour of Balboa Park and my father stood on the very spot where he had entertained, walked

57

the streets where he had signed autographs. Then he was invited to have lunch on the deck of a destroyer with the commander of the fleet, in appreciation for all the laughs Lou "Murphy" Brenner had given his fellow shipmates.

As I looked at the photos and read the article which appeared in the San Diego paper that he sent me I could visualize my father sitting in the Little Room with all those road maps, saying, "Kingy, someday I'm going to make this trip." Well, he did, and in a strange sort of way, I made it with him.

*More words of wisdom—when my mother told my slightly tipsy father that whiskey could kill as fast as bullets, my father replied, "I'd rather be filled with whiskey than filled with bullets!"*

## A SELLER'S MARKET

MY FATHER OWNED A lot of "clonkers," cars that made the property value go down even in a slum. At one point he owned five of them! He would sit in some and just hold onto the wheel, making believe he was driving cross country to San Diego or some other place. I never asked him about this behavior or commented on it, because it was none of my business. He got rid of three of the junkers when some neighbors complained that he had five spaces tied up on our street. They were right, otherwise my father never would've sold one of them.

Well, in many ways it's "like father, like son." I got into the clonker habit, only I did it one at a time. I'd buy a car for less than a hundred dollars, drive it a while and sell it for break-even money or a small profit.

One of the cars I owned for a while was a 1939 Dodge with a rumble seat. It cost me twenty-five dollars and I drove it for a few months. It was a real "clonker" but fun. When it started to fall apart even worse, I decided to junk it.

There was a junkyard near us which gave you twenty-five dollars if you had to tow the car to him but thirty-five dollars if you could drive it in. I was going for the former, until my dad came up with a scheme.

The junkyard was at the bottom of a long hill. My father stripped everything out of that poor car, including the entire motor. He then got in his car with several of my friends and I got into mine with several of my friends. He then pushed me to the top of the hill and over. I drove into the junkyard driveway at such high speed that when I slammed on my brakes (one of the few items my dad left on the car), hundreds of pieces of small gravel flew into the air. I blew my horn on the way in, too, so the junkman would see me coming.

He gave me thirty-five dollars and we left. We ran back up the hill and got into my father's car, watching hysterically as the junkyard man opened the hood of my car and saw no motor. He just scratched his head and kept looking for the motor, even under the car, just in case it had fallen out. Man, was that fun!

You know what else was fun? Being with my father.


## TO OWN A ROLLS ROYCE

IN 1981, MY PARENTS flew out to Los Angeles to appear on the Mike Douglas Show the week I was cohosting. It was their second appearance and they were as great as they were the first time. Naturals. This time, I wasn't sure they were going to come. While I was asking Lou about it on the phone, my mother was listening in on the extension.

"I don't know, darling," mom said quietly, "it's such a long trip just to be on the show and then come home the next day. Maybe some other time, dear."

"I'm eighty-five, Stelle. You tell me when is this 'other time'."

That line did it. They came. After the show, I had invited them to come to my opening night in Las Vegas. We drove to the airport. What I hadn't told them was that we were going in a private Lear jet. They had never been in one. I told my manager that my mother would admire the rich leather and fabrics of the interior while my father would hope to hit an exciting rainstorm. That's just what they said and that's exactly what happened.

There's another part to this story—the real reason why I brought my parents to Las Vegas.

When I was a little boy, my father always said, "You know you're really rich, Kingy, when you own a Rolls Royce."

In 1978, I had bought a 1976 Rolls Royce Corniche convertible. When I made the last payment and it was truly mine, I did two things. First I invited my father to Las Vegas to drive it. The reason I had waited until it was paid off was because my father said "own it," not "buy it." Anyone can buy. He drove it through the desert, and, after giving me the wheel, he said, "Now, I've lived. I've driven a Rolls Royce."

The second thing I did with the car after making the last payment, and my father had driven it, was put it up for sale. Why not? It had served its purpose.


## THE THERMOS

TO CELEBRATE MY PARENTS' fifty-fifth wedding anniversary, my brother, sister and I treated them to their first luxury ocean cruise. The event was full of surprises. First I went down to Atlantic City to pick up my parents in a limo and bring them back to spend the night with me in New York. Meanwhile, without telling them, my sister had flown in from Fresno, California, and my brother from Madison, Wisconsin. The following day my parents and I went to Atlantic City.

As my parents were about to get into the limo I asked to take their picture. As they stood together for the picture I told them to get closer for the "group shot." My father couldn't understand.

"What *group,* Kingy? Since when are two people a 'group'?"

"You've got to get closer together, if I'm going to get all of you in."

"What the hell you talking about—'all of us'? Just snap the picture, I'm sure your mother and I will fit into the picture."

It was at that moment that my brother and sister, who had been sneaking up behind them from down the block, put their arms around my parents and got into the picture. It was a great series of group shots and a wonderful surprise for my parents.

We spent the night having a great time in New York. It was the first time all of us were together at the same time in about eight years. The next morning we took my parents to the ocean liner. We checked out their cabin and took a tour of the ship, had a champagne toast and even danced a few. When it was time to leave the ship, we walked my parents back to their cabin. As we stood around talking my father started to unpack. Always in a hurry. I noticed a strange looking object in his suitcase. He saw me glance at it.

"You know what this is, Kingy?"

"No."

"This is the thermos I carried to work all those years in the neighborhood. Whenever your mother and I go on a special trip, like this one, I take it along to remind me of the poor days."

He needs no reminder. None of us do.

The funniest part of that day was when my brother, sister and I were standing on the dock, watching the ship start to pull out with streamers flying, a band playing, people waving. With all that excitement going on, my father pointed to his watch and mouthed the words "right on time." He just loves organization.


# LATE AT NIGHT, ALONE

WHEN I WORKED AT an amusement park during my teens, I often got home somewhere between two and four in the morning, depending upon what time the park closed and how lucky I was in making the connections between two buses and one elevated train. Not easy at that time of morning.

Very often when I'd walk into the dark living room of my house, I'd see a slowly pulsating glow of fire in the far left corner of the room. It was my father sitting in "his chair," smoking a cigar. The conversation always went the same.

"Hi, Lou."

"Hi, Kingy. How was work?"

"Same. Boring, hot, hard. The same. I'm gonna make a sandwich and get a glass of milk. You want something?"

"No, thanks."

I'd go into the kitchen, make a sandwich, either peanut butter or cream cheese on a bagel (my favorite), or tuna and cream cheese on a bagel or rye (my second favorite) and then I'd sit by the living room window eating it and drinking my milk. I never turned on a light and my father and I would never speak at this time. However, after I finished my snack, I would always ask him the same question and he would always give me the same answer.

"What are you doing, Lou?"

"Thinking, Kingy, just thinking."

I never understood what he meant but I never questioned him, either. Something told me that this was a very private, introspective time for my father. After I finished eating, I'd put my dishes in the kitchen sink and return to the living room.

"Good night, Lou."

"Good night, Kingy."

I'd then go upstairs and to bed.

Once I had completed my time in the army and graduated college, I was living in a small, one bedroom apartment in the same neighborhood I had grown up in, harboring an enormous feeling of frustration over not being able to figure out a way to escape the ghetto, seeing no light at the end of the tunnel. Once, in the middle-of-the-night darkness, I was sitting in an old chair in the corner of the living room smoking a cigarette, when I realized that were I to have had a son and were he to have walked in the room at that very moment and asked me, "What are you doing, David?"—I would have answered, "Thinking, son, just thinking."

It was then that I had the answer to the same question I had asked my father all those years; I knew what he was doing. I am my father's son.


## BRINGING IN THE SHIP

A COUPLE OF YEARS ago, when my comedy career was booming, my father asked me, "Do you remember when you were a little boy, Kingy? I would tell you that someday my ship was coming in? And then we'd talk about what we were going to do with all the money—buy a new house and a new car, a freezer full of ice cream, new clothes for everyone and all that stuff? We played that game a lot. You always knew my ship was never going to come in, didn't you?"

I nodded my head.

"Well, Kingy, you brought the ship in for me." It was one of my finest moments.

# FRIENDS

# NEXT TO FAMILY—FRIENDS

MY FATHER CALLED THEM "the gangsters." I called them "my friends." Some of them were both. They were the boys and girls I first met when we moved from South Philly to the West End towards the end of first grade. They were to become like brothers and sisters to me throughout all of my school years. A few have remained my very best friends to this day. They were and are very, very special people in my life, for they have shared it all with me, from the street fights to my success as a performer. More importantly, they helped mold me in many ways—intentionally and unintentionally, overtly and subliminally, positively and negatively, temporarily and permanently. Peer approval played a crucial role in my growing-up years. Next to my immediate family, my warmest memories are of my dear, dear friends. I owe them so much, because to me each of us is what we are today, in part, because of what each of us was or wasn't to each other back then, back when a smile from a friend could make anything seem better, back when you could say so much without saying anything at all, back when there were those you could count on 100 percent without qualifications—friendship as solid as the earth itself. Friends help you to grow, and when you have grown, they remain inside your very being forever. Perhaps my friend, Beb, said it best when he called me after seeing my television debut on the "Tonight Show."

"When you were standing up there, David, we were all standing there, weren't we?"

We were and we still are.

# DYING ON THE BEACH

THERE ARE MANY WAYS of having fun and passing the time on the beach for a group of thirteen-year-old boys. Girl watching ranks number one with most boys that age, but there's also pitching horse shoes, playing catch, foot races, horsemen fights, touch football, bury someone up to the neck, buck buck, imitate people's walks, toss someone up in a blanket, steal the fat kid's bathing suit, etc. One of our favorite beach games was War. This was played by dividing up into two sides, American and, let's say, Japanese. Then one army would charge attack the other army that was dug in on the beach. We fired imaginary guns, threw imaginary grenades and even had hand-to-hand combat with imaginary bayonets. One of the most prestigious achievements of the war was dying the best—sort of an Academy Award for acting. If you were to die real good, everyone back in the neighborhood would be talking about it for weeks.

The twenty of us who had gone to Atlantic City for the weekend had decided to spend the day on the beach in Ventor City, a more desolate part of the shore. There were less people, mostly adults, which greatly decreased the odds of fist fights and other annoyances. We arrived on the beach early in the morning and ran through the usual series of beach games before deciding to play War. I was chosen the general of the American forces and Gene Feldman was the general of the Japanese. We were to dig in and they were to attack first. When our foxholes and trenches were dug and we were braced for the attack, we signaled the Japanese, who waded waist high into the surf and then slowly inched their way back out of the ocean.

I waited until they were about knee high in the water before yelling the command to fire. We made our own gun sounds, of course. General Gene Feldman, the Japanese commander, led his men well. Only Bernie "The Buzzard" Lazowick was killed before hitting the beach. He floated face down right up to the shoreline and lay there, his plaid-bathing-suit-clad body rolling in and out gently with the surf. An excellent example of dying that probably would have won Best Death had he not gotten so concerned about sand getting in his horn-rimmed glasses and sat up.

David Linsalata made a break for the cover of someone's beach umbrella, but our Johnny Milliken leaped out of his foxhole and got "Linsey" in the back with a bayonet. We covered Johnny best we could but he was blown apart by a machine gun blast from Stan "The Dancer" Levinson. Johnny executed a series of death spins—good but too exaggerated.

I sent Morty "The Bird" Hoffman, my first lieutenant, with a message for Eddie "Dee-Dee" Romoff and Brian "Grab a Brush" Simons to sneak around the two ice cream vendors and come up behind the enemy. It would've worked fine if Dee-Dee hadn't decided to stop for an orange popsicle, which led to his and Brian's ambush by a heroic Japanese corporal, Bob "Bob O" Ominsky. The Bird avenged his friends' deaths with his forty-five pistol but was blasted out of his foxhole by a direct mortar hit. The Bird's right hand and leg twitched violently for about two minutes before his demise. Impressive!

Ellis "L.S.M.F.T." Jacobs and Stan Bluestein were chopped to pieces by a suicide attack in which Bobby Cott lost a leg and Harvey Feldcher had serious head wounds. Only one of their men, a brave Japanese sergeant named Micky "Big Micky" Zeitz, lost his life while screaming a combination Japanese death curse and prayer. My Segal, Herbie "Happy," and their Segal, Jay, fought it out hand to hand between our foxholes and their beach position, killing each other, falling dead into each other's arms. They would've won Best Death if they hadn't giggled while lying there.

The odds were against me. I had three men left, Kenny "Keat" Frost, Don "Captain Marvel" Miller, and Eddie Metelits. Gene had Stan the Dancer, Harvey Feldcher, Damon "Dame" Besinsky, Bobby Cott, and Barry "Beb" Black.

I was trying to figure out my strategy when Metelits, the putz, sticks his head out of his foxhole to look at some big titted girl walking on the boards. He got it with a hard sand grenade right on the top of his head. Even though he was killed instantly he ran out of his foxhole yelling and started a real fight with Dame who had thrown the fatal grenade. Bobby Cott got up to break up the fight and I shot him and Dame. Gene said it wasn't fair to kill men when they were fighting. I said they shouldn't be fighting when there's a war on. We settled with a compromise—Dame was killed and Cott was wounded in his arm.

Things got even worse for my troops. Beb called out to Captain Marvel that his mother was on the boardwalk looking for him. When Captain Marvel stood up, everyone shot him, including me, the stupid *putz!* Now it was only Keat and I. Five against two! I needed a plan and fast. That's when I got the big break. A very fat couple came by carrying beach chairs and umbrellas. When they were between me and the enemy, I stood up behind them and used them as a shield. As they passed the enemy lines I leaped out from behind them and turned my automatic on the exposed flanks. Stan the Dancer, Cott and Harvey dropped right away. As Gene started to get to his feet I leaped through the air, plunging my bayonet into his stomach. He died bravely. I would've been a goner if Keat hadn't charged Beb, who was aiming his rifle right at my heart. As Beb turned to face the screaming Keat I took off for the safety of one of my trenches. I rolled into a trench and caught my breath.

"It's only you and me, Brenner. I killed Keat. If you don't believe me, ask him."

"It's true! He got me, Dave! Sorry!"

"You did a great job, Keat. I won't forget you saved my life. When I get back to Philly, I'll tell your parents you died a hero."

"Thanks!"

"Could you guys hurry it up? I'm hungry."

"Me, too."

"Let's call it a draw and get some hoagies."

"No way! I'm going to kill Beb!"

"No, you're not, you Jew bastard!"

"Leave religion out of this, you Jap *putz!*"

"How about letting the dead get up?"

"Yeah, we can watch you guys better that way."

"What do you say, Dave?"

"I'll agree to let the dead rise, if Gene'll agree."

"Let the dead rise!"

The guys all stood up, shaking sand off their bodies.

"I think the dead should also be allowed to wash off in the ocean."

"No way! We all go in together after I blow Beb's head off with this extra powered grenade I've been saving!"

I peeked over the edge of the trench. Most of the guys were heading toward each other. It was just a stroke of luck that I saw Beb among them, making believe he was one of the dead. His back was to me, so I quickly scrambled out of my trench and rolled into the one next to it. Just as I had expected, Beb was casually ambling with the dead until he got within twenty feet of my former hideout and then, screaming like a wild Indian, he charged. When he was about five feet in front of my old trench, I stood up.

"Die, you bastard!" I yelled as I unloaded my automatic and threw my special grenade, a dead jellyfish. I got him. We won!

Well, Beb may have gotten faked out, but he did the next best thing to living—he died. And he died better than anyone had ever died before! As the bullets ripped through him and the jellyfish grenade exploded under him, he turned, ran toward me, did a somersault through the air and landed in a seated position, legs spread open, dead! Everyone—American and Japanese—applauded. Beb just sat there with his eyes open wide in a death stare, his hands stretched out stiffly holding his rifle.

"Great, Beb. The best!"

He didn't move or blink. I laughed.

"You can live again, Beb."

Nothing. I laughed and then looked down. When Beb had landed in his spread-eagle death position, his penis had fallen out of his bathing suit and was lying on the sand. I looked around. There was a woman, maybe as old as twenty-eight, sitting a few feet from us. She was looking down at Beb's crotch and laughing. I looked into Beb's face and nodded my head down to the accident area. Beb nodded his head in direct imitation of mine but saw nothing. I whistled. Beb whistled.

"Psst, psst," I whispered, looking down at his crotch.

"Psst, psst," Beb answered, looking down at *my* crotch.

"Your thing's out," I said softly through clenched teeth.

"Yor ting out," Beb mimicked.

I looked around for help, but all the guys were now swimming and body surfing. The woman, observing all of this, was now laughing quietly and I could feel my face getting red.

"Look at your putz, putz," I hissed through clenched teeth, wiggling my forefingers in the direction of his spread legs.

"Look at your pu . . ." Then Beb saw it. He slowly looked at the woman who was looking at him, then slowly turned his head and looked right at me. His face gave birth to a wide smile, and then he did something that was better than the great somersault dying, cooler than anything I had ever seen anyone do in my thirteen years of life—Beb reached down, cupped a handful of warm, soft sand and proceeded to bury his penis. The woman laughed aloud and joined me in applauding my smiling, coolest of cool friends.

## ALEX AND HIS COPS AND ROBBER

I BELONGED TO MY first street gang when I was four and a half years old, believe it or not.

Actually, I got into the gang by accident, which is exactly what I looked like I had been in the day I was accepted. I was walking down a side street near my uncle Jay's house, at 1431 South Fourth Street in South Philly, where we lived, when about fifteen boys ranging in age from five to fourteen started picking on me for being Jewish. They knew I was Jewish because above our door there was a big sign that read "Rabbi Jay Gerson Brenner." A pretty good clue. Anyway, they put their youngest member up to fighting me. I had never been hit in my life nor had I ever hit anyone. Well, this little blond terror swept the street with me, literally. I was filthy from being rolled around in the street and bloody from the punches in my mouth and on my then small nose. I cried and ran home with the gang in hot pursuit.

I charged into the house, where my mother was talking to my Aunt Belle. I told her, between sobs, what had happened. My mother held my chin up, looked me in the eyes, and, in her soft voice, said, "David, never run home to your mother. Fighting is wrong, but if you must fight, then fight and win!" She took my hand gently in hers, walked me to the front door, opened it and guided me out to the top landing of the steps.

I heard the door lock click behind me. I turned and saw my mother's face watching me through the lace curtain that covered the glass in the door. The gang was at the bottom of the steps, jeering and laughing at me. In the front was the kid who had beat me up, his fist clenched, a smile on his unmarked face. I leaped from the step landing on top of him, and, with all the rage I could muster, I pounded my fist into his face and body until I felt a couple of the bigger kids pulling me off him. He was the one doing the crying this time. Well, that was Moo-Moo, it was the day I became a member of my first street gang, and it was the day my nickname was changed to Duby *the Hebrew.* My father had nicknamed me "Duby," which is Hebrew for "Baby Bear." Supposedly that's what I looked like as a baby. The new addition was because I was the only Jew in the gang. Moo-Moo and I were best friends until we moved from South Fourth Street. Eventually I lost contact with my South Philly friends. When I was seventeen, I returned to the old block and was nostalgically looking at the house I had lived in when a handsome, blond-haired boy around my age popped his head up from the roof of my old backyard shed.

"Hi, how ya doin', Duby the Hebrew?"

I looked into the smiling face of this boy, trying to recognize him. He jumped off the roof onto the pavement in front of me and stuck out his hand.

"I'm your old pal, Moo-Moo."

As soon as he said his name his face melted into the past and we shook hands, hugged and laughed. We sat on the front steps of my old house and reminisced about the old days, including the time we fought each other.

I asked Moo-Moo about his brothers and different fellas in the old gang, what had become of them and so forth. Then I asked him about Alex, probably the strangest one of our friends.

In retrospect, I realize that Alex must've been slightly retarded. But when we were kids we just thought he was a little stupid and strange.

Alex had a favorite game he liked to play by himself. Whenever he wasn't in his parents' apartment we knew where we could find him—on his roof. Alex played a cops-and-robbers game. He would be the robber running from the cops after holding up a neighborhood store, during which he shot the owner. He had a tin cap pistol which he had broken in half—longways—so he would have two guns instead of one, a pretty standard procedure in a poor neighborhood. Anyway, Alex would hide behind the skylight on his apartment building's roof and shoot it out with the cops who were ducked behind other skylights and chimneys. The end was always the same. The cops would shoot Alex and he would die stretched out next to his skylight, the two guns in his limp hands.

When we'd go up on the roof to get him, we'd have to wait for Alex to finish the game.

Moo-Moo leaned his back against the brick wall and offered me a cigarette. I took it and we lit up.

"You remember that crazy game Alex used to play on the roof?"

I nodded, smiling.

"Well, a few years ago—Alex must've been about seventeen or so—he held up a grocery on Seventh Street. Shot and killed the guy. Well, the cops came after him. Right on his tail. So Alex ran up on his roof, behind his skylight and shot it out with them, a gun in each hand, and that's how he died."

I'm not a great believer in prophecy or ESP or anything supernatural but I've often thought of what Moo-Moo told me that day and have wondered whether, when we were kids, Alex was playing out, sort of rehearsing, his death as he knew it would be. Whether he was or not, it was still a damn shame!

## THE HUNTING CAP

WHO KNOWS WHAT STARTS a fist fight, sometimes even between the best of friends? Whatever it is, it isn't worth it. Somehow it happened one day between one of my best friends and me.

Beb, Dee-Dee and I always walked home together after school. We were the Three Musketeers. We had just whet our appetites for model airplanes by looking in the window of Don's Model Shop at Sixtieth and Spruce Streets, when some sort of disagreement flared up between Dee-Dee and me. The argument was intensified by a couple older guys in the neighborhood, and the next thing I knew Dee-Dee and I were circling each other, our fists clenched.

Now, I'd better tell you right here and now that Dee-Dee was one of the strongest boys in my class. At age seven he had started working in Cooper's Supermarket as a stockboy and this built his muscles (it also led to a teenage hernia but that's a different story). He hit very hard! My only advantages were that, unlike my opponent, I was graceful on my feet (Dee-Dee was a klutz), and I made up for not hitting hard by my speed and the rapidity of my punches. I also had a real good left jab.

We danced around for a few moments, I bouncing on my toes and Dee-Dee shuffling flat-footed, his arms cocked. The crowd around us was calling for blood. Finally, I threw the first punch, a left jab, which caught Dee-Dee flush on the mouth. His head snapped back and his hunting cap flew off. I was ready to move in with a follow-up punch, when Dee-Dee signaled me to "hold it" and bent down to pick up his hunting cap. He cleaned the pavement dirt off, put it back on his head and resumed his fighting crouch.

We danced, the crowd yelled. I feinted a left jab and when Dee-Dee moved to his left to avoid it, I lashed out a right cross and caught him right on the chin. His head flew back and his hunting cap popped off again. I was charging in with a left to the midsection when Dee-Dee threw up his hand, signaling another stop. I held my punches while Dee-Dee retrieved his hunting cap, cleaned it off and put it back on his head. This was really silly. I started laughing. So did Dee-Dee. We stopped fighting and never fought again.

You are most likely wondering why Dee-Dee was so concerned about his hunting cap and why I didn't take advantage of his move to retrieve it. Well, you see, when you grow up poor, you get a real strong respect for anything new. Dee-Dee's cap was new and there was no way he was going to let it get dirty or stolen, even at the risk of getting beat up. Actually, there was no risk of that happening, since I understood and would've done the same.

If you also are wondering if Dee-Dee holds a grudge today because I beat him, I'll answer that by telling you that he's the one who reminded me about this story for my book. Then he asked for a ten-dollar reminder's fee. Some nerve, huh? I wanted to slap his face for asking that but, luckily for him, he was wearing a new hunting cap at the time.


## THE TRANSFER

ONE OF THE MOST important values in street corner life is that you remain undyingly loyal to your friends. You do nothing—ever—to violate this bond. This is a story about someone who made the mistake of forgetting this part of the unwritten code.

The trolley car conductor would give you a transfer, a paper ticket which allowed you to ride for free on any trolley going perpendicular to the direction you originally traveled in. A time was punched out giving you up to two hours to use the transfer, and the color indicated the day of the week it was issued. The transit authority was kind but not Santa Claus. One of the things poor people always did was ask for a transfer, even if they weren't going to use it, so they could pass it on to a fellow poor person waiting for a trolley. This was either done as soon as one got off a trolley, or, if no one was waiting, then the transfer was rolled up and placed somewhere where it could be seen easily, like in the cracks of a wall or hanging out of a mailbox slot.

My friend, whom we'll call Howie in order to protect the guilty, and I hitched rides to Fairmount Park so we could dip our eleven-year-old bodies in the fountain, float dead leaves in one of the lakes, watch the boaters, sneak into the zoo or the Benjamin Franklin Museum of Science and just run around and have a great time on this Sunday in spring.

When it was time to start home, we hitched and walked our way over to Market Street. It would be dark in about an hour and we had about forty long city blocks to go, so we started looking for a transfer to use on the elevated train. We weren't too lucky. It was always difficult to find transfers because of the "blue laws" which at that time closed down most of the town on Sundays and opened the door to Philadelphia jokes. No longer true today in the new Philadelphia, thank goodness.

Anyway, there were no stops on the elevated line between Fifteenth and Thirtieth Streets, so we had to walk across the bridge spanning the Skuykill River. When we got to the other side I saw it, sticking out of a crack in someone's front step—a blue transfer! I checked the time. It was good for another fifteen minutes.

"Wow, David, you really are lucky. Maybe I'll find one, too."

"Come on, Howie, you don't think I'd use this transfer and let you walk all the way home, do you? You nuts? We both ride or we both walk. Here, you hold onto this transfer. I'm going to walk on the other side of the street. That way we'll have all angles covered."

I guess I walked another six blocks looking into every conceivable hiding place for a transfer but didn't find one. There were a bunch of sun bleached ones from previous days but nothing current. It was getting a little dark and I was tired. I looked for Howie. He wasn't across the street. I looked up and down the block, figuring he had either gotten ahead of or behind me. No Howie—anywhere! I became worried. There were a lot of street gangs in this neighborhood. Maybe some guys grabbed Howie and beat him up. I crossed the street and cautiously searched down every alley into every abandoned store, over yard fences. I searched everywhere—a friend always sticks with his friend. But there was no Howie and no transfer. I ended up walking all the way home, through all the "bad" neighborhoods until I reached my own "bad" neighborhood. It was dark and I was scared. A block from my house I stopped to tell the story to an older guy who said he saw Howie going into his house about an hour before.

The next day in school, I told my friends what happened, how Howie had disappeared. A few of the guys had had class with Howie that morning, confirming he was in school that day. At the lunch break I waited outside the main gate of the school. Most of my friends waited with me. Finally Howie came out of the school. He saw me and the crowd. Word had spread about what had happened to me. There was nothing he could do but come to me. He stopped a couple of feet in front of me while the rest of the fellas formed a circle around us.

"Hi, Dave."

"Hi, Howie. What happened to you yesterday?"

"Well, the strangest thing that's ever happened to me in my life! Right after you gave me the transfer, I blacked out. I swear! And I didn't come to until I was already on the el on my way home."

I smiled. He smiled.

"Well, Howie, if you think you blacked out last night, wait till you see this one."

I hit him flush in the mouth, hard, real hard! Then I followed it up with a flurry of punches, driving him backward down the street. He went down. I picked him up and kept hitting him, across the trolley tracks, up against a store window, down the street, punch after punch. He went down again and this time he didn't get up. I reached down, grabbed the back of his jacket collar and dragged him down the pavement, around the corner, up his frontsteps, across his porch and propped him up against the front door of his house. I rang the bell and left. My friends cheered, for I had done what had to be done—I'd avenged a breach of loyalty!

In spite of this, Howie and I remained friendly throughout high school and even into college. As a matter of fact, I was an usher at his wedding. Years passed and Howie became a successful CPA. Once after he helped one of our best friends from the old neighborhood out of a financial jam, I called to thank him. As he always did whenever we spoke, he asked to be my accountant. But as always, I thanked him and politely refused. This time, however, he didn't just drop it.

"You know, David, for years I've been asking to do this for you and you always turn me down. You know I'm good at what I do."

"One of the best. I know."

"Then how come you always say no?"

"You want the real truth, Howie?"

"Yeah, the real truth."

"The transfer, Howie. If you panicked and left me to drown once, you might do it again. I've never trusted you since that day."

"You know, Dave, way down deep inside, I've always known that was the reason."

"I figured you did, Howie, but I think you also know that we're friends enough that I would be an usher at your daughter's wedding, too, just as I was at yours."

I would, too—unless I had to take a trolley to get there, I was broke and only Howie and I . . .

Friendship is based on trust and loyalty. I'll always believe this!


## STRANGE VALUES

WHEN I WAS A kid, I'd ask to borrow a quarter from my friends to help me buy a pack of cigarettes. When they would give it to me, I'd throw it over the roof of a house. It would drive them crazy. I'd always ask why they cared what I did with the money just so long as I paid them back. For some reason it really bothered them. Not as much, though, as it did when I'd bum their last cigarette and then rip it apart and throw it in the gutter. They went even crazier! I guess a true friend is someone who'd rather see you get lung cancer than waste money.

# THE AUTO MECHANIC

HE WASN'T THE BRIGHTEST guy in the neighborhood. He might even have been a little mentally retarded. I'm not sure. He lived near me. He was about six years older than I, very friendly and I liked him a lot. We were pals. I learned two important lessons from him which I use to this day.

He couldn't read or write too well but he could fix a car better than anyone in the neighborhood, maybe even the world. Within moments of listening to or looking at a car engine, he could identify the problem and then he'd fix it. No failures. When it came to auto mechanics, Jackie was perfect!

One day, when I was about eleven years old, I was watching Jackie fix a neighbor's car. We talked baseball and girls and movies and television. Jackie carefully placed a clean chamois cloth on the fender of the car and then gently placed every tool he expected to use in a neat row on the cloth. I'd seen him do that lots of times but it was the first time I ever really paid attention. Each tool was individually wrapped in treated oilcloth and was in perfect condition. After he fixed the engine and had it purring like a jungle cat, he gently closed the hood of the car, wiped off his fingerprints from the hood and fender, then set all his tools on the pavement. As we spoke he cleaned and polished every tool, wrapped it in oilcloth and placed it carefully in its individual groove in the tool kit he had made.

Sure, being a car mechanic is a dirty job, not rated among the highest of professions, but to Jackie it was what he did and he did it better than anyone! That's why he cleaned his tools and that's what I learned from him—pride in what you do. No matter what it may be—self-pride!

The other lesson Jackie taught me was something that, to him, only concerned dating girls, but to me it had to do with everything in life. We were sitting on my front porch. Jackie was looking through an old Playboy magazine, going crazy over every girl's picture. I was still two years away from having girls replace trading baseball cards.

"Davie, when you grow up like me and start taking out girls, say, like you take her to a nightclub or something. You don't want her to think like you never been there before, you know. Like you're some kinda square or something, right? So, what you do is like you take her coat and you walk toward where you think the coat checkroom should be. With like confidence, you know what I mean? Now, let's say it ain't the coat room. Let's say . . . it's the men's room. You don't turn around or nothin'. No way! You don't act like you made a mistake. You act like you did it on purpose. You take a leak. Then you leave the men's room and head toward the second place where you think the coat room is. You just keep doing that, walking like you know what you're doing, until you really find it. See, that way, the girl and everybody else will think you know what the hell you're doin' and they'll have confidence in you. Then that'll give you confidence in yourself, too. You know what I'm talking about?"

Damn right I did, Jackie, and I've been using your system just about every day of my life. Thanks, pal.

## A DUMB ANSWER

ONE OF THE MEN my mother knew before meeting my father was an older gentleman named David Belasco, a successful Broadway producer who today has a theater named after him. He had signed his name in a script of William Shakespeare's *The Merchant of Venice,* which he was producing on Broadway, and gave it to my mother. She had showed it to me when I was a small child. When Mrs. Bishop, my fifth-grade English teacher, asked us who wrote *The Merchant of Venice,* I raised my hand and was called upon. I stood up in front of all my classmates and proudly announced that the author's name was "David Belasco!" When they laughed I called out, "I've got his autograph in a copy of the script!" Everyone laughed harder, even Mrs. Bishop. They all thought I said it for laughs. I didn't then—but I am now.

## THE BUZZARD

WHEN WE MET HIM, his name was Bernard Lazowick. He came to work at Woodside Amusement Park, where I was working when I was fourteen. He was assigned to me in Kiddie Land, where I was manager of the children's rides. As the busy Sunday went on

I forgot all about the "new kid" until I heard a soft voice behind me say, "When do we go to lunch?" I turned to see this sun-burned, fire-engine-red face with thick-lensed, horn-rimmed glasses. I couldn't help but laugh.

"Shit! You're the new kid I put on the rocket ship ride, right? Lunch was hours ago. It's even past dinner. Why didn't you say something?"

"I don't know."

"Okay, look, here's what you do. Go home and I'll ring out your time card later tonight."

"Thanks a lot."

"Forget it. And you'd better soak your face in Noxzema when you get home. Where is home, by the way?"

"Wynnfield."

"Oh, rich Jewish kid, huh?"

"Not too. My father owns a chicken store on the University of Pennsylvania campus . . ."

We became real good friends. I introduced Bernie to my street corner friends and he hung out with us from then on. He was crazy and a lot of fun, but my best story about him involves how he got his nickname.

We were at a party over some girl's house in Oxford Circle. I was sitting on the sofa when two girls came over, sat on either side of me and started talking. They were fairly attractive but not the brightest. Bernie was dancing and talking with the best-look-ing girl at the party. I really liked the way she looked, the way she smiled and laughed, which she was doing a lot of because Bernie was the second funniest guy in the gang. I wanted to be with Bernie's find, but how? The girls with me were babbling on. I interrupted them by thinking out loud.

"You'd never know it. Damn shame."

"What is?"

"What is what?"

"You said something was a 'shame'. What's a shame?"

"Oh, I must've been thinking out loud. Sorry. What were you saying?"

"No, I'm curious. What's a shame?"

"Me, too."

"Well, girls, I really can't tell you. It has to do with the fella talking to . . . eh, what's her name, there."

"Oh, you mean Harriet Gold."

"Yeah, of course, Harriet."

"What about him?"

"Who?"

"The fella with Harriet?"

"Oh. I told you I can't tell. Even if I did you wouldn't believe me. So, forget it. Although it is a real shame. Unbelievable!"

"What?"

"What? Please tell us! We'll believe you! Promise."

"Well, I really shouldn't . . ."

"Please!"

"Pretty please with whipped cream on it and a cherry."

"Well, since you put it that way, I'll tell you, but you've got to promise not to tell anyone! Swear to it."

"Swear!"

"On our lives!"

"Okay. Well . . . you know that Bernie's father—that's his name, Bernie—well, Bernie's father owns a chicken store on Spruce Street on the campus of the University of Pennsylvania. Well, when Bernie's mother was pregnant with Bernie she worked in the store right up until the moment she went into labor. Her job was plucking chickens. All day, sixteen, eighteen hours a day, seven days a week, she plucked chickens, pulling out feathers and throwing aside naked chickens, pulling and throwing, pulling and throwing! The doctors aren't certain if it was because of the sheer work or breathing in the feather dust, but . . . well . . . come closer and I'll whisper it. Okay, well . . . when Bernie was born, he didn't have any hair on his body, except for his head. Instead, all over his tiny little baby body were these tiny, almost microscopic black feathers, like buzzard feathers."

The two girls just stared at me, micrometers apart, eyeball to eyeball. They didn't say anything. It took superhuman will power for me not to laugh. Finally, I just closed my eyes slowly and nodded my head sadly, whispering ever so softly, "Feathers. What a shame."

"I don't believe you," whispered one of the girls.

"Me, neither. No one is born with chicken feathers."

"Buzzard feathers."

"Buzzard, chicken, what's the difference? I don't believe you."

"Me, neither. You made it up. You're the sick one."

"Okay, I knew I shouldn't've told you, but now you're forcing me to prove it. No one calls me 'sick'. You go up to Bernie and ask to see his legs and he won't show them to you. Go ahead."

I was counting on Bernie doing what I or anyone else would do if two strangers asked to see his legs, especially when talking to a girl he's trying to impress—I'd tell them to bug off. That's just what happened, and, when Bernie told them to get away, they began yelling, as I thought they might. Everyone was watching.

"We know why you won't show us your legs! Don't we, Marsha?"

"Yes!"

"What is it with you two? You got a foot fetish or something? Get lost! Go back under your rocks!"

"Show us your legs!"

"No! Now, get the hell away from me! Jesus!"

"Show us your legs!"

"Yeah, Bernie, show them your legs."

"Show all of us, Bernie!"

"All you guys can go to hell with these two scarecrows!"

"If anyone should know about birds, it would be you, wouldn't it? That's just why you won't show your legs!"

"Okay, I give up. Why won't I show my legs? Go ahead, tell me, tell everyone!"

"Because your whole body is covered with buzzard feathers, that's why!"

Everyone laughed and the guys started kidding Bernie about his buzzard feathers.

"Excuse me, Harriet. My name's David Brenner. I'd like to talk with you, but it's kind of loud in here with everyone yelling about the Buzzard, so let's go out on the front porch where we can . . ."

Yes, I got a new girl friend and Bernie got a new name—the Buzzard.


## EARNING EXTRA MONEY

WHENEVER AND HOWEVER WE could, we hustled to earn extra money even above and beyond our after-school jobs. We'd take out someone's trash cans, polish a car, babysit a kid, hold the leash of a shopper's dog, rake leaves, trim a hedge, cut a lawn, run some numbers or horse bets, pick up medicine at the drugstore, paint house numbers on the curb and side of houses, take in someone's dry laundry from the backyard, shine a doorknob. You name it and there was some kid to do it. The extra pennies, nickles, dimes, quarters, half dollars and dollars added up and bought some of our favorite things: a balsa wood model plane, a package of yo-yo string, a toilet chain to wear as a key chain, a real rabbit's foot, a real four leaf clover key chain, an Italian water ice, a roll of BBs, a string bag of marbles, bubble gum matching baseball cards, penny candy, or one of my favorites— a soft pretzel with mustard!

Beb and I were walking past Tony the shoemaker's when he came outside holding a brown paper bag. "Heya, one of yousa boysa taka dis shoes to disa lady at dis address I'ma giva you disa twenty-five cents."

Beb grabbed the bag, the note and the quarter. The woman lived about five blocks away.

"Man, this is a fast way to pick up a quarter, huh, David?"

"Sure is."

"Man, like all I gotta do is just drop off these shoes. I would've done it for a dime, wouldn't you?"

"Sure would."

"Why would Tony give me so much? I mean, you think the woman's in a big hurry or something?"

"For crying out loud, Beb, shut up already about the shoes! Just deliver them!"

"You're just P.O.'d because I grabbed the shoes before you did."

"Beb, the day I can't out hustle you on the street for money is the day I'll hand in my mouth."

Beb started to untie the string that was wrapped around the brown paper bag.

"What are you doing?"

"I want to see what's so special about these shoes that they're worth a quarter."

"Beb, that's private property."

"Shoes aren't private property, Brenner. They're just things you wear on your feet."

He opened the bag, reached inside and pulled out the shoes. They were black. One had a built-up heel and sole.

"Look at this, Dave. No wonder Tony gave me so much money.

He didn't want to take these himself, not after the way he screwed up this one shoe. Look at it. The sole must be four inches thick! The woman's going to kill him!"

"Beb, I don't believe you're that much of a putz. Tony didn't goof. These are shoes for a crippled person."

Beb screamed and threw the shoes into the street.

"What the hell you doing, Beb?"

"I'm not delivering no crippled shoes! Oh, God, I touched them!"

He started wiping his hands wildly on his pants legs.

"Beb! They're only shoes! You can't catch anything from a person's shoes!"

"Let's get out of here!"

"Beb, you got to deliver the lady's shoes."

"You deliver them!"

"No, you're the one who grabbed them out of Tony's hand real fast, so it's your job."

"I'll give you the quarter. Pleeeeease!"

"Fifty cents!"

"You bastard, Brenner! Thirty?"

"Forty-five or I tell Tony."

"Thirty-five is my top offer!"

"Forget it. Wait'll the guys hear about this!"

"Forty and you got to promise never to tell anyone!"

"Okay. Give me the forty."

I delivered the shoes and I didn't tell the guys. Until now. Now that I have, Beb, I owe you the nickle difference from your "top offer." The check is in the mail.


## BEB COULDN'T MAKE IT

HER NAME WAS BARBARA. She was sixteen and beautiful, long brown hair that fell down her back, dark eyes, full lips and lots of curves on a slim body. I picked her up on the Boardwalk in Atlantic City. I was fifteen lying that I was seventeen. She had a girl friend, Carol, not nearly as good looking, but Beb didn't care. We had dates and everyone would see that as we walked the boards, showing off. At that age, what else is important?

We had a wonderful Sunday night. We took Captain Starn's midnight boat ride in the Atlantic ocean and Barbara and I kissed hard, full and open the whole trip. At that age, three kisses could last two hours. When we got off the boat my lips were swollen. We walked the girls back to where they were staying with their parents, then went to the bus station for the first morning bus back to Philly. I told Barbara that we'd meet them next Friday night in front of the Chelsea Hotel at nine. I couldn't wait. Beb could. Seems he didn't get along that great with his date. She kissed with her mouth closed and wouldn't let him put his hand down her blouse, not even to the bra strap. I tried to persuade him that it would be better the next time, but he wouldn't go for it.

"I'm not going all the way to Atlantic City just to get a few Aunt Reba kisses."

"Look, Beb, I'll pay for both bus fares and half of everything we buy on the boards."

"No, man, she's zero city."

"I'm telling you, Beb, if you make the right moves you can score with her. I can tell."

"Forget it, Brenner, I ain't going. You go and make up an excuse for me."

"You're a real bastard, Beb! I'm always picking up girls for you or getting you dates and now that I've got a chance to get into one of the hottest numbers I've met in a long time you're going to beard me!"

"You can still go; just make an excuse for me."

"Like what?"

"I don't know. You're the fast talker. You'll think of something. Please."

"Okay, you bastard, but don't ever ask me to pick up a date for you again. From now on you're on your own."

"I knew you'd come through for old Bebby. Thanks, Brenner."

"Beb, I hope the next time you take a leak and shake it, it falls off."

I spent the following three weekends with beautiful Barbara, living out many of my youthful fantasies. I couldn't wait for the weekdays of work to pass so I could get to my beachside lover. Of course, I drove Beb crazy with stories of my summer escapades, feeding the blazing fires of his teenage horniness. I also made up stories about seeing his ex-date, Carol, making out passionately with some guys and what a hot number she was.

"Maybe I could sort of go to A.C. with you this weekend and like sort of maybe just meet, you know, maybe even, you know . . ."

"Beb, if you want to go down the shore with me, fine, but once we hit the boards, you're on your own. I'm not picking up a date for you, new or old, or spending any time with you, other than the bus ride home Monday morning. That's the deal, take it or leave it."

"All right, Brenner. It's a deal."

We hit the shore about eight Friday night and headed for the Chelsea Hotel on the boardwalk, where I was meeting Barbara. The boards were packed. Teenagers were all over the place. We said hello to guys and girls we knew as we made our way through the crowd. I spotted Barbara, even though her back was to me. I'd know that cute little ass in a fog. As always, there were several "older" guys talking to her, but in thirty seconds she'd be all mine.

"Look, Brenner, there she is. Carol! Wow, you're right. She does look like she puts out. I don't know how I missed noticing it when I took her out. I'm going to get laid, man! Great! Come on."

"Oh, no, man. I told you, Beb, you're on your own. Go pick her up yourself. I'm heading for Barbara. Ciao."

I started walking towards Barbara. Beb put on his cockiest walk and bounced along in Carol's direction. I stopped to watch. When he was about twenty feet from Carol, she looked up and saw him. He smiled and waved. She opened her eyes wide, her mouth dropped open, she pointed to him, both arms outstretched, let out a blood-curdling scream and fainted. Pandemonium broke out, girls screaming, people running, some trying to help the unconscious Carol. Beb came running over to me.

"What the hell excuse did you tell Carol?"

I smiled. "I told her you were killed in a car accident. See you on the bus Monday morning, Beb."

I sauntered up to my Barbara for another wonderful weekend in Atlantic City.

# CUTTING POTS

I'M NOT GOING TO use my friend's name in this because the only ones who should know about whom I'm talking are the guys from the corner.

We loved to play poker when I was a kid. We began at age nine playing for half-pennies and pennies. In our teens, the stakes got higher, but never enough to change it from being a friendly game. To avoid being arrested, we'd play inside someone's home. Most of the time we played in one particular friend's apartment, mainly because his parents would go to sleep early or stay in the "back." We'd play one or two games on old card tables in the living room. As customary, the host cut ten cents per pot. That is, after every hand was played, the winner gave him a dime. This was a good way to pick up some money with no risk.

All he had to do was supply the cards and some refreshments. It was with the latter that all the problems arose. We were always complaining to him about the refreshments, which always included stale pretzels and potato chips, since he always saved leftovers from the previous game. To wash it down, he'd put out a couple bottles of soda, and when they ran out, which they always did, he would give us tap water, no ice. We bitched and bitched about what a cheap bastard he was but nothing ever changed. His apartment was centrally located and we liked him a lot, so we never bothered to switch apartments.

I've been in touch with this friend all these years. The last time I saw him, I ribbed him about the lousy refreshments at the card games, as I periodically do. He laughed, as always, but then he got quiet for a moment before speaking.

"You know what I did with all that money I cut from the pots?"

I shook my head.

"I payed my father's medical bills."

I didn't say anything. I didn't have to.

I thought all you guys should know this.

86

# TIME FLIES

ONE OF THE ALL-TIME favorite pastimes among everyone in my neighborhood—even after the discovery of sex—was playing practical jokes. They were never intended to be cruel or humiliating, just fun—a release of the pressure valve. No one ever got mad—even, maybe, but never mad. One of my crowd's most ingenious jokes was pulled off in Atlantic City. It called for a combined effort and split-second timing.

One Saturday after work, I picked up some friends and we headed down to the seaside resort for the weekend. We got there around six-thirty in the evening. One guy checked into a hotel room and the rest of us sneaked in—the usual. There were Mutt, Linsey, Dee-Dee, Blaine, Joe Podolsky and I. After we unpacked and put away the few things we brought with us, someone suggested we "hit the boards and do some quail hunting" (take a walk on the boardwalk and try to pick up some girls). We were just starting to change into fresh clothes when Joe said he wasn't feeling too well and was going to sack out for a while. He got into bed and fell asleep. "Now here's my plan . . ."

One half hour later, Mutt screamed at the top of his lungs from under the covers next to Joe, whose eyes flickered open.

"Thank God, you're awake, Joe," I called out from under the covers in the next bed, "How you feeling?"

"Tired. Why?"

"Why?" remarked Dee-Dee as he came into the room from the bathroom, wet from his shower. "You sleep fifteen straight hours and you ask 'why'?"

"What are you talking . . ."

He was interrupted by Linsey staggering into the room, his hair all messed and his clothes completely disheveled.

"God," Linsey said as he flopped into a chair, "what a night! Girl liked to kill me! Scratched the shit out of my back. How about yours, Blaine? Bet she . . . Joe, how are you?"

"Fine . . . I . . ."

Linsey struggled up and put his hand on Joe's forehead.

"Fever's gone, thank God. Boy, you really had us worried there for a while."

"The doctor was right," Mutt added, swinging his legs out of the bed and stretching. "Wasn't easy getting those pills down your throat, Joe."

"What pills? What the hell are you guys talking about? We just got here."

"Now, Joe, you really were sick!" I said, getting out of bed and lighting a cigarette. "Really shouldn't light up first thing in the morning. They say that's the worst time to smoke."

"Come on, what time is it, really?"

"I don't know, Joe," answered Mutt. "Look at my watch. It's by the dresser on your side."

"Ten o'clock. Is this ten in the morning?"

"Of course. Look outside—it can't be ten at night."

I sat down on Joe's bed.

"Joe, do you remember last night when we got here, you said you weren't feeling so good? That you wanted to nap and we should come back for you? Well, we did and couldn't wake you up. We did everything. Linsey even poured some cold water on you. Not a lot. Only half a glass. You didn't budge. That's when we called the hotel doctor . . . and you're sure you don't remember any of this? You pulling our leg?"

"I don't remember anything! Honest!"

"Well, the doc came and said you had some kind of twenty-four- or seventy-two-hour virus and the best thing was to let you sleep it off which is what we did. Luckily, it must've been the twenty-four-hour one."

"I don't believe this. I mean if I slept so long, how come I'm still so damn tired?"

"The fever," suggested Dee-Dee.

Just then the door flew open and in bounced Blaine, wearing his bathing suit and carrying a blanket.

"The ocean wasn't that cold. You guys should've . . . Joe! How the hell are you? You look great."

"Fine, Blaine," Joe answered sadly.

"What do you say we all head for the beach?" Dee-Dee asked.

Linsey flopped down in the armchair by the window. "I'm too beat for the beach. What I need is food."

"Great idea," I agreed, "let's all go for breakfast. You up for it, Joe?"

"You know what else is funny? Here I haven't had anything to eat since those hot dogs we grabbed right before checking into the hotel last night and I'm full. I swear."

"Must be flu gas," I suggested, laughing. Everyone laughed. Good thing, because we were all holding it in and near the bursting point.

"Should we wear bathing suits?" Joe asked.

"No, we'll come back and change after breakfast."

"Yes, eggs!" Joe repeated to the waitress. "How many times I got to say it for you? I want eggs! Eggs! You know—those white things that fall out of chickens? And I also want bacon and home fries."

"And again, I'll tell you that we don't serve that *now*, sir."

"What do you mean—'now'? What do people usually eat at this time—hot roast beef and gravy?"

"Sir, it is half past . . ."

"Listen, miss," I interrupted, "this guy has been very ill. A bad flu. Doctor said he should eat lightly, so ask the cook to do us a special favor and make the eggs and stuff. Here's a dollar for you."

"Okay, thank you. Now what about the rest of you."

"Same thing. It was an epidemic."

The waitress shrugged her shoulders and left. Joe threw down his menu.

"What's happening? Eleven-thirty in the morning and they don't even give you a luncheon menu, let alone one for breakfast. A dinner menu! Is the world getting crazy, or what?"

Joe ate all his breakfast, complaining all the time about having to force it down. The rest of us sort of moved the food around our plates so it looked eaten. We left nice tips and went on the boards for a postbreakfast walk at eight at night.

"How come no one's on the beach? It's a beautiful day."

"Yeah, that is strange. Let me ask that cop over there."

I walked over to the cop, asked him what the boat was out in the ocean. He pointed to it. I nodded yes. He said he didn't know. I thanked him and left.

"Cop said there was a report of killer sharks."

"In Atlantic City?"

"Could be looking for kosher meat for a change. Well, should we keep walking?"

"Why not? Can't swim."

A man passed us carrying a portable radio, listening to a Phillies baseball game. Joe's ears perked up. He was an avid Phillies fan.

"Did you hear who hit the homer? I think—wait a minute. What the hell are the Phils doing playing at this time?"

Uh-oh!

"Ah . . . eh . . ."

"Oh, that's the makeup game for the rain-out with the Reds the last time they played."

"The Phils already made that one up last . . ."

"Look at the tits on that one!" I interrupted.

"Man, I'd love her to sneak up behind me, lay them over my eyes and say 'Guess who?' "

No greater distraction hath man than the mammary glands of a passing lass.

"Is it getting a little dark to you guys?"

"What are you talking about, Joe? Dark what?"

"Dark. Outside. The sky."

"At one in the afternoon? You sure you're all right, Joe?"

"No, I'm not all right! Would you be all right if you came down here to have a good time and spent most of it sleeping? Shit!"

I think it was Blaine who laughed first. Anyway we all cracked up.

"Sure. Laugh! To you bastards this is a joke! I sleep away my life, have to force food down my throat, can hardly stand let alone walk, and now my eyes are going bad on me and all you stupid jerk-offs can do is laugh! Well, go fuck yourselves!"

The more he yelled, the more we laughed. We were doubled up, holding each other from falling. People taking their evening walks stopped to stare at us. Joe continued ranting and raving, turning to the crowd.

"You see these guys, folks? They're supposed to be my friends! Been together since first grade! Friends? How'd you like friends who make fun of you 'cause you're sick? I'm real sick! Slept all night! Just woke up! Sick! Now my eyes are going on me! Everything's getting dark! I'm going blind and these idiots are hysterical! Darkness all around and . . . wait, a minute. How come the street lamps just went on? Why are the lights on?"

I don't know who the stranger was who yelled it, but it hit Joe like the Orient Express.

"Because it's nine o'clock at night! That's why the lights are on, you schmuck!"

Now I'm going to tell you the most unbelievable part of this story. We went back to the room to shower and get dressed for our first night on the boardwalk. Joe didn't go with us. He was sick. Really sick, and—this is the part you're not going to believe —he slept straight through until the next morning! I swear it's the truth! If you don't believe me, the next time you see Joe, or one of the other guys, ask him.


# JAY SEGAL

JAY SEGAL LOVED TO laugh and he had one of those contagious laughs. When he'd crack up, everyone would crack up. I always did my best to get him started. He was really tuned into my sense of humor, too.

While I was overseas in the army I received a letter from one of the girls in the neighborhood. She wrote me that Jay hadn't been feeling well for a while and finally went into the hospital, where they diagnosed him as having acute leukemia. The doctors gave him six months to two years to live. Jay didn't know what was wrong with him. All he knew was that he kept getting weaker and weaker. She wrote that everyone in the crowd knew what was going on but treated Jay the same as ever. Double dating, playing practical jokes on him, telling him off and maybe even punching him in the arm just like always, too.

One early summer evening, as thirty-odd friends stood on the street corner in front of Moe's Candy Store, which was a few doors down from where Jay lived, Jay came walking slowly down his front steps and up to the corner. Some of the guys and girls said hello, others nodded, some didn't do either. Normal. Jay stood listening to the conversations, milling among the small groups of friends laughing at the jokes. Normal.

Then, in a very quiet voice, he spoke. Everyone listened.

"I know what's wrong with me. I know how sick I am. I was just sitting in the house thinking that I'm only seventeen years old and that it may seem like a real bad break. But, I was also thinking about my life and that I've really done a lot in seventeen years. I've had a lot of laughs, too. And all of this was because of all of you. And I just wanted to come up to the corner and thank you."

He turned and slowly walked back to his house. No one on the corner said a word. A couple of hours later, Jay died. It was exactly six months to the day since the diagnosis.

The last time I had seen Jay was in Atlantic City. We were walking on the boardwalk. I was joking around and Jay was hysterical. He told me to stop making him laugh or he'd pee in his pants. He ran into the public bathroom, laughingly calling me a bastard, but he didn't make it. A strange way to remember someone—but a real good way, too.


## CARRYING IT TOO FAR

ONE DAY DURING A conversation at one of our poker games, Big Micky made the following statement while discussing his diminishing funds:

"I ain't got not much either."

That's verbatim and the reason I am so sure it is, is because I never let him forget those immortal words. Every chance I would get to use them, I would, as long as Big Micky was there, of course.

"I'm almost finished with my sandwich."

"Yeah, me too. I ain't got not much either."

"Hurry up, Bird, we're running out of time."

"Yeah, Bird, me too, I ain't got not much either."

Well, I don't have to tell you what a nudgy thing this got to be. I drove Big Micky crazy with it. One time too many and he punched me in the stomach. What a rotten sport.

One day when I was driving some of us to New York to have a blast of a time, I saw a sign reading THE GEORGE WASHINGTON MEMORIAL BRIDGE. A minute later, I commented,

"That's a pretty nothing bridge they named after George Washington."

Beb laughed. "You putz, that's just an overpass for pedestrians to get to the other side of the highway."

All the way to New York and then for an hour on the return trip, everytime we approached an overhead pedestrian walkway, Beb would announce: "We are now passing under the George Washington Memorial Bridge!" All right, it's funny once, twice, maybe five or six times, but forty, fifty times? I warned him to stop; I told him not to say it again. He did. I punched him in the stomach.

I can't stand it when someone carries a joke too far.

# NOT FUNNY

I GUESS IT'S REALLY a Philadelphia tradition. We *love* to dance! To this day, I go to discos. Well, when I was sixteen years old a gang of us, about ten couples, went to a nightclub in New Jersey that had a "hot" local dance band. The place was jumping and fast becoming the "in" place to go. The best dancers were showing up. I liked to consider myself one of them so I was anxious to compete. Showing off on a dance floor was a big status symbol.

We all sat at a table ringside to the dance floor. My date was a beautiful girl and one of the best dancers in West Philly. She loved to dance and people loved to watch her. Great body—great moves. The competition didn't look too tough—it was going to be a fantastic night. One of the guys came in with a date none of us had ever met before. She told a joke about a crippled guy trying to have sex with a girl. It was a very cruel joke. No one laughed but that didn't make the girl aware that we weren't amused by the tasteless story. I excused myself to go to the men's room, stood up and walked across the dance floor with one leg dragging behind me.

The girl finally got the point and felt badly all night. She couldn't even talk to me. Neither would my date, because we couldn't dance one dance or else the girl would've known I was faking my walk and might have lost her new found sensitivity to those less fortunate than she. To me, some things just aren't funny.


# THE BIRD FLIES AWAY

MORTY "THE BIRD" HOFFMAN came up to the corner and told us the news. He had joined the air force. A few of the guys had already been drafted or had joined the army or navy. We would really miss the little guy. I was shocked that he was accepted by the Air Force, the bird being only five feet tall.

"What are you going to be—a bomb?"

"Not funny, Brenner. With your nose, you could be a mine sweep."

It was tough to think of life on Sixtieth Street without the Bird for four years. A few of us got together and decided to throw a big going-away party for him. A big bash for the Bird! The biggest and best bash ever seen! Everyone chipped in. We had money for more food and booze than for any party ever given and plenty of cash left over to buy the Bird all kinds of going-away presents, like a genuine leather shaving kit, a matching suitcase, an electric razor, a gold-plated pen and pencil set, two gross of rubbers—all the stuff he would need.

The party was a huge success. I think every guy and girl in the neighborhood passed through the doors at one point of the night or other. About six in the morning, I stood by Stan the Dancer as he threw up all over Cedar Avenue. Then I took him home—or to a house that looked enough like his—and staggered back to my own house.

The Bird left. We were going to miss him but we gave him one hell of a send-off. Four years. Wow!

Six weeks later, a bunch of us were standing on the corner at Moe's when the Bird walked up.

"Hi you doin' guys?"

"Bird! What the hell you doing here?"

"What do you mean 'What am I doing here?'"

"You're supposed to be in the air force. You're not in any trouble are you?"

"No. I went in the air force and now I'm out. I went in on the six-week program. All I do now is summer camp and a few meetings every year, and then . . ."

"You little putz! Why the hell didn't you tell us you were only going for six weeks?"

"I wanted to see how everyone felt about me and I wanted the presents."

I think it was the only time that one person pulled off a practical joke on the entire neighborhood. I wished I had thought of it.

A few years later the Bird got married, and some of the neighborhood got together to avenge his going-away party scam. We'd had a great time at his wedding, acting crazy as we always did at such functions by stealing ashtrays and table lighters, tap dancing in a circle à la the Step Brothers, getting drunk, playing practical jokes—all the things that make men happy and wives pissed off. The Bird's wife, Marsha, was no different. She thought we were a bunch of wild animals.

During the next few months we heard from the Bird but hadn't seen him. A few of us were discussing this one night, so I gave the Bird a call and suggested that he invite his friends to his apartment Friday night. He held his hand over the mouthpiece of the phone and spoke to Marsha. I couldn't make out the words but I could tell he was pleading with her to change her mind.

"Listen, Dave, we'd love to have you guys over but we don't have any furniture and Marsha's a little embarrassed to have anyone over until the place looks nice."

"Tell her most of us spent our lives living without furniture."

"Yeah, well, that's the way she feels about it and I got to go along with her, you understand."

"How could I? I'm single."

"You know what I mean. As soon as the place is fixed up, we'll have . . ."

"Sure," I interrupted briskly. "Okay, keep in touch and say hello from all of us to Mrs. Bird."

I hung up and told the guys what he said. The consensus was that we should take some kind of action. I came up with a plan.

That Friday night, the Buzzard got himself invited over to the Birds. He was one of the closest to him and had been over the empty apartment several times. At exactly nine, he was to unlock the apartment door and then keep them occupied.

At eight-forty-five, about twenty of the guys with wives, fiancées and dates met half a block down from the Bird's apartment. Everyone was assigned to bring some sort of refreshment and a piece of furniture, any kind, but the more decrepit and uglier the better. Everyone showed up on time with everything from broken mirrors to two-legged dining room chairs. The worst stuff you ever saw—it would have made the Salvation Army in Peru throw up. The food was no better, ranging from chocolate-covered ants to pig knuckles.

With everything in hand, we stealthily maneuvered up the stairs to the Bird's apartment. At exactly five minutes past nine, we threw open the door and charged in! By the time the Bird and Marsha got to their feet, we were already hurrying around decorating the place, putting down the torn rugs, hanging the broken pictures of strangers of various ethnic backgrounds, putting the torn sheets on their bed, putting up the unmatched curtains, plugging in the smashed TV set. Some of the girls went into the kitchen and prepared the spread of food on the broken dishes we brought. Other guys set up the movie screen and projector to show the porno film Gene had made, intercutting stock footage of some of us.

We ate, talked, laughed, made long distance calls to Dee-Dee in Los Angeles and had one hell of a great time. Then we left.

It was many months before Marsha spoke to any of us. Now, we all laugh about it a lot! But you know, come to think of it, the Bird and Marsha have never invited me to see their new house. I wonder . . .

## PASSION PITS

ONE OF THE GREAT unsung heroes, especially to teenagers in America, is the man who thought up drive-in movie theaters. He put sex on wheels! When you asked a girl to go to the drive-in and she said "yes," you knew you were going to at least get heavy petting. No place, no where, no time was more fun than those wonderful "passion pits." During my teen years I must have gone to drive-ins more than a hundred times and can honestly and proudly say that I never saw one movie. Damn, we had fun!

Some drive-ins charged by the car, some charged by the number of persons. If it was the former, we would pack four couples in. You couldn't tell who was doing what to whom, but everyone was doing something to someone, so who cared? If it was the latter, we would hide people, sometimes on the roof, but most often in the trunk, which wasn't always the most pleasant experience.

"How many are you?"

"Just two, sir."

"Aren't you the same kid who was in here last week and a couple fell off your roof when you dug out?"

"No, sir." (LIE)

(MUFFLED FROM TRUNK) "Hurry, Dave! No air!"

"What'd you say?"

"Nothing, sir. May I have my ticket?"

(MUFFLED) "Dave, Lenore's goin' to throw up!"

"You sure you didn't just say something?"

"To tell you the truth I did. I'm a ventriloquist."

(MUFFLED) "God, Lenore, hold it in!"

"See. Pretty good, huh?"

"Not too clear but pretty good. Enjoy the show."

"Thank you . . ."

(MUFFLED) "You ass!"

"What'd you call me?"

"Only a joke, sir. Thanks again."

They had been going together for two years, since age fourteen. Beb and Lenore were in the front seat. I was in the back with my date, whom I had never taken out before.

"You know I really like these drive-in speakers. I'd like to have one."

"Oh, Barry, what would you do with it? I swear."

"I'd keep it attached to the window. That's what I'd do with it, Lenore. Do you mind?"

"Why should I mind? Do what you want."

"I want the speaker, that's what I want."

"Then take it!"

"How am I supposed to do that, Lenore?"

"How should I know?"

I had been making damn good progress with my date before all this bickering started and knew that I could get even farther if Beb and Lenore would keep quiet.

"Beb?"

"Yeah, Dave?"

"Just drive off with the speaker."

"Great idea! Now why couldn't you think of that, Lenore?"

"Go to hell, Barry."

"Go anywhere, Beb. Just stop arguing."

"Right, Dave."

Beb was always impatient about everything. He couldn't even wait for the end of the movie to get his speaker. He kicked over the motor, gunned it and "dug out, leaving rubber," and his window was ripped out by the speaker as we drove off.

I didn't "go all the way," but Beb did—he is still married to Lenore.

Again I was in the backseat. Again I was making all the moves. It was going to be a triumphant charge over the finish line! Dee-Dee and his date were in the front seat of my car. At first they were watching the movie, but then they started getting into it, too. Dee-Dee was always a klutz. His toe turned on the overhead light of the car and it took him five minutes to find it and shut it off. I had to start over again. Then he hit the horn with his foot. A slight setback. Another horn blast. Another setback. Then his foot got stuck in the horn and it was blasting and he couldn't get his foot out. Other cars started blowing their horns. Lights were shining into our car from annoyed neighbors. I had to climb over the seat and wrestle Dee-Dee's foot free. That was the end of that night!

The following weekend Dee-Dee took Corky to the Baltimore Avenue Drive-In. They were giving away an old car worth maybe five hundred dollars that night as a door prize. This was the first time Dee-Dee and Corky had gone out, so, to impress her, he handed her his ticket.

"Here, Corky, you can have my ticket, too."
"Suppose your number comes out?"
"Then you won a car."
"You mean it?"
"Sure."
"Thanks."
"Forget it."

It really worked. Corky was impressed. She also won the car. Dee-Dee couldn't "forget it." One weekend a "klutz" and the next weekend a "putz." I loved it!

There should be a monument built somewhere to the man who came up with the drive-in theater, and whatever shape it's in, it should definitely have a backseat.

## A MORNING QUIP

I USED TO SLEEP in the prenatal position, knees bent up to my chin, until I read a psychologist's claim that it was a sign of insecurity. I began sleeping with my legs straight. One morning, however, I was curled up in my bed, and a lady who had spent the night with me but had gotten up to go to work leaned over and whispered in my ear,

"David, it's time to be born."

I awoke laughing.

# THE GOLD RUSH

BOB "MOOSE" CARUSO LAID the parchment map on the table next to the open page of the *World Atlas.*

"See, it's the exact same mountain range! The gold is buried right here in Pennsylvania!"

"Come on, Moose. Gold in Pennsylvania? Forget it."

"Okay," he said as he gathered his map and book, "Cjedeski and I will climb the mountain ourselves and keep all the gold. You can go on rotting in the neighborhood."

"Moose, don't get pissed off. Give me time to think about it."

"We don't have time. I've got next week off and that's when I have to go. We start Monday. We're shopping for supplies tomorrow. If you decide to go, call me tonight. Don't say anything to my wife. Rita thinks we're just going hiking and camping."

Hiking, camping, mountain climbing. These are not for Jews. Shoveling, picking and sledge hammering aren't either. But, gold is! The next day I went shopping with them for supplies. Since I still had a lot of equipment left over from the army, Moose put me in charge of food supplies. I bought twenty-one breakfasts, lunches and dinners. At first, the Moose wanted to "live off the land." I told him that he could boil roots and suck flowers, but I was buying camp meals. Reluctantly, he agreed.

We left the Moose's Volkswagen camouflaged in the woods and set up a campsite at the base of the mountain. Then, with enough supplies for seven days, we set out climbing. At sunset, we had started a fire for cooking dinner and stretched out our sleeping bags inside small pup tents when I discovered my first mistake. I hadn't looked closely at the sleeping bag in the store. It was one of the few on sale, and I had little money, so I bought it. Now I had to figure out how to squeeze six feet two inches of person into four feet of a child's sleeping bag. The pictures in the lining of Mickey Mouse, Donald Duck and Goofy, I could learn to sleep with.

Cjedeski had been a short-order cook so he became our mess sergeant. I handed him three hamburger dinners. I was sitting by the fire reading a book when I heard Cjedeski yell:

"Where's the rest of it, Brenner?"

"The rest of what?"

"The food."

"It's all there. I handed it to you."

He and the Moose walked over. They didn't look too happy. Moose handed me one of the dinner boxes.

"This is all you bought?"

"What 'all'? Look at the picture on the box. You get a hamburger with gravy, mashed potatoes, carrots and peas—ah—it looks like a corn muffin with butter, a piece of chocolate cake and a glass of milk. What more do you want—the cow?"

"You idiot!"

"Brenner, they're only showing you what you can do with the hamburger patty that's inside the box! The rest of this stuff isn't in this little package!"

"Well, I'd say we got a pretty good case of false advertising on our hands."

"I'd say we've got a good case of starvation on our hands!"

"Well, fellas, if the false advertising is also true of the other meals, I'd say we have seven servings of scrambled eggs *without* the toast, butter, corn flakes, home fries and coffee, and seven slices of roast beef *without* the french fries, peas, rye bread, butter, hot chocolate and vanilla ice cream."

"Jesus! How dumb can you be?"

"Come on, Cjedeski, look at the bright side. You won't have to spend so much time in the kitchen now, and, if worse comes to worse, we can send out."

"Send out where? We're going up a mountain, you idiot!"

"You'd be surprised the places where I've found Chinese take-out restaurants. Once driving through Georgia . . ."

"I don't want to hear any of your Chinese take-out restaurant stories, Brenner! I don't want to hear anything from you!"

Cjedeski stormed away.

"Please make my hamburger medium rare, Cjedeski."

Only Moose spoke to me after that. On the second night, it poured. I was soaking wet. Cjedeski's tent got torn by the high winds, so he was really in a foul mood. As we were climbing on the third day I noticed that Moose was making $X$ marks in every fifth or sixth tree trunk.

"What are you doing that for, Moose?"

"Obviously, so we can find our way back."

"Could I ask one little simple question?"

"Don't be a pain in the ass, Brenner!"

"One."

100

"Okay, what is it?"

"Well, I'm not a big outdoorsman like you and Chef Cjedeski over there, so I'm pretty dumb when it comes to all these clever mountain-climbing and camping-out tricks and techniques you guys use. So, I . . ."

"Will you get to the fuckin' point, Brenner!"

"Calm down, Cjedeski. Your nerves are really getting shot. Maybe it's that high protein diet you're on."

"You son-of-a-bitch, I'm going to . . ."

The Moose stopped him from finishing his attack by getting him in a bear hug.

"Brenner, you're pushing him too far."

"Okay, I'm sorry, Cjedeski. I really like you and want to go to summer camp with you again next year, too, so let's shake hands and make up."

We did.

"As I was saying before schmuck-face interrupted me—only kidding, Cjedeski. Anyway, if these markings on the trees are to help us in finding our way back down, how come you're making them on the side of the tree which is facing us now, but won't be facing us as we come down? That's it. Finished."

The Moose didn't say a word. He just stared at the last *X* he made. Cjedeski threw his shovel down.

"I don't believe it! I'm with *two* fuckin' idiots!"

"I bet you say that to everyone you know. It's okay, Moose. I won't tell Rita."

It rained again all that afternoon and night. We were soaking wet. We were also hungry. I couldn't complain about that, as you can understand. Our bodies were getting thin and our tempers thinner. In the early morning of the fourth day, we reached the large, flat summit of the mountain. It was shrouded in fog. We stood side by side, hardly able to see one another.

"This is the top," whispered Moose. "The gold is buried here."

"Why are you whispering?"

"I don't know, but you just did it, too."

"I did it because I don't want to wake up the owner of the Chinese take-out place over there . . . see, you looked, Cjedeski!"

"Brenner, you're a sick fuck!"

"Now we're all whispering."

I let out a wild scream. Moose and Cjedeski both jumped out

of their pants. It was then that we heard it. A rumbling sound, like cattle on the move. Moose and Cjedeski took their rifles off their shoulders and cocked the bolts. We listened as the rumbling got louder, then it decreased in volume until it eventually faded away. The fog began disappearing quickly, and as it rose we saw them. Deer. Beautiful deer. Maybe thirty-five of them. They disappeared into a wooded area. I looked down at our feet.

"Well, if deer shit is worth money, we're millionaires!"

"Damn, I thought the ground felt kind of soft!"

"Okay, let's see the map."

The Moose took the map out of his backpack and we looked at it and then at the area. Nothing matched.

"What the hell is this, Moose? Where's the gold?"

"We'll have to dig."

"Dig? Where? It'll take us ten years with bulldozers to dig up this whole area!"

"Moose, where did you get this map?"

"I told you, David. In a bookstore downtown."

"What did it cost you?"

"Three dollars."

Cjedeski cracked. "Three dollars? You think some guy would sell you a gold mine map for three dollars? You stupid son-of-a-bitch, I'm going to . . ."

This time I grabbed Cjedeski in a bear hug and saved the Moose. When he had calmed down, I let him go. The three of us sat on our backpacks not talking for a while. Finally, I broke the ice.

"How about some eggs *with* roast beef for a change. Take it easy, only kidding. Well, I think we should head down. We could make it by sunset if we follow the pipe."

"What pipe?"

"There's a pipe over there that . . ."

"Come on, Moose, you going to listen to him and his pipe? I'll lead you guys down. Follow me."

"Wait a minute, Cjedeski, I think . . ."

"David, I've had enough of your thinking. The way down is the way the deer went. You coming or not?"

"Not. I'm going my way. Moose, who you following—the great Polish Pathfinder, Cjedeski, or the lineal descendent of Moses who led his people out of Egypt?"

"Took him forty years, too!"

"His guide was from Warsaw."

"See you guys down there."

"Wait, Cjedeski, I'm going with you. Come on, David."

"No, you go, Moose. I'm going to smoke a cigarette. I'll meet you at the campsite."

Cjedeski threw me the pack containing the food.

"Here, Brenner, you'll probably need all of these."

They left. I smoked my cigarette and then followed the pipe. It was a water pipe and I knew it had to be the easiest way down the mountain, simply because whoever had laid the pipe would have naturally selected the easiest way. I was at the campsite before sunset.

The following afternoon, Moose and Cjedeski staggered in. They got down the mountain before sunset, too, but then they had to climb up and go down the next mountain before coming to a highway where they hitched a ride in a chicken truck. They looked and smelled terrible. I offered to sell each of them a bite of my McDonald's cheeseburger, but they both just flopped down on the grass without saying anything, so I finished it myself.

That was our last camping and mountain climbing trip together. Matter of fact, it was *my* last camping and mountain climbing trip—period!


## THE BIRTHDAY SUIT

FOR THE MOOSE'S BIRTHDAY, his wife, Rita, had given him a couple hundred dollars to buy himself a suit. The Moose wasn't the least bit interested in clothes, but he did need "one good suit." Since his taste was horrendous and his wife didn't want to put up with his complaining, she asked me to go shopping with him to help him pick out his birthday present. I gladly accepted the invitation.

We went to a fine men's store on Chestnut Street in Center City. A salesman joined us right away. The Moose was already impatient and grabbed a suit off the rack.

"I'm going to try this."

I knew he just wanted to buy a suit real fast and get out of there. I had a responsibility to Rita to see that he got a fine-looking suit. I turned to the salesman, talking quietly.

"He's my brother. Mother always sends me with him. He's not all there, you know what I mean? Wacko! Don't get nervous. He's quite harmless. So, whatever I do, you'll understand it's because I know how to handle him, and I'd appreciate it if you would inform all the other employees so they're not alarmed by anything that might happen. Thank you."

The salesman scurried off and I could see him whispering in everyone's ear, pointing my way. The word spread throughout the store. The salesman returned.

"All taken care of, sir."

"Thank you for your kindness and understanding."

Just then, Moose came out of the dressing room and walked toward us wearing the ugly brown suit.

"What do you think? I like it. I'll take . . ."

"Get that off right now," I screamed at the top of my lungs, "before I rip it off you!"

The Moose stared at me. He had never heard me scream, let alone at him.

"What's wrong with you, David, are you . . ."

"What's wrong with me?" I continued screaming, "What's wrong with me? Look at yourself! Go ahead, look in the mirror! Now!"

"Calm down."

The Moose looked in the mirror, admiring the suit. I rushed up to him, grabbed the jacket by the back collar and pulled it down so his arms were trapped, as if in a straightjacket.

"There! Does that bring back memories? Get the point? The suit is crazy looking! You know 'crazy', I'm sure."

The Moose is a patient man, up to a point. I had passed his point.

"David, get me out of this, before I kill you!"

I turned to the salesman, who looked scared. Others were watching apprehensively.

"He's only saying that. Don't worry," I called out to everyone.

"Moose, I'll help you out of that, but I want you to try on this blue suit I picked out for you, it's more like mother would want."

"What mother? What the hell you talking about?"

I pulled his suitcoat up, freeing his arm movement again and slammed the blue suit into his chest.

"Put this on and do it quickly or no peanut butter sandwich tonight!"

"Jesus, what the hell's wrong with you?"

The Moose stormed away and went into the dressing room. I turned to the salesmen who had witnessed the whole scene and called out, loud enough for them to hear, but not loud enough for the Moose,

"Everything's okay. Doesn't remember his own mother. Loves peanut butter. Keeps him out of the institution. Thank God for Skippy."

I saw one salesman cross himself. The Moose walked out. The blue suit was way too small.

"Off! Off! Off! Right away! Go! Go! Don't even come a step closer!"

The Moose was livid. He pivoted and headed away. In his anger he made a slight mistake. Instead of going through the dressing room door, he opened the door leading outside to the loading dock. He was so angry that he didn't even notice and took off his pants. It was at this moment, standing there in a shirt, suit jacket, knee-high gym socks and jogging sneakers that he realized what he had done. There were several truckers unloading shipping crates of clothing and pedestrians walking through the wide alleyway. Everyone was just staring at this Sicilian giant standing there with no pants on.

The Moose was so cool. He reached into his shirt pocket, took out his cigarettes and lighter, lit a cigarette and calmly smoked it, suit pants over one arm and eyes looking with feigned interest at the sights in the far-off distance.

I guess you can figure out that the Moose left the store after finishing his cigarette. I tried to get him to try on another suit, but he just looked at me like I was crazy and walked out. As I followed him several salesmen passed their condolences on to me. I nodded my deep gratitude.

As you can also guess, the Moose was not in the mood for any more clothes shopping that day. He did, however, buy something else with his wife's birthday money—a hunting rifle! He stuffed it into one pant leg and walked stiff legged into his apartment, telling her that he'd pulled a ligament. It took him nearly a month to confess to what he did. Rita was as understanding as the fox is in the hunt.

# FIRST TIME IN L.A.

AFTER A VERY SUCCESSFUL year and a half as a television writer/producer/film director, I decided it was time to make the move to Los Angeles. My plan, regardless of career choice, was to live in L.A. and Chicago before settling down in Manhattan. I took two weeks off from work and made my first trip West. I was going to stay with Dee-Dee, who was now living in La Ventura. He picked me up at the airport. I was in my heavy winter topcoat and he was in his short-sleeved Hawaiian shirt. It was great seeing him.

As we left the airport I asked him the typical first-time-in-L.A.-tourist question: "What stars have you seen?"

"No one."

"You've been in Hollywood three and a half years and you've seen no one? You're kidding."

"Well, Mim and I aren't exactly on the stars' party list. 'Say, Duke, call Eddie and Mim Romoff and see if they can make it Saturday night! Ask them if they'll pick up the Gregory Pecks on their way over.'"

We drove for about ten minutes, catching up on the news from back home. We stopped for a light.

"Dee-Dee, don't look now, but in the white Rolls Royce next to you is Rex Harrison and his wife."

Naturally, Dee-Dee looked right away.

"I don't believe it! I'm here all these years and see no one and within fifteen minutes you see Rex Harrison! Wait'll I tell Mim!"

To explain what happened next, I have to take you back to the neighborhood and two seven-year-old boys named Dee-Dee and David who were already becoming best friends. Both were poor but Dee-Dee was poorer. Once when David knocked on the door to pick up his friend, his leg went through the rotten wood of the porch and ended up dangling in the cellar. When Dee-Dee's mother opened the door, a midget David asked if her son could come out to play. She laughed and from that day called him "meshuga," or "crazy."

From when they first met right up until the time Dee-Dee moved to California, David used to tease Dee-Dee about how much poorer he was in one particular way. It always went something like this:

"So, Dee-Dee, how much money you got on you?"

"Leave me alone, David."

"I'm not trying to bug you. I'm just curious."

"Forget it."

"Okay, but I'll bet you I got more than you."

"I'm not interested."

"Probably way more."

"Who cares?"

"Even though someone just got paid last night."

"Okay, you nudge, here's what I got!"

"Let's see . . . wow . . . forty cents . . . sixty . . . a dollar fifteen. Wow!"

"Okay, now let's see yours!"

"What's the difference who has more? Forget it."

"Oh, no! I showed you mine. Let's see it!"

"This is really stupid. Let's go . . ."

"Show me your money!"

"Okay, okay. Calm down. Jesus. Here. Two fifty. Got you again. You'll always be poorer!"

And so it went like that all through our youth and into adulthood. I always beat him, sometimes by only a few pennies, but I beat him.

Dee-Dee turned the car onto one of the freeways. We went from reminiscing to talking about the present, our families, our jobs, our lives.

"So, David, you're doing pretty good for yourself, financially, I mean."

"It's a beginning, but I'm still after my dreams."

"Still want to be rich, huh?"

"I told you when you got me my first job working for Sobel the butcher when I was nine years old that I was going to make the big bucks someday. I still mean it, Dee-Dee."

"I wish you luck, too. You know that. But for right now, you're bringing home a nice dollar, right?"

"Yeah, but why all this talk about money?"

"Nothing. I just want to know you're all right."

"I'm all right. Thanks, Dee-Dee. So what kind of house you . . ."

"I mean, if you're not all right, if you need a few bucks, well, you know what I mean."

"You trying to tell me that I can borrow money from *you*?"

"Yeah. Why do you say it that way—'from *you?*'"

"No reason, Dee-Dee, except, I appreciate your offer and all, but you know since we were kids that I . . . forget it."

"No, what were you going to say?"

"Nothing. Just something stupid from the past. So how's Mim and the baby?"

"Fine, thanks. What stupid thing?"

"Come on, Dee-Dee, forget it. I was just thinking of that dumb thing we used to do about who had more money on him. Stupid kid's stuff. Anyway, are you . . ."

"Why, you think you still have more than I have?"

"Of course, but let's not go into that now. So, how . . ."

"No, let's get into it! Go ahead ask me, David!"

"Ask you what?"

"How much I got on me."

"God, you still talking about that?"

"Ask me!"

"All right, take it easy. How much you got on you? Happy?"

"I'll show you!"

Dee-Dee swerved his car off the road onto the service lane and screeched to a stop. He reached in his pocket, took out his wallet, whipped it open and pulled out a bundle of one-hundred-dollar bills.

"Twenty-seven hundred and fifty-five dollars! I took every dime I own out of the bank this morning just so I could beat you once in my life! And I did it!"

When he got done laughing hysterically and slapping me on the back, we got back on the freeway. Dee-Dee began telling me about his son. I didn't say anything. After a couple of minutes, I casually slipped my hand into the inside pocket of my sportcoat, removed a thick bundle of one-hundred-dollar bills and gently laid them on the dashboard in front of Dee-Dee's face. I spoke in a soft, slow whisper.

"Three thousand . . . two hundred . . . and eighty . . . five . . . dollars. I, too, took everything out of the bank. I figured you'd try to pull off a fastie."

"You bastard!"

Dee-Dee started throwing fake punches and I started to slap his head. We almost got killed swerving in and out of traffic, but we would've died laughing first.

\* \* \*

108

On his way to work, Dee-Dee would drop me off in Hollywood at my first interview appointment and then I would just take buses or hitch rides for the rest of the day. After spending a few days at his house, I moved into a hotel and rented a car, but for the first few days I wanted to be with my friends and have time to learn the freeways and streets. The way we would work the pickup at the end of the day was that I would call his wife and tell her where I was, then Dee-Dee would call and find out where to pick me up after work.

At the end of my first day of interviewing, I was standing outside ABC studios when I saw Dee-Dee drive up real fast. I could tell he was happily excited. I got in the car and we took off.

"What's up?"

"You'll never guess what happened to me today. I had some appointments late today so I stopped at a phone booth to call Mim to find out where to pick you up, right? Well, there's some guy in the booth. He's talking and talking, and it's not like back east where you got a phone booth on every corner. Out here it's every few miles, and I'm not sure where there's another one so I just stand there. Finally, the guy finishes and steps out of the booth and says to me, 'Sorry I kept you waiting'. Now guess who it was . . . Rex Harrison! Isn't that unbelievable?"

"That's nothing!" I laughed. "Can you imagine when he goes home tonight, he'll say to his wife, 'You'll never guess what, darling. I saw Dee-Dee Romoff for the second time in two days!' "

We shared the same kind of belly laughs we used to enjoy back in the old neighborhood.

When I knew I was going to L.A., I asked my brother if he wanted me to bring him back anything from the land of our father's dreams, and he replied, "Some Pacific Ocean water so I can keep it on my desk and in the gloom of winter or whatever I can escape to exotic lands." Moby Dick was always such a romantic. And why not?

I had my most important interview the last day I was staying at Dee-Dee's. Twentieth Century-Fox was thinking of setting up a documentary film department. My first interview with the man who was to be in charge had gone very well and he wanted me to come back and meet with some of his superiors.

The day started off disastrously. While brushing my teeth I smelled smoke. I checked my cigarette and it was out. While shaving, the smoke got stronger, so I opened the bathroom door and asked Mim and Dee-Dee if they smelled it. They said no, so I continued shaving. I removed my suit jacket from the hanger it was on above the towel rack and put it on. Well, put it half on, because that's all that was left of it. Only the front half. The back half had burned away, melted, actually, from being hung in front of a California electric wall heater. We never had those in Philly. Luckily, I had brought one other suit with me, so amid the hysterical laughter of my friends, I changed.

Dee-Dee graciously took the scenic Pacific Coast Highway into Los Angeles. As we drove along the beach I remembered my brother's request and asked him to help me. We bought a small bottle of Vitalis hair tonic in a drugstore and then parked at the beach. I took off my shoes and socks and carefully rolled my suit pants up to my knees. I told Dee-Dee to keep an eye on me and waded into the surf. I emptied the hair tonic into the water, which took forever because of the small opening. It would take forever to fill, too. It was my mistake for not checking the bottle, but what's the difference? It was a beautiful, sunny day; I was in California; I had an important interview; I'm doing something for my older brother; one of my best friends is with me—what more can anyone ask of . . . I didn't see it, I heard it! Roaring! The familiar sound of a wave cresting, about to crash. I looked up in time to see the wall of water a minisecond before it covered me. Standing waist deep in the ocean, I turned to see my friend Dee-Dee staring at a bikini-clad girl lying on her blanket. I was about to scream at him, but what good would that do? I just waded farther out into the ocean until the water was up to my chest and held my little Vitalis bottle under until it was filled. Then I casually walked out of the ocean, got into Dee-Dee's car and went to my interview.

No, I didn't get the job! But my brother loved his gift from California.

## WYNN OR LOSE

ONE OF MY BEST friends is Wynn Katz. He didn't grow up with me. Matter of fact, we met only five years ago. But, as my old street corner friends said about him when we were all together at my parents' surprise sixtieth wedding anniversary party—"He could've been one of us!" He really could've. This is to his credit, because he grew up in an upper-middle-class family and has money from his family business. Somehow, though, his soul grew up in the streets. So, as with the friends I grew up with and anyone else I love, I play practical jokes on Wynn. Wynn and I also share a lot of laughs as results of bets. We don't bet money, usually—we bet "humiliation."

The very first bet was while we were going to sailing school together on Captiva and Sanibel Islands off the west coast of Florida. Wynn lost the bet and the consequence was so humiliating, he made me promise that I'd never tell anyone what it was and I haven't. However, I didn't promise not to write about it, so here's what happened: Wynn and I were sharing a beach house on Sanibel and I bet Wynn . . . I only did this so he'd shit in his pants reading it here in this book. I can't tell you what it was. A promise is a promise. But I'll tell you about some of the others which are damn good. First, some practical jokes.

Wynn's real name is Irwin, Irwin Katz. One of the great bad names of all time. Matter of fact, it was because of his name that I didn't want to meet him. Someone wanted to introduce us.

"Irwin Katz?" I said. "You got to be kidding. What could I ever have in common with a guy named Irwin Katz and a business executive on top of that? Forget it!"

Come on, what kind of person does the name Irwin Katz conjure up for you? A short, fat guy who is bald or balding, wearing a three-piece gray plaid suit, a Cartier tank watch alongside a thin gold bracelet, a wide gold bracelet on the other wrist, cordovan shoes with thick soles, Canoe aftershave, a sapphire ring on a pudgy pinky, neck creases, sweat beads on the brow, white boxer shorts either plain or ones with red hearts, hairy chest, pot belly, spindly legs, a duck walk and lots and lots and lots of Yiddish expressions. Right? I thought so, too.

Couldn't be further from the truth. Wynn is short but that is where the comparison ends. He's handsome, muscular, well dressed and hip. He, too, hated his name and was aware of the image it created in people's minds, so one of the first things we set out to do was get him a new name. There isn't too much that goes with Katz, but we kept trying. Finally, his mother suggested Wynn. Perfect! Why didn't she think of that thirty-five years ago?

Wynn loved his new name. You could see his eyes light up whenever he was introduced to someone as Wynn or whenever someone addressed him by his new name. The ladies also took to it. He was always getting compliments from all his dates about his name. Well, it wasn't too long before he was acting like a Wynn all the time, instead of an Irwin, until he really became Wynn Katz. This love of the new name gave me fertile soil for planting a practical joke.

It began at the Tavern on the Green restaurant in Manhattan's Central Park. The Crystal Room, named after the magnificent crystal chandeliers which hang from the ceiling, seats about a hundred and twenty people. We were on a double date having a great time. After dinner, about twelve waiters gathered around our table carrying a large cake with candles and sang.

> Happy Birthday to you.
> Happy Birthday to you.
> Happy Birthday, dear, *Irving.*
> Happy Birthday to you.

The diners joined in the applause.

"Thank you, but it's not my birthday and my name is not Irving. My name is . . ."

"IrVING," I interrupted. "The accent is on the VING. Ir-VING!"

"Oh, I'm sorry, IrVING. May I get anyone coffee or something? How about you, IrVING?"

For the rest of the night, the waiters, maitre d's, customers and I called him IrVING. It didn't end there. Every time we've gone to the Tavern on the Green, which must be a dozen times, at least, I've arranged for another birthday celebration for my friend IrVING. As soon as he walks in now, all the employees greet him as IrVING, which means he must tell the whole story to his new date, in order to explain the name.

When Wynn was going to Los Angeles and mentioned that he was going to have dinner with a mutual friend, I had a birthday cake and song arranged for IrVING, just so he wouldn't be too homesick.

One of the birthdays was the final stroke of a great practical joke. I'd loved to take credit for it, but its conception belongs to Charisse Brody, a beautiful lady with a beautiful sense of humor. I only helped with some of the execution. Wynn owns, or rather owned, several sailing hats which he kept on his sailboat in Connecticut. Throughout the summer, I slowly boiled his hat collection down to a total of one, kindly taking a couple apart so they'd dry faster in small pieces, sinking one with rocks when Wynn did something to disgrace the title of captain, using one for practicing "man overboard," hoisting one up with the mainsail, etc. The survivor was his favorite hat. He had purchased it in Japan and it looked the best on him. I respected that—so did Charisse, but she took advantage of it.

I couldn't make the sailing one day, but Charisse and her girl friend went. While Wynn prepared some refreshments below Charisse was at the helm. She was wearing Wynn's favorite hat. As Wynn was making his climb up the ladder to come on deck Charisse screamed and looked behind at the dark waters of Long Island Sound.

"What's the matter?"

"Oh, Wynn, I feel terrible. It just blew off my head. I . . . ."

"My hat? My favorite hat?"

"There it is!" called out the other girl. Wynn ran to the stern and searched the waters.

"I don't see it!"

"There! There!" yelled Charisse.

"Where? Where?" yelled Wynn.

"I'm 'coming about'," replied Charisse. "Ready to come about!"

Wynn helped with the maneuver and the boat turned heading in the direction of where the hat was last seen. He ran below, got his binoculars, charged back on deck, ran to the bow and searched the waters.

"Do you still see it?" he cried.

"No," screamed Charisse, "so let's come about again. Ready to come about."

Again Wynn charged back to help with the maneuver. As soon as the boat settled into her new direction, Charisse called out, "I think I see it over there. Ready to come about!" Wynn pulled the sheets and they turned again.

"I'm wrong. Sorry, Wynn. It's a lobster pot. Ready to come about!"

Again the exhausted Wynn made the maneuver.

"It's gone, Wynn. I'm really sorry. I'll buy you a new one."

"You can't, Charisse. I got it in Japan. It's one of a kind."

Wynn plopped down on the deck, looking dejectedly into the

water as if hoping the hat would float by.

"Maybe they have them in Chinatown."

"Come on, Charisse, the Chinese aren't the same as the Japanese. Forget it. Thanks anyway."

"I really feel badly. How about a cowboy hat? You'd look good in it."

"Charisse, people don't wear cowboy hats when they go sailing. Just forget it."

"Baseball caps are cute, Wynn."

"Very."

"1950s porkpies are real macho. White painter's cap? How about those floppy golf hats or an Israeli Kibbutz cap, or . . ."

That night a broken-hearted Wynn told me about how his favorite sailing cap was lost at sea, gone forever and irreplaceable. He was really crushed. For some reason, this cap was like family to Wynn. I consoled him.

That night, Charisse told me how she slipped the cap into the back of her T-shirt and about her plan for returning it. It was ingenious and I volunteered to help, of course.

A couple of weeks later, Wynn, Charisse, my manager, Steve Reidman, and I went to Joanna's restaurant in downtown Manhattan. Slowly I maneuvered the conversation into boats and mentioned to Wynn that I had just received my new boat supply catalogue and all the great things that were in it, "including beautiful spinnaker sails, improved self-tailing winches, great rain gear, sailing caps, deck shoes, French . . ."

"Don't mention sailing caps, if you don't mind," lamented Wynn.

"Still miss it, huh?"

Wynn nodded sadly.

"Missing what?" inquired Steve as I knew he would.

"My favorite sailing cap, I lost . . ."

"It was my fault," confessed Charisse sadly. "It blew off my head and sunk to the bottom of Long Island Sound. It was terrible."

In the mirror against the far wall behind Wynn, I signaled the waiter by nodding my head. He approached our table.

"Tell Steve what it looked like."

"Oh, it was a blue cap with special trim on the beak. It was very much like a street cap, but unique because of the leather . . ."

"May I take your drink orders?" interrupted the waiter.

Wynn looked up. "How about some wine, everyone? A bottle of Pouilly Fuissé."

"I'll have a Virgin Mary," I said as Wynn continued to describe his hat to Steve.

"It had this great leather band inside, but what really made it special was the way it fit me. It was so . . ."

"Excuse me, sir, did you want the wine now or with dinner?"

"Now, thank you," Wynn replied, looking at the waiter. Then Wynn's eyes opened wide, his mouth fell open. He screamed, "My hat!" and leaped to his feet pointing at the blue cap on the waiter's head. As he got up his chair fell and knocked over a bucket of champagne at the table behind us. The whole restaurant was looking.

"What the hell's wrong with you, Wynn?" I asked with fake embarrassment.

"That's my sailing cap! Where'd you find that?"

"I bought it, sir, in a store at Eighty-second and Columbus. Matter of fact, my father-in-law sails in San Francisco so I sent him a couple. They're only twelve dollars."

"Unique, huh, Wynn? Do they have any more of those *twelve dollar* caps?" I asked the waiter.

"Lots of them."

"Impossible!"

"Wynn, sit down. You've caused enough of a scene already. Waiter, please send that table a bucket of champagne and put it on our bill. Sorry, folks! Let's forget your damn *common* cap, Wynn. I can't believe how badly you made Charisse feel about losing one of the four hundred caps you can buy at Eighty-second and Columbus. Let's eat."

Wynn sat down but kept staring at the waiter and the cap.

"Could I see it?" Wynn asked the waiter and when he got it, he looked inside.

"No, it's not mine. Mine had Japanese writing on the label and . . . wait here it is! This is mine!"

"Come on, Wynn, buy it from the waiter for twenty dollars, and . . ."

"Oh, no! You and Charisse did this. Now, waiter, I'm going to give you seventy-five dollars to tell me the truth. Here it is. Seventy-five dollars. Now . . ."

"Take back fifty-five and buy the cap."

"David, you tell the waiter that he should tell me the truth."

I looked at the waiter. "You can tell him the truth."

"Now, tell me the truth. Where did you get this cap?"

The waiter looked at Wynn.

"Eighty-second and Columbus."

Before Wynn could close his gaping mouth, the waiter swooped the cap out of his hand, along with the seventy-five dollars and walked away. Good thing Charisse had told the waiter that he was to stick to his story of where he bought it, no matter what was said or done, and I reinforced it by giving the waiter fifty dollars.

We ate dinner. Well, Charisse, Steve and I ate—Wynn "picked." When we left, the waiter nodded and tipped his cap. Wynn forced a weak smile. He wasn't his usual peppy self all night.

A couple of weeks later, Wynn invited Charisse and me to join him and a date for dinner. He suggested Tavern on the Green and I said it would be fine. After dinner, during which Wynn was definitely "up" and all of us were having a good time, a group of waiters carrying a small cake with a single candle approached the table. Once they'd gathered around us they began singing:

> Happy birthday to you,
> Happy birthday to you.
> Happy birthday, dear IrVING

The smile left Wynn's face. "IrVING?" he screamed.

> Happy birthday to you.

As we and the rest of the audience were applauding Wynn turned to the group of waiters.

"I told you to sing it for David! David, not IrVING!"

When Wynn had suggested that particular restaurant so readily, I got suspicious and called them. They confirmed that he had ordered a birthday cake for me. I requested that they go along with the whole scheme, except to change the name to IrVING.

"Well, IrVING," I said, "I wish you a happy birthday."

We toasted Wynn.

"Thank you, gentlemen," I said to the waiters.

"Thank you, Mr. Brenner, and again, may we wish you a very happy birthday, IrVING."

Upon saying these words, the headwaiter removed his blue Japanese sailing cap and bowed, sweeping the cap back around his waist. Wynn looked at his Japanese sailing cap, then at Charisse, then covered his face with his napkin.

"Shit!"

Wynn wears his sailing cap whenever we go to sea, but it is never out of his sight for a moment.

Not only is Wynn "easy" when it comes to practical jokes, he is butter in the hands of a bettor. The loser's payoff is always in some form of humiliation. Wynn has paid off such losses by standing on the bow of my little sailboat in Lake Mead, Nevada, and screaming at the top of his lungs—and you know how far sound carries over water—in the direction of all the pleasure boaters: "I am an asshole! I am an asshole! I am an asshole!" For a bet he lost on the island of Saint Maarten he had to go shopping with me wearing his clothes on backwards and only one shoe. Of course, I didn't make things easier by pointing to him and asking the locals and tourists, "Isn't there something strange about that man limping over there?"

It got to the point that no matter how "sure" the bet seemed to Wynn—such as, we just passed a man standing on the corner back there at Fifty-ninth and Fifth holding onto a llama (which there was, even though he was not there by the time we circled the block)—he will not bet me. He has never won and is completely gun-shy. Well, not completely . . .

Wynn came over to my place to pick me up for a Saturday night on the town. We were all dressed up. I made drinks for us and we sat in my living room talking about this and that. Then I mentioned the weather, which got Wynn talking about going out to his boat that afternoon to clean her. This led to his telling me that he got the stains off the deck and could've won the bet when I said they couldn't be cleaned off. That bet was only a setup for the following:

"What's the difference, Wynn, you wouldn't bet me about anything, anyway."

"I wouldn't bet you 'humiliation.' I just couldn't go through being humiliated again. But I'd bet you money."

"Bull! You're even too afraid to bet money. Change the subject. So tonight . . . "

"Wait a minute, David! Don't make me out like a scared putz.

I would bet you, say, a hundred dollars, on something."

"You wouldn't have the guts to bet me a hundred dollars on anything, no matter what it was! Like you wouldn't bet me right now that . . . that . . . let's see . . . okay, that I'm wearing two sets of underwear shorts now."

"That's a bet!"

"Which way you want it? That I am wearing two pairs of underwear or that I'm not wearing two pairs?"

"This is one time that con won't work, Brenner. *Not* wearing two pairs. Here's my hundred and my hand. It is a bet."

"Bet."

The two one-hundred-dollar bills were on my coffee table. I stood up, opened my belt, unzipped my fly and slowly lowered my suit pants—one pair of bikini underwear.

"Ha! I won! I beat you at last! Ha!"

Wynn bent to pick up the money. I waved my forefinger motioning him to stop. He looked at me quizzically, still hunched over, as I slowly pulled down the side of my bikini shorts revealing a different colored, second pair of shorts.

Wynn didn't move a muscle. Didn't blink an eye. He just stared at me like the RCA Victor dog. Finally, in a very weak voice, he spoke, deliberately:

"Why . . . are . . . you . . . wearing . . . two . . . pairs . . . of . . . underwear?"

"To win a hundred dollars!"

I picked up the money, excused myself, went into my bedroom, took off one pair of shorts and came back to where Wynn was now flopped on the sofa, his face buried in his hands. He was muttering to himself.

"Two pairs of underwear. The guy's sick. Sick!"

I gave the hundred dollars to our waiter that night and when he thanked me I told him, "Thank Mr. Katz, one of America's foremost authorities on underwear." Wynn's date didn't understand. Now she will.

Wherever I have traveled, I have fulfilled my brother's request to bring back a little piece of the country I have visited. I mean that literally. I collect stones and rocks from the soil and send them to my brother who, in turn, keeps them on his desk for those moments when he wants to escape. He merely holds the rock or whatever in his hand and—bam!—he's there. It might sound a little crazy, but it makes more sense than some stupid Statue of Liberty paperweight, or a T-shirt that reads MY GRAND-MOTHER WENT TO TEL AVIV AND ALL SHE BROUGHT ME BACK WAS THIS LOUSY T-SHIRT. Groan.

Anyway, when Wynn and I went to Tokyo, I traveled to Mount Fuji. Fantastic! I gathered petrified lava rocks for my brother. When Wynn asked me what I was doing with a bag of rocks and I told him, he thought my brother was crazy and I was crazier.

"You're going to schlep a bag of rocks all the way to Hong Kong?"

"I'll decide which ones I'll keep after they dry off. Some were in the snow and they change when they dry."

"But in the meantime, you're going to carry all that weight? What a schmuck!"

Wynn didn't get off my back about me carrying the heavy rocks to Hong Kong. Fifty times he commented on it, calling me a schmuck each time.

When we got to our rooms in Hong Kong, Wynn unpacked *his* suitcase and pulled out my bag of rocks which I had hidden in there. He was right—only a schmuck would carry a heavy bag of rocks to Hong Kong.

I knew that someday, somehow, Wynn would have to try to get back at me for the years of losing, even if only once. I kept my antennae up whenever I was around him, constantly listening for anything irregular. Wynn even tried to recruit some of my street corner friends to help him set me up, but each one told him that, although they'd like to get back at me for some of the things I'd pulled on them, they knew that my retaliations were always worse than my attacks. No one would help. Wynn was on his own. I could tell he was plotting. Actually, I could hardly wait.

For years Wynn had been inviting me to join him on one of his many business trips to Tokyo and Hong Kong. Finally I said yes. I had to work so Wynn left before I. He said he'd have a car pick me up at the airport in Tokyo and take care of everything. Wynn speaks pretty fluent Japanese so I relaxed, knowing all would go smoothly.

When I arrived in Tokyo, a driver did pick me up. On the long ride to the city from the airport we talked, the driver speaking broken English fairly well. After about an hour he said:

"You do television, isn't that so?"

"Yes, how do you know?"

"Hotel manager tell me."

I ran down a list of programs on which I've appeared, asking the driver if he had heard of any of them. His answers were negative, and now I was seeing the red alert sign going off inside my head. Wynn is up to something and has the advantages of knowing the country, the people and the language. I'll have to stay on guard.

When I entered the Tokyo Hilton I was welcomed by Wynn and, following closely behind, the manager, who asked if he could have his picture taken with me. I agreed. Wynn asked the manager how he knew me and he answered that I was a popular TV star in Japan. Very suspicious. The flashbulb went off. I suggested we take another. We smiled and took it. I registered and checked into the second bedroom in Wynn's suite.

That night Wynn first took me to a popular little bar for predinner drinks. We sat and talked a while and then headed for the nearby restaurant which Wynn suggested. On our way there, two Japanese teenage girls called my name and waved to me. I smiled and returned the wave. Wynn commented on how great it was that I was known in Japan. I agreed, smiling inside.

After dinner, we went to a disco. A Japanese girl dancing on the floor waved to me and a young Japanese man shook my hand and welcomed me to Japan. Sure. I was now certain that Wynn was setting me up for something, but what?

A couple of days later, I received a call from a Japanese man named Mr. Urgami. He said he represented Channel Five and would love to have me appear on their TV talk show with an interpreter. I asked how he knew I was in Tokyo and he said the public relations office at the hotel had informed him. I then asked him how he knew who I was and he replied that they had seen me on TV in Japan, and knew that I've worked with Susan Anton, who is very popular in Japan. The latter is true but the whole thing rang off-key. I suggested that he give me time to think about it and call me at five o'clock the following evening.

As soon as I hung up, I called the hotel's public relations department, who had heard neither of me nor Mr. Urgami. I called Channel Five and asked someone who spoke English if he ever heard of Mr. Urgami or me or if they ran any American TV shows I had done. Negative. I had caught Wynn! Now I had to figure out how to tell him.

I put a small peanut in everything he owned, and I mean *everything*. As soon as he would ask me why there were nuts in everything, I would reply, "Why am I doing a TV show that doesn't exist?"

Wynn came back from his office and came into my room. He had changed out of his suit and tie into his jeans and sweater. He was talking about work, when he reached in his pocket and pulled out a nut. He looked at it and put it in the ashtray. Nothing. He continued talking. A few minutes later, he pulled another peanut out of another pocket and again placed it in the ashtray without comment. Finally, I decided to open the subject and told him about the call and the offer to do the TV show. He listened as though it was all new to him, but I knew him well enough to detect the slight smile on his face . . .

"Say, I've got a great idea, Wynn, why don't you do the show with me? You speak Japanese and it could be good for your business dealings here in Japan."

"No, I don't think they'll want me, but thanks."

"I'll talk to this Mr. Urgami when he calls! By the way, I was signing autographs like crazy in the streets today. A few people even stopped praying at the Holy Shrine to get an autograph. Never thought I was even known in Japan."

"That's wonderful, David. Well, I think I'll shower and get ready for dinner. See you soon."

He left and not once that night did he comment about the nuts he found in his soap, socks, shoes, sport jacket pockets, shirt pocket, or jockey shorts. More drastic measures had to be taken. The next day, while Wynn was at work, I squeezed the toothpaste out of the tube and meticulously squeezed in shampoo. I figured that evening's conversation would go:

"How come there's shampoo in my toothpaste?"

"How come I'm doing a TV show that doesn't exist?"

But, it didn't happen. He said nothing! Nothing!

The following day he came back from work, changed into his jeans, came into my room and flopped in a chair, his head held low. He was holding a message slip from the hotel in his hand. His voice was low.

"I'd better come clean. I saw the grapefruit in my toilet."

Yes, I put it there. I knew he couldn't *not* say something about a big grapefruit in his toilet bowl. I just looked at him as he raised his head and started reading from the note.

"Dear Mr. Katz: I talked with David Brenner. I think we have him one hundred percent. Make sure he does not telephone TV station to check. I said I would call him back at 5 P.M. tomorrow. Tell him in Japan it is impolite to telephone when they say they will call back. I think we got him cream. Most Respectfully, Mr. Mawada."

Wynn crumpled the message paper into a ball and threw it into my wastepaper basket. He looked at me dejectedly.

"I worked on this for months right down to the finest detail. I was going to have you driven to the TV studio and told to wait. No one there would know who the hell you were. You'd just be sitting there surrounded by Japanese, trying to explain you're a star and going on one of their shows. I paid all those people to wave to you and ask for your autograph. I arranged for the hotel manager and the photographer. Everything. This cost me a small fortune! When did you find out I was trying to set you up?"

"The very first time I ever set you up. Well, since I don't have any TV show to do tomorrow night, I'll treat you to dinner. What do you say?"

"Great," Wynn smiled.

"But let's make it someplace where I won't be hassled by fans."

Wynn laughed. We had a fantastic time in Japan and Hong Kong.

Two months after we returned home, I handed Wynn a package. He tore open the paper and looked at the crumpled Tokyo Hilton message in the frame with a brass placard underneath which reads, "You Cannot Con King Con!"

Today it hangs in his apartment. He's a great sport and a terrific friend. I almost feel a little guilty about the next one I'm setting him up for, but it's sooo good . . .

# FLIGHT 668

IT WAS A LONG, rough climb from the street corners of Philadelphia to where I am today. I'm a very, very lucky man! I know it and I appreciate it. I also know life is fleeting and one should enjoy every precious moment of it. This was reinforced for me one night coming back from Saint Maarten to New York, my town house, my career, my family, my friends. "The good life" almost ended.

"We're not going fast enough."

"What are you talking about, David?"

"For takeoff. We're not getting enough speed out of the engine on our side."

Wynn and I had just completed two glorious weeks sailing in the Caribbean. We were tan, relaxed and happy, heading back to New York aboard a commercial jet. I've done a lot of flying, as much as most pilots I guess, so I sort of have a sense if something is wrong. Something was wrong as we sped down the runway on the beautiful tropical island.

"David, you're crazy. It just might seem . . ."

The explosion sent the plane veering off to one side! The pilot turned down the flaps, hit the brakes, and did whatever else one has to do to abort a takeoff.

I looked at Wynn. Then I put my head between my legs in the crash impact position, although I was certain that we wouldn't make it. I had already been in one small crash and a few aborted takeoffs. This one seemed to be the worst—we were going too fast and had too little runway and were carrying a full load of fuel. Then it happened—we screeched to a stop. I felt Wynn's hand rub the top of my head.

"We made it, man," he said in his quiet voice.

I picked up my head and looked out the window. We were no more than ten feet from the end of the runway and the ocean. The pilot came on the P.A. system. His voice was low and shaky.

"Ladies and gentlemen. It's been a very bad day—a very bad day."

Later, in the airline's private office, we overheard the pilot talking to his office back in the States. He informed them that he was less than two seconds below V-1, which is the point of no return. After that a jet must take off regardless of the situation. In other words, if the engine had blown two seconds later, we would have had to lift up and that would have meant that we would have crashed and probably exploded in the ocean. The pilot then told them to call Lockheed and thank them for making a plane that did exactly what the manual said it would do.

Now, I've always been a guy who has lived his life as fully as possible, wasting little time, appreciating every minute of every day, not taking any shit from anyone, doing it my way and seeing that I stay on the roads I want to travel. However, there have been times when situations or circumstances have interfered with my philosophy, at least until the night of the aborted takeoff.

From that moment on, because I truly feel I was given a second chance to enjoy a life I am so fortunate to have, I've promised myself that whenever anything or anyone is trying to push my life in a direction I don't want it to go in, I just superimpose in my mind over the situation or the person, "668," which was the number of that flight. It reminds me of how short life is and I hurtle over or sidestep the problem and go on my way—*my* way! Everyone should have his or her own 668. It works! If the problem or obstacle doesn't have anything to do with affecting your health or shortening your life, it isn't worth your precious, fleeting time. I want to be able to enjoy my good life—I paid a heavy price for it!

## THE LAST TIME

GOOD FRIENDS ARE LIKE special treasures. They enrich one's life immeasurably, and I believe it's important to let them know this.

One day I started thinking about how I would have reacted, were I to have known that something I was doing was to be the last time I'd ever do it. How would I have played that last stickball game, taken the last roller skate ride down the street, played football and baseball and boxball, raced my friends to the corner and back, ate that orange fudgesicle, sledded down the hill, raced the bike into Upper Darby, chased the girls across the schoolyard, eaten a double order of french fries with gravy on them, gone to a Saturday matinee with my friends, and all the hundreds of other things that are gone from our lives before we even realize it.

Carry it a step further. What about all the things I do now that one day will also be for the last time? And what about all those special people in our lives who leave us before we get the opportunity to tell them exactly how we feel about them? God, I wish I had told so many of my aunts and uncles how much I truly loved them.

If we knew it was to be the last time for anything or anyone, we would live our lives with much more fervor, determination and will, and with much more love and appreciation for those around us. I decided that even if I had neglected to do it in the past, I could make certain not to continue making the same mistake in the future.

One night I was walking up First Avenue on my way to practice some new material for "The Tonight Show," when I was stopped by a young lady I had dated for about six months. I had quit seeing her because she was becoming emotionally involved with me and it would not have led to what she would have liked. I felt that the more time we spent together, the stronger the hurt would be when we finally stopped dating. I hadn't seen her since our last date about four months previously.

She was sitting at an outdoor cafe with two girl friends, fellow models. We chatted about the usual superficial things and then, motivated by my new philosophical theory about "what if you were to know this is the last time . . . ," I decided to tell her how much I liked her, and all the wonderful things there were about her. She sat with her mouth open, not believing what she was hearing. After all, I am the man who never opens the door leading to his innermost feelings even a millimeter, let alone two feet wide with a lighted sign blinking "This way in." After expressing how I felt about her, I saw that there were tears in her eyes. I said a quick good-bye to her friends, kissed her and went on my way.

It was the last time I saw her. The next night, she was murdered.

This made me feel even more that we should tell or show people how we really feel about them! It isn't easy. I still have my own problems doing it, but I'm trying.

# NEIGHBORHOOD

# THE STREETS WHERE I LIVED

IN WEST PHILADELPHIA, IT ran from the elevated train stop at Sixty-third and Market Streets, along Cobbs Creek Park to Washington Avenue, down to Fifty-six Street, back over to Market and back up to Sixty-third Street. It was "the neighborhood." We lived there, and for most of us, it was the only world we knew, and, for a few, it was the only world they would ever know. It was a lower-middle-class to middle-class, basically Jewish section of West Philadelphia. I say basically, because interspersed within these boundaries one could find small pockets of other minorities, including Greeks, Armenians, Slavics and Irish. Bordering it were two large, heavily populated ghettos, one Italian, the other black. I moved to the West End from South Philadelphia when I was seven and a half years old and remained there until after I had graduated from Temple University.

In the time I lived there, I either knew everyone by name or could recognize them as someone who lived there. It was as though in some strange way all of us were related, joined together in some kind of human cause. We were as one. It was a comfortable feeling. It was security. You knew that, if something happened to you, someone would come to help you while someone else would tell your parents. Sometimes, of course, it was a dirty, often violent place, but you still felt good being there—you knew you belonged and were a part of it—the neighborhood. I loved it and I hated it. I felt good every time I went back to it, but while there I spent most of my time trying to figure out how

129

to get away. I'm glad I grew up there, but I'm more glad I didn't stay there. Part of the reason I am who I am today is because of that neighborhood. This also includes some of the ways I wish I wasn't. What I have achieved in life I must also partially attribute to the neighborhood, for it made me strive to get ahead in life, to succeed, to obtain all the possessions I now have. Back there in the streets, I paid for all that I have today—a big price, but well worth the prize. To know better the man, look at the neighborhood.


## THE CAFETERIA

WHEN I ATTENDED ELEMENTARY school, everyone went home for lunch. I had an hour and a half to walk the ten city blocks to my house and then the ten blocks back. It was fun to get away from the school, to run in the streets, push and shove, "pantsing" some new kids or a smaller kid (the art of removing someone's pants and hiding them), splashing in a puddle, sword fighting with garbage can lids and sticks, racing someone to the corner, hopping on the back of a trolley or sneaking inside of one, teasing the girls, looking in the gutters for money (I always found some and still do), stealing a piece of candy, sharing a cigarette in an alley, playing with a stray dog, watching the deli man cut thin slices of baloney, laying pennies on the trolley tracks to flatten them into the size of nickles, imitating an old man's walk, talking to the blind broom salesman, getting nickles from a neighborhood mafioso to play the pinball machine in Babis's drugstore, making fun of the underwear hanging on backyard clotheslines, seeing who could hold his breath longest, having a cinder throwing fight, playing catch with a rock wrapped in plumber's black tape, hiding from each other, scaring each other by suddenly leaping out of an alley, looking at the naked women in National Geographics, giving a sleeping man on a bus bench a hotfoot, scaring shoppers by pressing our noses against the window of the Woolworth's five and ten cent store, betting who could hit a telephone pole wire with a stone, testing who could skip the fastest, walking past a store window like stiff-legged zombies, placing an old wallet on the pavement and pulling the attached string as soon as someone stopped to pick it up, floating home-made popsicle stick rafts down the gutter in either the rain water or the urine from a vendor's horse ("Quick, Stan, get the rafts! The fruit man's horse is pissing on Addison Street!"), watching the old Italian man sharpen knives and scissors, whistling at some couple who acting like corny lovers, being mesmerized by the shoemaker as he makes an old scuffed pair of shoes look almost brand new, giggling at the drunks who are arguing over a bottle of whiskey wrapped in a brown bag, staring in bewil-derment at the dope addict teenager who is trying to walk nor-mal, cheering on two fighting alley dogs, tossing stones at cats perched on backyard fences, walking all the way without step-ping on a crack so we wouldn't "crack our mother's back," studying a long row of ants as they move in single file across the pavement and up the wall, poking carefully at a hornet's nest in a neighborhood tree, following a flock of birds flying south, sneaking a quick peek into the "haunted house," arguing over who is the better baseball player, comparing arm muscles, see-ing who could kick a can stuffed with rags the farthest, avoiding the "older guys" who had nothing better to do than fight us, begging for some loose change, throwing a soda bottle into an empty lot and running away before it hits and breaks, tearing the new sneakers off some kid's feet to tie the laces together and throw them over telephone wires, making believe we're a motorcycle gang on big Harley's, extending our arms and mak-ing believe we're fighter planes diving for the kill, putting a blade of grass between our thumbs so it turns into a whistle, falling dead into high bushes, lining up for a game of buck buck (in New York it's called Johnny on a Ponie), just having fun and growing! Nothing in the world was as exciting and as much fun as those city streets and alleys. Nothing!

One day in school, it was announced that a cafeteria would be opening. Food was to be sold inexpensively so students could relax with their lunch at school. The first day the cafeteria opened, we all went into the basement and looked through the large plate glass windows as three students passed through the line with trays to get their food. We watched them pay, take their seats and then left to walk home for lunch. Every day for one week we watched the same three kids go through the cafeteria line and then we walked home. You see, they were three of the few rich kids who went to my school. The rest of us couldn't afford to buy lunch no matter how cheap it was. Matter of fact, some of my friends didn't even have food for lunch at home and would either play in the streets or just sit in their house or apartment until it was time to return to school. Besides, who in their right mind would ever give up the adventure of the trip home and back?

On Monday morning of the second week, the cafeteria closed, never to reopen. No one missed it, except maybe those three kids.

"Yo, you guys, what do you say on the way home for lunch today we play a game of touch football and then climb to the top of the brickyard smokestack or maybe get a couple of pink high bouncers and . . ."


## BUMS, GHOSTS AND GROWN-UPS

IN A POOR NEIGHBORHOOD, Halloween means a human flood of child-sized bums, ghosts and grown-ups on the streets, because they're the cheapest costumes to make. For the bum, you put on your own clothes or your father's, mark up your face with burnt cork, tie a workman's handkerchief over a mop handle which is slung over your shoulder and you've got it. The ghost is real simple—a sheet over the head with holes for the eyes, if it's an old sheet, or without eyeholes and a friend to guide you by the hand if it's a good one. The grown-up costume was simply putting on an adult's clothes.

The whole idea of this holiday was stupid to me as a child. Most holidays were. On top of dressing up silly and, worse, looking just like everyone else, there was always the danger of the "big guys" coming after you with their homemade blackjacks, made out of wool socks stuffed with large chunks of coal, trying to steal your treats. Halloween? Who needs it?

When I was about eight years old, my mom did something real special for me. She actually bought me a store costume! A wolf. It was complete with feet and head and paws and a long tail, just like the kind the rich kids from past Cedar Avenue wore. Well, I was a shoo-in for best costume at the Halloween party being held at my classmate Michael Weinstein's house. My friends would flip out!

I got dressed and showed my family. They cheered. I think it was the first store-bought costume in our family, ever, dating back to Moses. My ancestor is the one in the painting "The Parting of the Red Sea," who's wearing the three-piece suit and tie. I was so proud. I really felt like a wolf. I growled and slinked out of the house. I moved through the neighborhood like a real wolf, passing all the bums, ghosts and grown-ups. I tricked or treated a half bag of candies and other good stuff on my way to the party.

About two blocks before Michael's house, six "big guys" came out of an alley. They were swinging their weighted socks.

"Well, look what we got here. A wolf."

"One of them rich kids."

"I'm not rich. I'm from Sixty-first and Spruce and don't go fuckin' with me!"

"Well, well, well, the big bad wolf."

They laughed and I started to back away, trying to figure out how to get away, but in the damn costume with the padded paws for shoes, I didn't have a chance of outrunning them. Only talk could work.

"Listen, you guys, this is my first store-bought . . ."

The first blow caught me from behind and was square on the top of my head. I saw stars but swung out, getting one of them in the groin. I heard him yell but couldn't take the time to celebrate because it began raining socks. I couldn't see too well out of the tiny holes cut in the mask, so I just swung wildly. I did catch one of them in the mouth, but it was a losing battle from the beginning. They really beat me up and took my treats.

When they ran away, I checked the damage. My snoot was bent out of shape, my chest was torn open, my tail was ripped off and missing, my real nose was bleeding and my mouth was swollen. I walked slowly to Michael's house. When I came into her living room, everyone just stared at me.

Some bum asked me, "What are you supposed to be?"

"A beat-up wolf."

Everyone laughed and I won first prize for best costume. I never went to another Halloween party and to this day I hate costumes.

# A PERFECT REPLY

ONE MORNING I DROVE into Philly from New York to join childhood friends for breakfast at a famous deli on Gerard Avenue. We had gone there as kids, so it was going to be a nostalgic reunion. The reason it was famous was because it had been there a long time and retained the atmosphere of delicatessens as they used to be. All the waiters were older Jewish men who had worked in delis all their lives. As was typical with these characters, sometimes they would actually tell you what you should eat, rather than simply take your order.

"What are you talking, a cold sandwich on a night like this? I'll give you a hot bowl of beef barley and a hot brisket of beef sandwich. Now, what about you, *boychic*?"

Our waiter walked over to us and slapped the cloth napkin he carried slung over one arm on the table, killing an imaginary fly.

"So, what is it? We ready or is the United Nations still in session?"

"No," I answered, "we're ready to order. I'll have a heated, not toasted, bagel with a double order of cream cheese and a couple eggs . . ."

"We're out of bagels. So, rye or challa?"

"Out of bagels? You're kidding."

"This to you is a joke? We're out of bagels."

"Do you realize that I came all the way from New York City to have one of your bagels?"

Without losing a beat, the waiter answered, "Do you realize that I came all the way from Europe to tell you we're out of them?"

The perfect reply! Those men in white aprons are a dying breed, unfortunately.


# BROOMHOLDERS AND KNISHES

HOW CAN YOU BEST a knish? (pronounced kā-nish) You can't! Potato or meal filled, it is one of the greatest treats in this world. For those of you who have never had a knish or have no idea what it is, it's a delicious dough, shaped like a doughnut without a hole, that is filled with potato, rice or chopped liver and is served hot. It is orgasmic! To the eyes and taste buds of a ten-year-old, it is splendiforously delicioso. It is also too expensive.

Dash's Deli was on Sixtieth Street, only a block from our elementary school. Mr. Dash made the best knishes in the world. You could smell them in Camden, New Jersey, and possibly in Kansas City. Just to walk into his store was to stand as close to the Gates of Heaven as most of us ever would.

My school couldn't afford a wood shop setup and teacher, so we walked six blocks to a nearby school for our classes. We made the usual wooden things all school children make—a broomholder, bookends, tie rack and telephone table. Most of the projects turned out to be disasters, because most of us were Jewish and Jewish kids are not into using their hands, except to turn book pages or scribble numbers on a balance sheet. It's our heritage. Believe me, the pyramids were our greatest miracle. We forgot the windows, but still . . .

One day, a few of us were standing in Dash's getting our nostrils titillated by the smells and aromas, when Mr. Dash asked to see the wood pieces we were taking home. We showed him and he bargained with us as to how much they were worth. My broomholder garnered two knishes and a slice of lean corned beef.

This was the beginning of a wonderful tradition. We would crank out our wood projects in shop and trade them in at Dash's for his delicious foods. Our craftsmanship improved as well as our productivity. I'm sure Mr. Johnson, our shop teacher, proudly took all the credit for our progress. He wouldn't have ever believed it was deli food pushing us on to greater and greater feats of carpenter mastery and productivity. We were making things in wood shop like our lives depended on it, and each of us ended up with a long line of credit at Dash's.

I never understood as a child what old man Dash did with all of our woodwork. Someone suggested that he sold it for a big profit and that seemed to satisfy all speculation. One of the dictates of city life is to look for someone's angle—especially when they are being nice to you. However, looking back on it as a man, I now know that the reason Mr. Dash bartered for all our wood stuff was simply because he was a very nice man. It was simple, everyday men such as Mr. Dash who made my old neighborhood anything but simple and everyday. Mr. Dash's knishes were special—so was Mr. Dash.

# THE ROOFERS

SOME OF THE BIGGEST heroes to children in the city ghetto are the roofers, the men who fix roofs. When we smelled the pitch cooking in their street stoves, we would search the neighborhood until we found the house they were working on. Then we would stand on the pavement and call up to them.

"Yo, roofers! Roofers!"

Suddenly, one or two of those giant men, standing precariously close to the edge of the roof, muscle-bound in their white underwear shirts, would call down, "What you kids want?"

"Can we chew some of your pitch?"

There was a rumor that chewing pitch made your teeth white.

"Yeah, but watch you don't burn yourselves!"

"Would you also throw down the balls?"

This is what made them our heroes. They had access to every ball and half-ball that was roofed during the street baseball and stickball seasons. The roofers would disappear and then balls and half-balls would come raining down on the street. Sometimes fifty or sixty of them! We'd keep the best and sell or trade off the rest. Roofers were the greatest!

A few years ago I was walking in Center City, Philadelphia, a commercial and residential part of the city, considered one of the "better" neighborhoods. As I turned a corner and headed down Delancey Street I smelled it—hot pitch. There in the center of the block was the pitch-splattered iron stove, boiling the black liquid. I smiled at the wonderful memories it brought back.

"Hey, mister, you got the time?"

I looked around. No one was there. I continued walking.

"Yo, mister. Up here!"

I looked up. There he was—a roofer. Not the muscular, brave hero of my childhood, but a man in his late fifties, bent from the years of hard labor, a filthy black undershirt that hung loosely from his tanned but somewhat frail body, his face blackened by the pitch, hands that hung purposelessly alongside baggy trousers that were spotted with globs of dried pitch.

"Hi," I smiled.

"You got the time?"

"Yes, it's . . . eleven-forty-five."

He waved slightly and started back from the edge of the roof.

"Thanks for the balls!" I yelled, still smiling.

"What?" he asked weakly.

"The balls!"

"What balls?"

"Forget it," I said quietly, waving him off.

He disappeared and I headed down the street to my appointment at the TV studio. Some images are better off locked away in a young boy's memory.

## MRS. DEAD PIGEON

SHE WAS A MEAN, middle-aged woman who lived behind us, on the other side of the wide alleyway which separated the nicer homes from ours. You know the kind of person—tells you to play in front of your own house and then turns the waterhose on you when you don't; keeps your ball if it rolls onto her property. She had three of mine. I had batted each of them through her kitchen window. I worked hard to save money to pay for the windows I broke but she still didn't give back my balls.

One spring afternoon in my tenth year I was sitting at the kitchen table eating a piece of bread and butter when my father, who was looking out the kitchen window, called to me.

"I don't believe this. Come look, Kingy."

Well, there's the old mean witch from across the way sweeping something across to our side of the alleyway.

"What is it, Lou?"

"A dead pigeon."

"You're kidding."

I looked closer and my father was right—the woman was sweeping a dead pigeon onto our property. My father handed me a broom.

"Okay, Kingy, push it back."

I laughed and went outside with my long-handled broom and swept the dead pigeon back to the woman's property. As I was heading back to my house she came running outside.

"What the hell you think you're doing sweeping a dead pigeon onto my property?"

"Lady, we watched you from our kitchen window. You pushed it over to us first. It's *your* dead pigeon!"

137

"Like hell it is!"

Next thing I knew she was whipping by me, pushing the dead pigeon with her broom. My father came running out of the house.

"Stop her, Kingy!"

By the time I went after her she had already redeposited the pigeon on our property and was walking away. A few neighbors had come out back to see what the yelling was all about. That's all I needed—spectators. Like a champion ice hockey player, I swooped the pigeon up with the ends of my broom's straw and delivered it onto her property. Some neighbors applauded and I bowed. In a rage, she swept up the bird toward my house.

"Block her, Kingy, block her!"

I met her at half court and wrestled the bird out of her broom and headed for her goal. More neighbors had come outside and were cheering me on. Before I let the bird go, she blocked me and stole the bird, heading for my goal. I caught up quickly, bumped her off balance, stole the bird and started back for a point. She was quick to recover and was hot on my trail. The stands were going wild! I reversed field, passed her other side, raised my broom high into the air and let it fly, and fly it did— through the air flew this dead pigeon on its last flight, up, up, up and right through her open kitchen window.

The neighbors screamed with delight, applauding wildly. Philadelphians have always loved hockey. The woman stood perfectly still, her stare frozen on the open window. I ran and threw my arms around her.

"Good game, Mrs. Dead Pigeon, good game!"

The name stuck until she moved out of the neighborhood.


# HUNKS, HALFIES AND WHOLIES

NO MATTER WHAT YOU bought, from a double meat and double cheese cheesesteak sandwich to a strip of candy dots on paper, if anyone, friend or foe or stranger, yelled "hunks" or "halfies" or "wholies," before you yelled "no hunks," they would be entitled to break off or bite off a "hunk" or a "half" of whatever it was you had or take the "whole" darn thing! It must have seemed very strange to any outsider who was in the neighborhood when he heard somebody screaming the words "no hunks!" at the top of his lungs, but it was a rough world we lived in and you could never play it too safe.

## ICE CREAM

I AM AN ICE cream addict. I have been since birth. When other babies were on the bottle, I was on the cone. Maybe it comes with growing up in the ice cream capital of the country. Philadelphia produces, sells and consumes more ice cream per capita than any other city. Whatever did it to me, I am wild about it. I'm not a fancy flavor man, either. I consider myself a purist. I prefer vanilla, chocolate and, maybe the killer of all time, peanut butter and chocolate. I never let one day pass without having ice cream. That stems from a promise I made to myself as a kid, when I could afford an ice cream only once or twice a month: that, as a grown-up, as long as I had a few dollars in my pocket, I would treat myself to an ice cream. Another one of my idiosyncracies concerning ice cream is also traceable back to the same deprivation. Whenever I have an ice cream in a restaurant today, no matter how fancy the place, no matter who is having dinner with me, as I eat my ice cream I shield the dish with the other hand, so no kid can "dig in" and eat some of mine. I really look stupid doing this, but you never know when someone is going to jump out of the shadows with a fast-moving spoon and swoop down on your last few bites of ice cream! You have all been duly warned that I am always on my guard!

## THE COLDEST DATE

SANDY WAS ONE OF the prettiest girls in my seventh grade class. She had dark hair, almost black, brown eyes, a small waist and big breasts. What more could a twelve-year-old kid want? On top of that, she was probably the wealthiest girl in my school. I asked her out for a Saturday night and she accepted.

The big night came and I put on my best pair of pants, powder blue with dark blue saddle stitching up the side, my blue suede shoes, my pink silk shirt and my blue blazer. Too much! I counted out my life savings put away week by week from my earnings as a supermarket bag packer. I had enough for the trolley fares to Sandy's house, to the movies, back to Sandy's house and back to my house, and enough for the movies and some candy. Perfect! I whipped the comb through my long greasy hair one more time, pulled up the collar of my shirt, winked at my image in the mirror and stepped out into the night—and sub-freezing weather!

An unseasonable cold front had moved in unexpectedly and I didn't own a winter coat. Last year's coat, a hand-me-down from my brother, had fallen apart. I hated the cold! I still do. Anything under seventy-five degrees is like the Antarctic to me. I literally shiver and my teeth rattle.

Standing on the corner that night waiting for a trolley, I nearly turned into a statue. My hand shook so much when I finally got on the car that I could hardly get the change out of my pocket for the conductor. At Sandy's street, I got off the trolley and ran as quickly as I could to her house. Catching my breath, I rang the bell. When a light came on in her vestibule, I controlled my shivering and stood casually, a smile on my face.

"Hi, David."

"Hi, Sandy."

"Well, I'm all ready. We can go."

God, she already had on her coat. I wouldn't have a chance to even warm up in her house for a few minutes. My luck—not only was she beautiful and rich, she was punctual! She came outside and we started walking—slowly—up the street to catch a trolley. She held my arm and I did every mind-control trick I could think of to keep from shivering.

"How come you're not wearing a top coat?"

"Cold doesn't bother me."

"But you're even wearing a thin silk shirt."

"So?"

"Wow, I'd be freezing. I'm even cold with this fur lining."

"Guess I'm just lucky."

The movie was great. I don't remember what was playing, but I do remember the theater was heated. After the movie, we walked to get a trolley back to her house. The temperature had dropped even further. I remembered the carcasses of cows hanging in the meat freezer in the butcher shop where I once worked. Now I understood how they felt. I did a few physical kind of jokes just to keep warm. Nothing worked. Finally, the trolley came and we got on. I let my hands hang in front of the heater under our seat and let them warm up before I held Sandy's hand. I didn't want to frighten her by handing her a frozen lamb chop. The trolley was warm and I starting to thaw out. We were halfway to her house when we stopped at the corner of Sixtieth and Locust Streets where Murray's Deli was located, a local hangout.

"Let's get a bite to eat," Sandy screamed, grabbing my hand and dragging me off the warm trolley and into the North Pole.

As we looked over the menu I quickly calculated what I could afford. I had to talk Sandy into ordering something that cost three trolley fares, two fares if possible. There aren't many things in a deli that sell for that little.

"I'm telling you, Sandy, the bowl of borscht and the chicken fat on rye are killers. Much better than the corned beef special. Trust me! Gertrude, give the young lady the fantastic borscht and the supersensational chicken fat on rye sandwich."

"What about you?"

"Nothing. Thank you."

"Nothing? You took up a seat in a booth for a nothing?"

"I'm with an eating customer. Now would you put in the order?"

"Are you sure you don't want something, David?"

"I ate before I left the house. *Boys* do that."

"What do you mean, '*Boys* do that'?"

"For some reason, girls always get hungry on dates. I don't understand it. Don't your mothers feed you? My mother feeds my sister."

"I ate dinner. I just thought it would be nice if we had a little bite. Sorry."

"I'm only kidding. Listen, get all you want. You want a steak or something? I'll order it for you. Hey, Gertrude!"

"No, everything's fine, David. Thank you."

"You sure, Sandy? Sky's the limit for you."

"You're sweet, but no thanks. The borscht and rye bread will be fine."

"With chicken fat."

"With chicken fat," she smiled. Perfect teeth. All rich kids had perfect teeth.

We hung out in Murray's for about an hour, talking with friends, laughing, staying warm. I paid the check and then told Sandy I had to go back to the table to leave a tip.

"Gertrude," I whispered, "I'll come in during the week and tip you. Don't make a scene. I like this girl."

"I hope you get the clap!"

"Me, too, Gertrude," I smiled. Gertrude smiled and hit me with her clean-up rag. She was a doll.

Sandy and I walked outside. The temperature had dropped a few more degrees. I was now not only cold, I was flat broke.

"Let's walk home."

"Are you crazy? It's freezing!"

"Come on, Sandy, I'll keep my arm around you. You'll be warm."

"Some other time, David, right now I'd . . ."

"At least let's start out walking. The minute it gets too cold for you, we'll hop on a trolley. There's none coming now, anyway. Okay?"

"Well . . . okay."

We walked. It was easy to keep my arm around her shoulder because it was frozen there. I let Sandy do most of the talking, because the cold air hurt my teeth too much. Now, she was beginning to shiver a little.

"I'm getting cold, David. Let's take the trolley that's coming."

"Come on, we're only a few blocks from your house. Let's run!"

Before she could answer, I started running. It's not easy running with your arm around a girl's shoulders and your other arm frozen by your side, but I did it. When the trolley passed us, I stopped running.

"David, what everyone says about you is true—you are strange, without a doubt."

"And you're the prettiest girl in the class."

"You really think so? What about your old girl friend, Cicely, or Rhoda or Susan or Toby or all the others you've taken out?"

"None of them could run like you."

Sandy laughed and snuggled close to me. I was glad. Her body heat felt real good. When we got to her house, she kissed me good-night. I think she did, anyway, because my lips were too frozen to feel anything. Then she went inside her big, warm house. I walked down the steps, looked to see if Sandy was watching. She wasn't so I let out the bundle of shivers that were stored in me and shook as I walked eighteen city blocks home.

I dated Sandy quite a bit, on and off right into high school. We had some great times together. She got prettier. Then she decided it was time to date older wealthy boys, so we stopped seeing each other socially. Right after high school, she married one of the well-to-do boys and I didn't see her again until I was performing at a nightclub in New York City a couple of years ago.

I was handed a note in my dressing room. It was from Sandy. She and her husband were in the audience and wanted to say hello. I told the maître d' to tell them I'd join their table when the crowd thinned out after the show.

She was still pretty and her body was still sexy. We talked about the old days, of course, and brought each other up-to-date on what had happened to whom. It was real good seeing her. Then, as I was about to say good-bye I felt it was time to tell her the truth about that first date.

". . . so the real reason was because you didn't have a winter overcoat?"

"Couldn't afford one."

"Well, you can now. You did exactly what you said you were going to do, didn't you, David? You're rich now, aren't you?"

I nodded. We both smiled.


## THE HARDWARE STORE

I THINK I WAS a pretty likeable youngster, especially before my teens. The adults in the neighborhood seemed to like me, except for a rare few, among whom, maybe even at the top of the list, was the owner of the neighborhood hardware store. But that wasn't entirely my fault. I wasn't the one who gave him his name, and I wasn't the one who painted his store sign. I'll explain.

The man's last name was Crappe, rhyming with "trap." His first name was Isadore. He owned the neighborhood hardware store. I had nothing to do with any of this.

He had a sign stretching the entire width of his store, above the double windows and door. He had his last name up there, of course, followed by the word hardware, naturally. However, instead of using his full name, because there just wasn't enough room, he used only his first initial, "I." Therefore the sign read, "I. Crappe Hardware." I had nothing to do with any of this, either.

What I did do was at least three times a week—sometimes twelve or fifteen times—I would go into the hardware store with some of my friends and call out to I. Crappe Hardware—"Let's see you do a few bolts." Sometimes, I'd say "nails" or "a hammer" or "a screwdriver" or "a plumb line," etc. Well, Mr. Crappe would curse me, run around his counter, whether he was waiting on a customer or not, and chase me down Sixtieth Street, swearing that he would kill me if he ever caught me.

All he had to do was change his sign, which he didn't do, or wait for me to grow up, which I did do. God, I would've loved to have seen him crappe even a tiny thumb tack.

## DR. LASKIN

THERE ARE ONLY A few outstanding heroes in a poor city neighborhood. There's the bookmaker, the candy store and delicatessen owners, the roofers, the handsome ladies' man, the best dancer, the best pool shooter, the toughest street fighter, the first stringer in any high school sport, the honor roll students, the guy who "made it" and got out of the ghetto, the kid who can eat three pizzas without throwing up and the doctor. Among Jews and Italians a doctor is revered.

Dr. Laskin was a tall, rather handsome, nonsmiling, very serious man and an excellent general practitioner. He always tried to collect the money owed him but eventually would settle for a jar of homemade jellies or an IOU. He was every family's doctor; he was everybody's hero; he was also a lifetime of embarrassing situations for me.

My first recollection of Dr. Laskin was when I was about eight years old. My mother took me to him for a general examination. After weighing me, measuring, listening to my heart, taking my blood pressure, checking my ears, nose and throat, he handed me a glass beaker with red measurement lines and numbers on its side.

"Go in the little boy's room over there, David, and fill this with water for me."

"Yes, sir!"

I walked into the bathroom, shut the door and leaned against a wall thinking. After a moment I opened the door and took a couple steps out. Dr. Laskin was talking with my mother.

"Excuse me, Dr. Laskin, how much water do you want?"

"As much as you can get in."

I returned to the bathroom, thinking to myself, "Boy, for a doctor, he's really a little dumb. I can fill it to the top."

I opened the bathroom door again and poked my head out. "Excuse me, doctor, do you want hot or cold?"

The doctor did what he rarely did—he laughed hysterically. So did my mother. When they finally explained what they really wanted, I was too mortified to do it, which then led to embarrassment number two.

When we got back home, my mother stopped laughing long enough to tell me that she was going to put an empty Gulden's mustard jar in the bathroom, and, when I next went to the bathroom, I was to fill it, put it in a brown paper bag and take it to Dr. Laskin.

That afternoon, I played stickball with Linsey, Mutt Feldman, Carl "Oogie" Weinberg and Johnny Milliken. When you play hard, you drink hard, so I must have had two quarts of garden hose water to drink, plus a large lemon-flavored water ice that Tony the Italian Water Ice Man had given me. That did it. I had to go and real bad. Normally, I'd just duck down an alley, relieve myself and continue playing. This time I had to make up a wild excuse for leaving a game right in the middle and run home, and I mean run!

By the time I got to my house, I was ready to burst. By the time I charged up the stairs into the bathroom, I was seeing large yellow spots in front of my eyes. I just about got the Gulden's mustard jar opened in time. Unlike in the doctor's office, I had no trouble filling the jar. Matter of fact, I could've filled the Gulden mustard factory.

I screwed the lid on the jar which I'd filled to the brim, put it in the brown paper bag and headed for the doctor's office. I guess the lid wasn't on exactly straight because I noticed the bag was getting wetter and wetter. I panicked and for some reason decided that the sooner I got to the doctor's office, the better it would be, so I started to run. Naturally, the faster I ran, the more the jar spilled, the wetter the bag got, the more I panicked, the faster I ran . . .

At my full running speed I burst into the doctor's office, sped through his packed waiting room and up to his receptionist/

nurse. I slammed the soggy bag on her desk blotter, which immediately began soaking up the spilling contents. I gasped, "Here's the mustard the doctor ordered," whipped around and charged out and home as fast as my white, high top, canvas Ked sneakers could take me.

A few years later, my friend Beb was bitten by a dog. He hurried to Dr. Laskin's office. The nurse told him that if he couldn't find the dog that bit him he'd have to get those painful rabies shots in the stomach that we had all heard about. Beb found me playing in the brickyard and begged me to help him find the dog, a black-and-white spotted terrier, with one eye scarred, probably from a street fight. At first we searched together, but as time passed we decided that we'd better separate so we could cover more territory.

I was looking for nearly an hour when I saw a dog that fit the description. He was eating out of a garbage can in an alley. I sneaked into the alley, moving closer and closer toward the unsuspecting dog. When I got within ten feet, I could see the dog's face clearly. The eye was scarred. This was the dog. In the alley, I saw a meat bone covered with green head flies. I shooed away the flies, picked up the bone and whistled for the dog. He growled, baring his teeth. I smiled and "made nice," throwing the bone a few feet in front of me. The dog inched his way toward it, growling all the way. I let him smell the bone and picked it up, but when he turned his back on me I leaped on him, lifting him up by his neck. I ran full speed ahead to Dr. Laskin's office.

Again I charged into his office. It was lunch hour, patients were there but the nurse wasn't, so I made a beeline for the doctor's office. The door was slightly ajar, so I kicked it open with one foot. Dr. Laskin was looking in the ear of an elderly lady. I threw the dog into the room.

"Here's Beb's mad dog!" I screamed.

I slammed the door shut, ignoring the woman's screams, the doctor's curses and the dog's barking.

To this day, I still don't believe it was my fault that things got out of hand. Beb hadn't told me that Dr. Laskin didn't know anything about his being bitten. Well, everything turned out okay in the end. The dog was not rabid, which was very good news for Beb, the elderly Jewish lady, Dr. Laskin and for all the other patients whom he had bitten.

When I was twelve years old, I started getting terrible pains in my legs. My mother was afraid I might have contracted polio so she asked Dr. Laskin to make a house call. He knew it must be serious, because house calls were a couple dollars extra and people only asked for them when they were close to death or, better yet, if several family members were simultaneously close to death.

Dr. Laskin walked into my bedroom, murmured a quiet hello, pulled down the covers and examined my legs. He then bent my legs back, pressed them against his chest and asked me to push him. I did. He asked me if that was the hardest I could push. I said no. After all, I had been playing football and running track all my young life. My legs had always been the strongest part of my body, long and powerful. I was holding back because I knew Dr. Laskin had developed a bad back and wore a brace. Besides, he hadn't talked to me more than a few necessary words since the dog attack. I was trying to get back on his good side.

"Push as hard as you can."

"But, doctor . . ."

"As hard as you can! Push! Now!"

I did and watched as he flew back and flipped over the foot-board of the bed, crashing to the floor, out of sight. I froze, afraid to look, afraid I broke his neck and killed him, or worse—I broke his neck and didn't kill him! The top of his head surfaced slowly from behind the foot-board. His hair was disheveled, his silver-rimmed glasses were hanging on one ear, his face was distorted in pain. His hands held on unsteadily. He glared at me; his lips curled in anger. His voice was a hoarse whisper.

"You don't have polio. They are growing pains. You are becoming a man. God help us all."

"When . . . when can I get out of bed?"

"Whenever you want, unfortunately!"

He got to his feet slowly, painfully, and limped out of my bedroom and down the stairs. I waited until I heard my mother close the front door before I got out of bed.

The whole family got it again. Food poisoning. It was a rather common ailment in the neighborhood, since the food in ghetto supermarkets is of the worst quality. Dr. Laskin came to the house and examined all of us, confirming what we feared and informing us that the best thing to do was to vomit, then drink warm milk, take aspirins and rest.

I had already emptied my stomach so I came downstairs to join my mother, father and Dr. Laskin. I was on my best behavior, determined not to humiliate myself in front of the doctor again. Everything was going perfectly. I sat in an overstuffed chair by the radio as Dr. Laskin talked over some neighborhood news with my parents, then he picked up his hat.

"Okay, Lou, Stelle, if you or the kids aren't feeling better by morning, give me a call."

"Thanks, Dr. Laskin."

"You're welcome. Good night."

"Good night, Doctor Laskin."

"Good night, Doctor Laskin."

"Good night, Uncle Laskin." That's what I had called him—"uncle." "Uncle." Why "uncle"? It was so stupid! Oh, God, I did it again!

Dr. Laskin turned, looked at me, shook his head slowly and left. My mother and father looked at me and simultaneously cracked up. I tried not to laugh but couldn't hold it back. I'm laughing as I write about it now. What a little putz I was.

When I got discharged from the army and returned home, I spent my first few days and nights on a nostalgic tour of the neighborhood I hadn't seen for two years. I decided to visit the old family doctor. Besides, it was time for my flu booster shot. I walked up to Dr. Laskin's office entrance. Nothing had changed. I opened the door and went inside. The waiting room had a lot of people as always. Everything, the pictures on the walls, the furniture, and I'd swear even the magazines were the same as the last time I was there. Only the nurse was new.

"May I help you?"

"Yes, I'm here to see Dr. Laskin."

"Have you ever been here before?"

"More than I'd like to think about. Since I was a kid."

"May I have your name and the nature of your illness?"

Just then the doctor's office door opened and he was leading a patient out. He spotted me. I smiled warmly. I was truly happy to see him. I wondered if he would even recognize me, for I had become a man.

"What the hell do you want?" he growled.

"I . . . it's me, Dr. Laskin. David Brenner. Lou and Stelle's boy. I just got out . . ."

"I know who you are. What do you want?"

"Well, I came to . . . I . . . I need a booster flu shot."

"Give him one," he said to the nurse. "Next."

He pivoted and went into his office, followed by the next patient. His door slammed shut. I never saw Dr. Laskin again. I was sorry I didn't. I wonder if he was?


# THE IRVING STREET AUCTION HOUSE

MY PARENTS RAISED ME not to let anyone take advantage of me. I believed in this very strongly and still do.

Someone took over an old trucking company's garage on the 5900 block of Irving Street. Stadium benches were put in and it was opened as an auction house on Friday and Saturday nights. It gave everyone something to do and was a lot of fun. I was eleven years old at the time and went quite often with my friends. We didn't have much money, but sometimes we'd start off the bidding just for the thrill of it.

One Friday night, we were at the auction when the auctioneer asked who would bid twenty-five cents for a pair of work gloves which he held up. I had a quarter on me and figured I could resell the gloves to a workman in the neighborhood for at least a dollar, so I shot my hand up in the air.

"I will!"

"Sold to the little fella with the reindeer leg sweater!" (When you're poor you often buy irregulars if you ever get anything new, and I'd gotten such items as a reindeer sweater which only had the reindeer's legs going across the chest, with a reindeer head at one end and a reindeer ass at the other.)

I was so excited. It was the first time I had ever bought something at an auction. My friends thought I was crazy but they didn't think like a big business man. The man who worked the aisle, handing out the purchased items, gave me the gloves in exchange for my quarter and walked away. As the bidding started on the next item, I examined my purchase only to discover that the gloves were both left-handed. My friends laughed. I stood up, waving the gloves over my head.

"Hold it! Hold it! Both of these are left-handed!"

"What do you want for a quarter?" answered the auctioneer. The audience laughed and the bidding began again, but I held my ground.

"I want my money back!"

The man who had handed me the gloves walked over to me.

"Shut up, kid, and sit down!"

"Wait a minute, mister. What am I supposed to do with two left-handed gloves?"

"You'll figure out something. Now sit down or I'll throw you out!"

I sat down. I was despondent. How was I going to explain to my parents how I was conned out of a quarter? My friends were still laughing at me and I knew that by noon tomorrow the story would be all over the neighborhood. I'd never hear the end of it. I had to think of something fast and I did.

"Hey, mister," I yelled, interrupting the auction and getting everyone's attention, "you're right—I thought of something to do with these two left-handed gloves."

The people laughed.

"What?" asked the aisle man.

"Come here and I'll show you," I said with a cute boyish smile. The aisle man came over to me.

"Okay, kid, what can you do with two left-handed gloves?"

"This!" I screamed, smacking him across the face with them.

He smacked me in the head, hard enough to knock me off my feet.

"What are you doing hitting a kid?" someone yelled out.

"What's it your business!"

I was on my feet and let a punch fly, hitting the man, whose back was now to me, right on the ear. This time when he swung, I ducked. All hell broke loose! A couple of men came to my defense which led to the other auction men coming to their man's defense which led to others coming to my defenders' defense which led to one helluva brawl with punches flying every which way, benches flying through the air, one of which went through the front plate window. Within a few minutes there was just about total destruction of the auction house. The following morning it was boarded up with a sign: "Closed for alterations. Will reopen soon." Some wise guy in the neighborhood added the words, "With a special sale on left-handed gloves." I wonder who?

# SELF-EMPLOYED

SOMETIMES, I HAD TO work very hard in order to fight against those who tried to take advantage of me.

During the summer of my thirteenth year, I decided that instead of getting another lousy job in a neighborhood store, as I had been doing since age nine, I would open my own business. I talked a few neighbors into loaning me their lawn mowers, scythes, rakes and other lawn equipment. In exchange I agreed to maintain the equipment and to cut their lawns for free. Then I talked four of my friends into working for me for 50 percent of the take. The David Brenner Lawn and Backyard Maintenance Service was open for business.

We started doing real well right away, averaging about eighty bucks a week. We charged whatever the market could bear and business continued to boom. I was giving money at home and had enough left over to buy some "firsts" (as opposed to reject clothing or hand-me-downs) and take some girls to the movies, to the roller skating rink, as opposed to walking and talking. It was turning out to be a real good summer, and I was enjoying my initial experience being self-employed.

One day I walked into the neighborhood Radio Shack. It was a small store surrounded by a large empty lot, created when neighboring buildings had been condemned and razed by the city. The huge lot was another eyesore in a neighborhood of eyesores. The lot had grass-covered spots, but there were mounds of dirt and piles of debris tossed there over the years. I offered to clean up the lot, level the ground, cut the grass and plant new grass for one hundred dollars. The owner agreed.

I put my whole company on the job. I even worked! We worked from eight in the morning until five at night but the job was done and it was a good one. I wiped the sweat from my face, put on my T-shirt, smoothed out my hair with my fingers and entered the store for our pay.

"Well, the job's all done. You can look out your windows. Class A, huh?"

"Took you less time than I figured. Not too hard, huh?"

"Plenty. I put all my men on it. Even I did some work. Usually I just hustle the business. White collar," I smiled warmly.

"Well, here you go."

"Thanks. Anytime you . . . hey, wait a minute, there's only fifty bucks there. We agreed on a hundred!"

"That's when I thought it was a real tough job. Take the fifty and be thankful."

"Wait a minute, mister, we agreed on a hundred and a hundred it's going to be, or . . ."

"Or what, punk?"

He was a big guy and his two brothers were even bigger. I was all of five foot six inches, one hundred and twenty-six pounds. If I had a baseball bat . . . but I didn't.

"My pals ain't going to like this one bit, mister."

"Tough shit. Now get out of here. I got to close up. Unless you want to buy a nice fifty-dollar tape recorder."

He and his two brothers laughed. I crumpled the bills in my hand and left the store. When I told my friends what happened they wanted to attack the brothers with the scythes, but I talked them out of it. I had a better idea and one that wasn't dangerous.

I put the word out for a meeting. That evening about thirty-five of the gang met at Moe's. I told them my plan. We spread through the neighborhood, gathering all the junk we could find and used it to completely cover the Radio Shack's "new lawn." When the brothers arrived at the shop the next morning, they were greeted with piles of beer bottles, car and truck tires, crates, rags, automobile parts, bricks, newspapers, tin cans, broken furniture, ripped mattresses, rusted piping, boards, dog shit and dead pigeons.

I greeted them, backed up by about fifteen of my gang. This time we had baseball bats. I was wearing my best clothing.

"Morning. I am David Brenner, president of the David Brenner Lawn and Backyard Maintenance Company. I couldn't help noticing that your lot is in desperate need of a cleaning. Looks like it hasn't been done in years. Well, I can get the job done for you for two hundred dollars—cash in advance."

"Why, you little bastard, I'll . . ."

The owner started advancing toward me but stopped when everyone raised his bat over his head. He knew, as I did, that my friends would use them.

"If you don't want to hire us, I'd like to inform you that we also remove sugar from automobile gas tanks, repair broken store windows and help put out store fires."

I bought my first "real" leather jacket with my share of the money. Whenever I put it on, I felt a great sense of pride and accomplishment. Sometimes you have to work real hard for your principles.

*Once in a blue moon, a new Cadillac would come down Sixtieth Street and, as it drove past Moe's, I would wave and smile, hoping that the rich owner inside would think to himself, "My, that certainly is a cute lad. Let me stop and give him a few thousand dollars." Sure!*

## CARRY A BIG STICK

I HAD A LOT of weird teachers during my twelve years in public school, ranging from Miss McConnell in seventh grade, who was so cockeyed you couldn't tell at whom she was looking, to Mrs. Hitz, my tenth grade French teacher who, when she became angry at your mispronunciation of the language, would swear in French, pull fingerfuls of hair out of her head and throw them on your desk. In four short weeks, I almost made her go bald. However, the strangest one of all was a metal shop teacher in ninth grade.

My junior high was a tough school. The kids who went there were mostly tough Jews and black kids from the surrounding ghettos. Fights were commonplace. Even the teachers were terrified. If they showed the slightest bit of fear, they were overrun by the students. About half of the student body were preparing for college while the rest were preparing for prison.

One of the most popular courses was Metal Workshop because this is where thirteen-year-olds could manufacture their homemade knives, brass knuckles, zip guns and other weapons. These classes were overcrowded and unruly. The shop teacher was horrified and silent.

One day we entered metal shop as we always did, yelling, laughing, shoving, pushing and punching. We headed for our work benches, picking up our shoe boxes containing our individual projects and began setting up for work. No one had even bothered to look around for the teacher or we would've noticed that he was gone and a new teacher had taken his place. Well, actually we didn't have to look for him, he got our attention.

"Okay, let's knock off the shit! Shut the fuck up!" The room sounds died like an LP pulled off a turntable. No one had ever heard a teacher curse before. He was a short, very stocky man in his mid-forties. His barrel chest was bursting out of his shirt and you could see the mass of graying hair on it. His arms filled out his shirtsleeves and his neck was too thick for the collar. His face was deeply lined and weatherbeaten. His eyes were a piercing blue, small and deepset. He was almost completely bald but you could tell he had to shave his face a few times a day. He stood in front of his desk with his legs spread wide open.

"I heard you were a bunch of hard asses but those days are over! I'm the hardest ass you'll ever meet in your life! You fuck with me and I'll splat you against the fuckin' wall, run your bleeding ass through my buzz saw and then throw your remains out the fuckin' window! Your mother'll have to pick you up with a sponge. My name's unimportant because you're all going to call me "Sir." You've just met the toughest motherfucker you've ever met."

He then picked a large metal tip hammer off his desk, and with full force he swung it high into the air and brought it crashing down on his leg! The leg rang out like a large bell. He hit it again and again! The room reverberated like a church tower on Sunday morning.

"It's aluminum! I made it myself!"

He then threw the hammer across the room and started down the aisle, his artificial leg now obvious as he swung it along with him. For the next four months, no one ever messed around in Metal Shop as we made ashtrays, inkwells, magazine stands and other harmless household items, as taught to us by "Sir."


## THE BALLERINA

SHE'S IN EVERY HIGH school. The girl nearly everyone can't stand. Ours was Pita. That's not her real name, not to save her feelings, but she may be married to some killer giant and I don't need the aggravation of an attack. So we'll just call her Pita, which stands for Pain In The Ass.

Pita acted like God's gift to God. She was, in her own humble estimation, the perfect human. She was beautiful, but she acted more beautiful. Smart but acted smarter. Rich but acted richer.

154

You get the point. If there were a superlative for "snob," she was it. Everything about her was the best and the latest. She was Beverly Hills before Beverly Hills. A Pita before her time. She didn't dance—she studied ballet.

Every year, each class participated in a school show given in the auditorium for students, teachers and parents. Students with raw talent and no talent performed. I didn't participate because I didn't have any talent and besides I thought the whole thing, like most school activities, was stupid. I made certain my mother never wasted her time with it and tried to get out of going myself.

In our senior year, Pita was once again doing her solo ballet dance. She even had musical charts made specifically for the school orchestra. Once again, our little Miss Perfect was pirouetting across the wide auditorium stage. Boring! Then it happened. She must have taken wider spins or too many because she spun into the stage curtain and was spinning so fast that she wrapped herself up like a salt water taffy in its waxed paper covering.

Those students who couldn't stand her, which was almost all of us, leaped to our feet giving her a standing ovation, cat whistling and demanding an encore. She stayed wrapped in the curtain with the orchestra playing the rest of her chart better than I had ever heard music played by them. When the song ended, we stopped blocking the aisles so a couple of teachers could get up on the stage to unravel her. Pita wasn't such a big Pita from then on. It was moments like that which helped prove to me that there is a God.

# THE PHOTOGRAPHER

HE WAS IN HIS mid-sixties. His baggy suit made him look like he had "just gotten off the boat." His white shirt was wrinkled and frayed, his tie was too wide, too colorful, too stained, his shoes were too worn, but you could tell he tried to be neat, tried to have personal dignity. He had a stubble of beard on his face. His eyes were blue and friendly. He was carrying an old studio box camera with a three-legged tripod over his shoulder. All in all, a strange looking character.

There were about twenty-five of us twelve-year-olds. We were going home for our lunch break from school. We were all friends and, like all groups, could easily assume a mob mentality, a one-ness of thought or action. That's what a street gang is all about.

Some of the boys started giggling as soon as they saw the old man. A few comments flew. The old man smiled good-naturedly and spoke with a thick Italian accent.

"You boysa wanna picture?"

He took the camera off his back and set it on its tripod. It was the oldest, most ridiculous camera I had ever seen. It looked like he had stolen it out of a museum. Being the leader of the gang and the class comedian, I had to do my usual—show off the humor.

"Will it come out as good as Abe Lincoln's?"

Everyone laughed, as they always laughed at me. I had an audience now, so I kept rolling.

"What was it like working with Moses, huh, pop? Did you get a shot of the Red Sea parting? How's that camera operate—with steam?"

As usual, others joined in with the quick one-liners, and, as often happens, the jokes became crueler until it turned into harassment. Some of the boys started to touch the old man, making fun of his clothes. Others began messing around with his camera. I looked at the old man. He was frightened but not angry. His face was still pleasant and kind. He spoke gently as he asked to be left alone and his moves were gentle as he tried to protect his old camera. Suddenly, I felt sorry for him and regretted starting the trouble. I knew that what I did, I could undo.

"Wait a minute, you guys," I said. They stopped and looked at me.

"Tell you what, old man. You can take my picture."

"Aw, come on, Brenner, this camera can't take no pictures."

"Even you said so yourself. Let's take it home with us and play Hollywood."

"No! I said I want my picture taken! Any objections?"

It really wasn't worth anyone fighting over, so they just called me crazy and things like that and watched as the old man smiled at me, ducked his head under the black cloth that hung off the back of the camera, focused the badly bent lens and put his arm up for silence.

"Okay, boy, smile for your mama."

I smiled, the boys laughed and the old man pulled the string.

"Bravissimo!" The old man applauded and we all applauded.

156

All of us laughed. I started to walk away but the old man touched my sleeve.

"I needa your name and address so I canna deliver your pictura. Itsa dollar."

I smiled and gave him my name and address. He offered me his hand and I took it.

*"Grazia."*

*"Prego."*

We walked away, waving to the old man who smiled and waved back to all of us.

About a week later, I came home from work and was standing at the kitchen sink washing off the grime from unloading the supermarket supply truck, when my mom walked over to me.

"Why didn't you tell me you had your picture taken?"

"What picture?"

"The one I payed a dollar for from that old Italian photographer."

"You're kidding. Let me see it."

Today, it is one of the very few pictures I have hanging on the wall of my den. I don't like the way I look in photos, but this has always been my favorite picture of myself. I've included it in the photo section with pictures of my friends.


## BENNY'S POOLROOM

IT WAS LOCATED ABOVE Gollub's Supermarket, formally Cooper's, at Sixtieth and Locust Streets in West Philly. It was called Benny's Poolroom, even during those times that Benny didn't own it. Maybe the explanation of this strange statement is as good a place as any to start a story about the neighborhood poolroom.

Benny did own it. That is, he was the one who paid the rent and owned everything in it. His name wasn't on the window overlooking Sixtieth Street or on the glass door at the bottom of the stairs, but everyone in the neighborhood knew that the official name was Benny's Billiard Parlor.

Benny didn't just own and operate a pool hall, he used it. He was one of the best pool players in the neighborhood. The stakes were always high, and Benny usually walked away with every shooter's money. Plus, he still charged them for the use of the table. Benny was a tough man. There was one man who was tougher—sometimes. And that was the man who owned the luncheonette diagonally across the street from Benny's on the corner of Chancellor Street. It was called Douvry's Luncheonette, even during those times that Douvry didn't own it. Oh, here we go again—another guy with a business named after him that he doesn't own.

Well, the explanations are relatively simple. Benny and Douvry were pretty evenly matched in pool. Sometimes one would win; sometimes the other. When either one of them ran out of cash, a watch, gold pen or whatever else he had of value, he would then bet his business. Sometimes Douvry owned Douvry's and Benny's and sometimes Benny owned Benny's and Douvry's. Then there were those times when Benny owned just Benny's and Douvry owned just Douvry's, or when Benny owned Douvry's and Douvry owned Benny's.

I started going to poolrooms (not Benny's) with my father when I was about six years old. My father would introduce me to all his cronies, as he called them. Then he would put me up on a high seat (the one usually used by judging officials) and would shoot pool or craps or both. I loved the poolroom: the smoke filtering around the lights, the tough-looking men, the spitting in the spittoons, the cursing, the dirty jokes, the attention I got. Maybe what I liked best was doing something with my father, just being with him, hearing how he made the men laugh, seeing how much everyone liked him, realizing that he was as much a man as anyone and more so than most.

It was only natural that at about age nine I started going to my own pool hall—Benny's. Oh, I wasn't allowed to shoot, but I would do favors for the older guys, like get them a sandwich at Douvry's or run some number bets to the cop at the corner of Sixtieth and Spruce Street, who would take off his hat to wipe his brow so I could drop the slips of paper in it which he would in turn give to the local bookie who stopped his car to ask directions. I got paid for doing all this but I loved doing it anyway. My first job at age nine was in the supermarket right below Benny's so I hung out in the poolroom a lot. Stay in a neighborhood poolroom long enough, you'll see a lot and you'll learn a lot, some of it might even be about shooting pool. By the time I was fourteen, I had passed a lot of courses in life at Benny's Pool and Billiard University.

My first job, at age nine, was for Mr. Sobel, the butcher, in Gollub's Supermarket. Above it was Benny's Billiards where I learned a little about pool and a lot about life.

This is the elevated train stop at Sixtieth and Market Streets, where I got off. When it continued, it ran right past my bedroom window.

I worked, worked, worked; saved, saved, saved and bought this 1956 Belaire; then I made out, made out, made out!

Moe's Candy Store at Sixtieth and Locust Streets was where my "gang" hung out. For a long time, this was our whole world.

The Hot Shoppe Drive-in
Restaurant in Upper Darby,
Pennsylvania, was the Friday and
Saturday night spot for picking
up girls. Great double-thick black
and white milkshakes, too.

At age eleven in Bryant Schoolyard, I had my eyes on something. See the next picture...

I was the first boy in my class to realize that girls were a lot more fun than baseball. That's me to the left, making my approach.

This is the photo taken by the old
Italian man with the ancient box
camera. My smile tells the whole
story.

At fifteen I was the manager of Woodside Amusement Park Kiddie Land, stood over six feet tall and was cool enough to wear my belt buckle on the side.

Here I am in my late teens in a rented tux, about to attend a friend's wedding. One by one the guys got married and so ended the street corner life.

What better way to pass the time with friends than by beating the hell out of them?

Ninth grade: Me, Bernie "Getz" Getzenburg, Damon "Dame" Besinsky and Norman Shoor (who I'm still convinced switched his old trench coat for my new one later that semester).

Yours truly, Stan Bluestein and Barry "Beb" Black at age fifteen. The reason Beb is screaming is because I'm pulling his ear off. Good friend, huh?

As you can see, by ninth grade we were already a very serious lot thinking about our futures.

One of my two best pals from age seven, Edward "Dee-Dee" Romoff as he looked at age ten (cute) and a few months ago (disturbed).

My other best pal from first
grade on, Barry "Beb" Black as
we looked at ages ten and
recently in St. Maarten—still
"hanging out on a street corner."

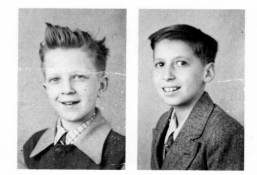

From the bottom up, here's Morty "The Bird" Hoffman, Don "Captain Marvel" Miller, Bernard "The Buzzard" Lazowick and me at age twenty-one still acting stupid.

Bernie the Buzzard trying to stretch a few more inches in height for Morty the Bird, who remained five feet (Stan the Dancer, his best friend, will argue that The Bird is 5'3". Who knows?).

Morty "The Bird" Hoffman, twenty-one, looking very tall (because nothing else is around him).

Far left to right: Bob "The Moose" Caruso, Gene "Bottles" Feldman, David "D.B." (or "Kingy") Brenner, Morty "The Bird" Hoffman, Barry "Beb" Black and Stan "The Dancer" Levinson at a recent get together. Old friendships never die—they don't even fade!

Yours truly at the helm while over my left shoulder George "Georgie Starr" Schultz, owner of Pips, does some of his obnoxious fishing and on my other side Steve Reidman, my manager, prepares to throw up. Miami Beach, 1982.

The former street corner kid not as frail and weak-looking as he appears in clothes.

Irwin "Wynn" Katz and I
happily sailing the Caribbean,
enjoying the good life!

A long way from Sixtieth Street—
the Nevada Desert, October,
1982. Beb, Brenner and Dee-Dee.

They came up the stairs. Six of them. Older than I was, maybe nineteen or twenty. Very mean looking. They were strangers, so everyone kept an eye on them. They spread out a little which meant they were there for trouble.

"Who's Crazy Jake?"

"I am," answered Crazy Jake. "What's it to you?"

"You were warned not to mess with my sister!"

They pulled out their guns so fast that all of us were caught off guard. When the first bullets were fired, I slammed myself to the floor. I was two tables down from where Jake was playing so I could see him and his friends pull out their guns and return the fire. You could hear glass crashing as windows, mirrors and overhanging table lights were hit by bullets. I decided that being so close to the shootout was not the best thing, so I belly-crawled toward the back of the poolroom. Besides, that's where the fire escape was. Seems like a lot of others had the same idea, including friends of mine, as well as Benny, Crazy Jake and his boys. Great! I'm trying to get away from Crazy Jake and he's crawling right behind me. The firing became more sporadic as everyone was pausing to reload. I thought I heard laughter. Well, that crazy son-of-a-bitch would laugh at anything. Figures that he'd find this funny. Then there was more laughter. More. Jake and his friends were standing up laughing. I peeked out from behind one of the pillars. The strangers were also standing and laughing.

"Get up you dumb fucks! It's only a joke. They're blanks!"

What a stupid joke! Firing blanks. Throwing light bulbs! Benny didn't think it was funny, either. He didn't let Jake's crowd play there for a week. If the bullets had been real, Benny would've kept them out a whole month—maybe.

"Who's Crazy Jake?"

Here we go again. Same joke a year later. I was at the table right next to Jake, but this time I kept shooting. I wasn't going to fall for the same joke twice.

"I am! What's it to you?"

I laughed and sunk a combination shot in the side pocket.

"I'm here to collect the money you owe me!"

At least they were using a new bit. I missed a bank shot on the eight ball and stepped back to watch Beb try to catch up.

"I don't have any money. Come back another day. Only next time, bring your mother!"

159

The guy Crazy Jake was talking to threw a round house right that caught Jake on the side of his jaw. The guy was good. The punch looked real. Jake was good, too. He spun around just like he was really hit. The other two guys grabbed Crazy Jake's arms and pinned them behind him as the puncher made believe he was hitting Crazy Jake right in the mouth. Crazy Jake cried out and then let the catsup or Easter egg dye or whatever he was using to look like blood run out of his mouth.

I laughed. I was surprised at what a good acting job they were all doing. "Beans," the guy Jake was playing was moving around the table taking shots. He was Jake's best friend. I felt he should have gotten into the fight or acted a little concerned to better pull off the charade. Beans was the one weak link in the fake brawl, but it was still entertaining.

The puncher threw two or three more punches into Crazy Jake's abdomen and face. I was going to applaud but decided to wait until the end. A cut opened above Crazy Jake's eye and blood started running down his face. How the hell did they arrange that? And what about the blood coming out of his nose, too? Beans had to use the space at the end of the table in order to shoot the next ball but the fake fight was in the way. Beans tapped the puncher on the back.

"Move it, Fatso! You're blocking my shot!"

"Who the fuck you think you're talking to?"

"You, you big load of shit!"

"Why you . . ."

Before the puncher's hand got back into throwing position, Beans brought the handle part of his poolstick down on the puncher's head. It sounded like a home run coming off the bat. BAM! The guy slumped unconscious on the floor; the stick broke in half. Jesus, this wasn't acting! This was for real . . .

The two guys let go of Crazy Jake's arms. Crazy Jake slid down the pillar. The two guys moved in on Beans. A big mistake. There was only one offense against Beans, one of the toughest and strongest street fighters in the West End, and that was to run your ass off! Beans held onto his title by hitting those two guys so hard and so often that they must've felt like someone dropped them off a building. They joined their unconscious friend on the floor.

Beans turned to Crazy Jake, who was wiping the blood off his face.

"All right, Jake, you want to finish this game, or what?"

Crazy Jake nodded. Beans took a new stick off the rack on the wall, chalked it, stepped over the three guys he had knocked out and made the next shot.

I guess you can say that Beans was a very strange kind of friend to have. I mean, what would've happened to Crazy Jake if that guy had never been in the way of Beans's shot? Some people have strange value systems, don't they?

I was sixteen years old and was shooting at the front table by the window overlooking Sixtieth Street. It wasn't my shot, so I was looking down on the street. I saw the unmarked cars pull up and the men in suits getting out of them.

"Cops!" I yelled, dropping my stick and joining everyone who was charging toward the back to go down the fire escape. Over the running footsteps and the yelling, you could hear the weapons and drugs being dropped on the floor. They came in the fire escape door, too! No sense running. All exits were blocked. They showed their badges, which wasn't necessary because most of the "older guys" knew the vice detectives personally, unfortunately. They lined us all against the wall and made us stand spread eagle as they ran their hands all over us, looking for everything that was already all over the floor. The cops were frustrated. The raid was foiled. Well, it was their own fault, driving up in unmarked cars with phone radio antennas sticking out of the roof, not to mention the dumb business suits they wore and short hair—all of it was a dead giveaway. Come on. No one could be arrested. The only thing they could've gotten me for was playing pool as a minor, but that would've been Benny's problem, not mine. But, as I said, the police were frustrated, so they started pushing around some of the guys who would take just so much before fighting back. Now arrests could be made and were. One policeman grabbed me tightly by the arm.

"You use dope, kid?"

"No."

"Nothing?"

"No."

"I think you shoot H."

"You crazy?" I smiled.

"I think you're a full-fledged junkie."

"Only cream cheese and peanut butter," I answered nicely with a smile on my face. The cop didn't smile back.

"Let's see those tracks!"

He ripped both sleeves off my shirt, a good shirt, too, looking for heroin needle marks on my arms. Of course he didn't find any. I told him the truth—I didn't do drugs. He could've believed me. Maybe he did. It wasn't easy being a kid growing up in a drug culture. I guess it wasn't easy being a vice detective there, either. Then again, what the hell is easy?

# DO UNTO OTHERS

A FRIEND OF MINE, an older man also from my neighborhood, was giving me a lift in his Cadillac one day when he told me about how, as a poor kid driving a truck in the neighborhood, he used to spit on the rooftops of Cadillacs as he drove past them. This was a long time ago because he ended up buying the truck, then another truck and another until today, when he operates one of the largest trucking firms in Philadelphia. As we were driving along all I kept thinking was "I wonder if the driver of the truck stopped next to us is spitting on the roof of this Cadillac?

# THE ULTIMATE WEAPON

IN WEST PHILADELPHIA ACROSS from Cobbs Creek Park, at Sixty-third and Cedar Avenue, there was a parochial school, Saint Carthage. Some of the students who attended this school had a favorite game. I'm not certain what they called it but the rules were as follows:

1. No fewer than four could play, and the more the merrier.

2. The playing field could be any street, although alleys were preferred.

3. No ball was used. In its place was a Jewish kid, but only one or two of them, unless there were at least ten Saint Carthage kids, and then three Jewish kids were allowed to play.

162

4. It was also important that the Jewish kids were at least two years younger and the more physically frail the better.

5. The objectives were to a) terrify the Jewish kid; b) steal his money, school books, religious symbol, and/or any articles of clothing; c) curse his heritage as meanly as possible; d) beat him as violently as possible; e) spit or urinate on him after the beating.

Points were given for all the above, but I'm not certain which were worth more.

The game was played as often as possible but was particularly popular during Christmas and Easter.

Reports were that it had the full approval of many of the Saint Carthage faculty, who were often seen watching the matches.

Jewish kids avoided the Saint Carthage school and its students, unless they were with enough friends. One day I made the mistake of walking alone across the street from the school. I was going over to a girl's house on whom I had a bit of a crush. I guess I was thinking of her, not paying attention to the six older boys who were crossing the street.

"Hey, Jew boy!"

I didn't have to look up to know what was going on. I just spun around, ran and leaped over the railing into the park. I figured that there was a good chance I could hide in some bushes or climb some tree or meet up with some of my friends. I also was very fast on my feet and knew the park, so I had a fairly good chance of escaping. As I ran I glanced over my shoulder. They had fanned out, so that killed the idea of hiding. I decided to gamble on my speed and started running full speed down the high hill toward the Fairmount Park Mounted Police Guardhouse and horse stables.

Even though I was fleet footed with long legs for my eleven years, the Carthage boys were older and, therefore, faster. They were gaining on me. My only hope was to beat them to the bottom of the hill and get into the Park Guard Horse Stable where the police would protect me. I got to the bottom of the hill first, ran to the other side of the stables and up to the door. It was locked! I started pounding on it. It was too late. The six boys came around the corner of the building and stopped. They laughed and started walking towards me slowly.

"Well, looks like we got us a skinny little Jew."

To my right, maybe six feet away, I saw it—a pile of horse manure balls, some still steaming. I ran to the pile and picked up maybe fifteen manure balls. Now I was a damn good hardball pitcher, displaying pretty good speed and even better accuracy. The first ball of horseshit got the kid who had done most of the talking right on the forehead—splat!

"Shit!"

"Right," I yelled and attacked.

They started running for their lives and I stayed right on their heels, stopping only to take aim and let a ball fly through the air. I chased them out of the park and into their school. I threw the last three balls of horseshit through an open classroom window, figuring that whoever they hit was probably as guilty at one time or another as they were.

I went over to Sandy's house. Even though I rubbed my hands with grass, I guess I didn't get everything back to normal because the first thing Sandy said to me was "You smell kinda funny." I answered, "Maybe, but I *feel* damn good."

There was a lot of anti-Semitism when I was growing up. Maybe there is as much or more today, but I live in a rather protected and isolated world now so I rarely see it. I was raised to be proud that I am a Jew. I would have been raised to be proud of whatever I was, for that is how my parents are. I learned no prejudices. I also learned that it was not a choice but an obligation of every Jew to fight anti-Semitism and all forms of prejudice. It is my generation's, and all subsequent generations' *duty* to see that the senseless murder of six and a half million Jews during the Nazi holocaust are best remembered by seeing that it never happens again—not even to one Jew, anywhere, anytime. That is the least we owe them. I strongly believe this! So, you see, even what started out as a funny story isn't that funny after all.


# BRICKYARD HELEN

THAT'S WHAT EVERYONE CALLED her—Brickyard Helen. She got her nickname because that's where she used to do anything the boys wanted for whatever they wanted to pay her—lying inside the smokestack in the abandoned brickyard.

The first time I saw her was when I was ten years old. I was coming home from work, and noticed a bunch of the older guys —ages fourteen to sixteen—gathered around the doorway of one of the stores on Sixtieth Street. They called me over. I thought they were watching some guys flip baseball cards or shoot craps in the doorway. When I got there, one of the older guys said, "Come on, Brenner, Brickyard Helen is giving head to everyone for nothing and it's great 'cause she got no teeth! Get in line."

There was a break in the crowd and I could see this skinny girl of maybe thirteen sitting spread legged with her back against the store door. She smiled. I saw her red gums. Then she went to work on the next guy in line. Everyone cheered. I walked away and went home. I never did do anything with Brickyard Helen, although through the years I did see her in plenty of action.

The day they tore down the old brickyard smokestack to begin excavation for the junior high school I would eventually attend, the older guys hoisted Brickyard Helen up on their shoulders and marched her around the brickyard for the last time, although she would continue her work wherever she found the action.

One summer evening a few years later, I was standing at Moe's corner with fifteen or so of my friends and some of the "older guys," when someone spotted Brickyard Helen. She was about half a block away, coming toward us. With her was a young sailor in uniform and they were pushing a baby carriage. There had been a rumor, after Brickyard Helen had disappeared from the neighborhood, that she had married a sailor in Virginia, but no one believed it. As they approached us Helen looked worried. I didn't blame her. The neighborhood slut passing all the guys to whom she had done everything and anything for any price or no price, anywhere, anytime. I figured they were going to verbally attack her and make fun of her and . . .

"Hi, Helen, good to see you. How are you?"

I don't remember who was the one who said it, but he said it, God bless him, and then everyone followed suit, asking how she had been, admiring her baby, shaking her husband's hand in congratulations, telling him what a wonderful girl he married, and wishing them well.

After she left, no one said anything about her, not even a comment on the fact that no one called her "Brickyard" or that when she smiled, her false teeth were perfect, but I'll bet every-one thought it. I know I did. I'll tell you something else I thought

165

that night and never said—I was real proud of all the guys on the corner, real proud!


# HAIRCUTS

MOST KIDS DON'T LIKE to get haircuts. I was no different. One time my mother asked me when I was going to let her take me to the barber's for a haircut and I answered, "Christmas." It was July at the time. She made me wait. I think I was the first long hair in America.

The worst part about getting a haircut was handing the barber the note which read, "Please cut the chewing gum out of David's hair. Thank you. Mrs. Brenner." A heavy price to pay for falling asleep with chewing gum in my mouth.

I also didn't like the neck powder, the little hairs down my back, the stinko perfume, the stupid way the barber combed my hair and, of course, "swats." This was a neighborhood tradition, I guess. When someone got a haircut, if you yelled the word "swats" before he yelled "no swats," you could smack him real hard on the back of the head at the hairline. I hated swats.

When I got to my teens, haircuts got to be fun because you went with your friends instead of your mother and the talk in the shop was fun. Most of us went to Emil's Barber Shop, right around the corner from Benny's Poolroom. Emil was a good character. A short Italian man, he was bald (of course), looked like Elmer Fudd and loved to gamble. He'd gamble on anything but craps was his passion. After the haircut, you would step in the backroom with Emil and roll him once for the haircut, double or nothing. It was almost always nothing, because Emil had the worst luck of almost all crapshooters in the world.

Emil's was a great place but the greatest barber shop in all of Philadelphia was the one located in the Bellevue Stratford Hotel on Broad Street. This was where all the politicians, sports players, business tycoons and gangsters had their hair cut. My dream was to someday go there. I knew it would be a while before I would want to or could afford to spend five dollars for a haircut when Emil only charged thirty-five cents and that was before the crap shoot.

The day came after I turned sixteen. I was working real hard, gambling pretty good, and saving a few bucks here and there. I decided to treat myself to that special haircut. I got on the bus and went into Center City, to the Bellevue Stratford Hotel Barber Shop. It was everything I had thought it would be: twelve chairs, barbers all dressed in bright white jackets, a man to shine shoes, a man to brush off your suit jacket, two manicurists and a cashier. Like in a movie!

I walked up to the cashier's desk. One of the barbers walked over to me.

"May I help you?"

"Yeah. I'd like a haircut."

"We're all booked up today."

"Oh. Well, then, tomorrow."

"Tomorrow, too."

I didn't like the way he was looking at me. I knew he had sort of studied my long, greasy hair and my clothes as he walked over to me, but now he was looking into my face with a bored, arrogant expression on his face.

"How about next week?"

"Booked."

"Next month? Next year?"

He shook his head. I looked past him. Other barbers and some of the businessmen sitting in the chairs were watching the scene now. I looked around at everyone and announced:

"My name is David Brenner. Someday, I'll be back!"

I spun around on my heels and stormed out of the shop, letting the door slam behind me. I was so angry that I almost chipped my teeth from grinding them together. I pushed past people in the lobby. I was just hoping someone would say something to me, anything, so I could beat the hell out of him and get it out of my system, but no one said a word and I went back to my neighborhood.

When I was a successful writer/producer/film director with my own documentary series in Philadelphia, after my name and picture had appeared often in the local papers, after I had been seen regularly in the company of the city's leading citizens, I made a standing weekly appointment at the Bellevue Stratford Hotel Barber Shop—every Friday at four in the afternoon. Every time I walked in everyone greeted me, someone took my suit jacket and hung it up, and I sat in the "first" chair with their best barber, Al Stavola. I tipped big and gave expensive

Christmas presents to everyone in the shop.

One day, after I had been going there for two years or so, I told Al the story of my first trip to the shop.

"Guess it must make you feel pretty good now, huh, Dave?"

"No, Al. I wish it did. It still hurts."

I knew that Al understood—he was also from my old neighborhood.


## TOO FAR TOO SOON

I ONCE MET A rich girl whom I liked a lot, so we made a date. I used my American Express card to buy a whole new outfit, top to bottom, just for that night. As I was driving the girl's Cadillac convertible on the Pennsylvania Turnpike with the top down, I called to my friend, Joe, who was in the backseat with his date.

"This is the life, huh, Joe?"

"Yes, it is, but if right now you had with you only what you *own,* you'd be running down this road in your underwear!"

He was right.

*I've always said that weddings and funerals make me sad—weddings even more so, because at least when a man is dying, he knows what's happening to him.*

*When I was in my late teens, someone once told me that we pay for our sins, so I got a second full-time job.*


## GOING HOME

A COUPLE OF YEARS ago, on impulse, I rented a car and drove to Philadelphia to see all the many houses and apartments where I had lived and left personal landmarks. I even took a leak in the alley behind Dee-Dee's house as Beb, Dee-Dee and I had done so often throughout our childhood. It was much smaller than I had remembered—the alley, wise-guy, the alley!

I saved the best for last—the house on Sansom Street where I had moved when I was nine and lived in the longest. I parked the car and looked at the house. It looked a lot better than when we had lived there. It was freshly painted and had newer porch furniture. Why not? I got out of the car, walked up the front steps and knocked on the door. A middle-aged black man pulled open the venetian blinds.

"Yes?"

"My name is David Brenner and I used to live here. I wondered if I might come in and look around for a second or two?"

He eyed me suspiciously. In today's world, I couldn't blame him.

"If you lived here, tell me what's strange about this house?"

"A lot," I laughed.

"Like what?" he asked, seriously.

"Well, let's see—oh, yeah, the arches above both dining room entrances are crooked. My father did them himself to save money. And, if no one has changed the wallpaper in all the rooms, then it's peeling, because he did that himself, as well—or as poorly, I should say."

"What else? In the cellar."

"The cellar? Well, all the heater pipes are covered with asbestos and my name and the name of my last girl friend might still be written there . . . oh, there could be lots of little holes in the wall under the back window from my BB gun target practice . . . the old coal bin . . . I can't think of anything else."

"As you go down the steps."

"There's a shelf where my father stored the winter rugs and I once hid a radio microphone and . . . I can't think of anything else."

"On that shelf. You can see it the moment you open the door and . . ."

"The horseshoe! I hung a horseshoe there when we moved in. Found it in the park. But I hung it upside down. 'The luck will run out', my father told me. Is that it?"

"That's it," he smiled and opened the door. He extended his hand. "My name is Howard Johnson, as in the restaurant, but I don't have their money, and this is my wife, Kathleen."

"Glad to meet you and thanks for letting me in."

"We heard a family named Brenner once lived here."

"Then why . . ."

"All the questions?" he laughed. "Come on. Let's see it together and then I'll tell you."

As we walked to the dining room my eyes seemed to be able to "read" more information than normally. I could see so many things, existing now and in the past, as though I were looking through a wide angle lens: the crooked arches, my father's chair, the sofa where we all napped, the stair landing from which Lou threw water to break up a fun wrestling match between Moby Dick and me, which resulted in ruining the ceiling wallpaper, the little table where Bib kept her record player and LP collection, the strategically placed pictures to cover the cracks and holes in the walls, the rug where Moby Dick and I played card games he made up, the mantel above the fake fireplace where mom placed the ceramics she made in her kiln, the dining room table where I sat to do my homework, the spot where my dog Duke curled up to nap, the dining room cabinet in which mom kept her "good silverware and good dishes for company" and on top of which were framed family photos, the little window where I looked to see what the weather was like because at one particular angle you could actually see a piece of the sky; the telephone table I made in shop and kept instead of trading it for knishes, the spot where we all stood with my father and threw money into the air when he hit the numbers real big, the marks in the rug when I forgot to take off my roller skates before coming into the house, the chairs my childhood friends sat in waiting for me to come down-stairs, the outlet for the old vacuum cleaner whose bag some-times exploded with dust, the wall which had the mirror on it that I finally became too tall to see my face in without stooping down, the path across which I pushed my two-wheeler bike on the way down the cellar . . . the bombardment of these and so many other images from the past, superimposing themselves over one an-other, miniseconds of vivid memories, sounds and sights and feelings intertwining, pulling at the memory, touching the emo-tions, crashing out of retirement . . .

"There it is—the horseshoe."

"Sure is. Just the way I left it."

"Exactly, which is what I'm going to tell you about. Now, this is going to sound real strange, crazy, actually. When we moved in here, I kept looking at that horseshoe wondering who put it there the wrong way, and . . . well, I had this strong feeling that I shouldn't remove it or paint over it, because one day I was going to meet the person who put it there and it would be important to him."

I looked at Mr. Johnson. I didn't know what to say. It was such a strange story in an already too strange day. I looked at the horseshoe and could clearly remember the day I put it there. It was the lowest point in my family's life. We had gotten evicted and moved in here. I wanted to change our luck, so I hung the horseshoe. Mr. Johnson was right. It was important that I saw it again.

"You can paint it now, Mr. Johnson, and I hope it brings you and your family as much happiness and luck as it brought to mine."

"Thank you. Eh . . . look, why don't you kinda walk around by yourself for a while and . . . eh, take your time."

"Thank you."

I liked him but was glad to be alone. One should be alone during such a rare and special moment. I went into the kitchen. They had busted out the wall, combining the dining area and cooking area. A good idea, but I missed seeing that little window in the wall through which mom passed the food. I could hear all the laughter that once rang in this room. It has always been a Brenner family tradition that all meals should be accompanied by lots of laughter. Everyone saved his or her funny stories until we were dishing out the food.

I looked at the overhead fixtures and wondered if Mr. Johnson had corrected the problem created by my father when he some-how connected the breakfast room light to the bathroom light upstairs, so when one went on, the other went off, making it a standing rule that one had to announce when one was going to the bathroom, so anyone in the breakfast room would be pre-pared to be in the dark a few moments or call out to anyone in the bathroom when one was going into the breakfast room. I still have the stupid habit of announcing to people, even strangers, when I'm going to the bathroom.

I looked at the refrigerator and remembered how, when we first moved in, we didn't have enough money to buy one and used to have a wash basin on the floor with a big chunk of ice in it, and how I used to watch the margarine and the food floating around in the ice water. Then there was the kitchen where we stood to eat, until my friend Linsey's mother gave us an old kitchen set she had.

The kitchen where mom created great ceramics in her kiln and terrible food in the oven. Memories, memories, memories . . . the doorknob around which I would secretly tie my mother's apron string, so when she walked away, the back door flew open and hit her in the rear end. It always made her laugh.

I stood on the little back porch looking at the shed that was still on it, the shed I used to climb on top of and then boost myself up to sneak into my bedroom through the window. The backyard where I forgot to take in my pet turtle during a blizzard and at the end of winter found only the string that was tied around his neck and an empty shell, where my mother tried to plant tomato bushes, where I handed mom the wooden clothespins out of the canvas bag slung over my shoulder to help her on washday, where my dog would dig holes and bury the bones I stole from the butcher shops, the iron fence I used to leap over when I was taking off in my sneakers to run up to Moe's and hang out with the gang.

It was all gone, but, for the briefest of moments, it was all still there.

I walked back into the house and into the living room. I couldn't bring myself to go upstairs. I guess bedrooms are such a personal part of everyone's life, the Johnson family's and mine, that I wanted to keep our bedrooms just as I remembered them.

"Thank you, Mr. Johnson, I really appreciate it. You've kept the house in a lot better shape than we did," I smiled, but Mr. Johnson didn't smile. He was looking deeply into my eyes, deeply enough to know my kidding around was only a thin layer of disguise floating on top of the real emotions I felt. He took my hand in both of his, squeezed it, and said in a voice so soft that even his wife, who was only a few feet away, could not hear.

"Anytime you want to come home again, David, you are welcome."

"Thank you," I whispered.

I said good-bye to them and left. I sat in my car a moment, reflecting on what had happened. I started the car and pulled out of the parking space. As I passed the house I looked at it and saw Mrs. Johnson with one hand holding open a few venetian slats on the door window and her other hand waving exactly as my mother had done every night I left my house. I waved back.

Yes, a lot of people have felt that Thomas Wolfe was correct when he wrote you can never go home again, and I have to agree, but you *can try*—and it's worth it—I think.

172

# ONLY ONE TRULY LIKE ME

I DIDN'T LIKE SCHOOL; I didn't like teachers and teachers didn't like me. I was what today is called a "disruptive student." This means I was bored to tears and was well liked by my fellow students.

My first recollection of dislike for school was the first week in kindergarten when I refused to return, explaining my reason to my mother:

"This woman makes us eat milk and cookies when I'm not hungry, lie down on a blanket on the floor when I'm not even tired and gives us clay and blocks to play with—all silly stuff. I'm not going back!"

Of course I had to and did but kept thinking how stupid it all was. I still think so.

Many of my problems stemmed from being raised properly. You see, in my home we were allowed, even encouraged, to express our individuality. Freedom was a major value. So was laughter. Crazy concepts, aren't they? Well, in school they teach you freedom as an important value by not letting you enjoy any of it. I found this out my first day in first grade. I stood up and started out of the room.

"Just where do you think you are going, young man?"

I thought the teacher must be kidding. No one ever asked me this question at home, so I just kept going.

"Young man! I said, 'Where are you going?'"

She was serious. "To the bathroom," I replied.

"Well, you must raise your hand and ask permission to go. Now return to your seat and do it!"

Now this was the craziest thing I had ever heard! Asking permission to go to the bathroom? That's like asking permission to breathe. I kept walking.

"If you walk out of this room, you can just walk right home and don't come back without your mother or father!"

That's exactly what I did. After I first went to the bathroom, of course. My mother came in the next day and tried to explain the family's belief in freedom to the teacher, which failed miserably, as did the teacher's attempt to control me. Throughout all my days in school, I never raised my hand to leave the room. It caused me to be "kept after school" or to be expelled a lot but it was a small price to pay for personal freedom.

I got expelled a lot for various other reasons, too. Miss McConnell expelled me once because she thought I was joking around when I misspelled the first simple word given me in a class spelling bee game. I can't spell.

In sixth grade, Mrs. Cantor expelled me because I had all the right answers in a math test without "showing my work," so she concluded I was cheating. My mother came to school and explained that, like my father, I had an uncanny ability with numbers (which was one of the reasons my father was a good numbers bookie. He could memorize all the plays for the day.) Only after my mother insisted that Mrs. Cantor give me a test with no other students in the room and I got all the correct answers without showing my work, was I given my one hundred and returned to class.

Ironically, in spite of the too-numerous-to-mention expulsions from school, I still managed five achievements of which I am still proud:

1. I was never late for school or to a class.
2. I was elected class president from fourth grade through twelfth.
3. I always made the honor roll, all As and Bs.
4. I was voted Class Comedian.
5. The system never beat me!

My only regret was that my mother had to stop her housework or shopping, put on her one nice dress and come to my school to get me out of trouble so often, but I finally worked that out in eighth grade. I told my mother that we were studying handwriting analysis in school and asked her to write her name at the bottom of two hundred sheets of tablet paper. All I did after that was write above her signature an apology for my actions and an excuse of why my mother could not appear in person. I covered myself further by making sure that whenever a notice for Parent-Teacher Day was sent, I got to the mail before my mom did. The only time after this that she ever had to come to my school was graduation night, which saved mom a lot of time, aggravation and gray hairs.

In spite of my roller skating down the study hall aisle, stealing the crayfish in biology class, having a "who can scream the loud-

174

est" contest with Beb, imitating over the P.A. system the principal's voice to get me and my friends out of class, charging into the vice-principal's office with a stocking over my head and making believe it was a robbery, rolling hundreds of marbles down the assembly hall floor, throwing all the board erasers down the air chutes, switching the Boy's Room and Girl's Room signs, taking the whole school out with me when I got expelled by setting off the fire alarm and then exiting last and bowing from the waist, making money bets that I could close the alligator's eyes at the zoo by spitting on their heads, marking up Billy "Eppis" Berger's face with a ballpoint pen so he looked like a road map, making a large wooden penis in wood shop and putting it on Mrs. Bristol's desk, smoking cigarettes, spitting, cursing, making out in the fire escape, ad infinitum, there were a couple teachers who *sort of* liked me.

They were my fifth grade teacher, Mrs. Bishop, who let me tell my Tarzan episodes in front of the class every day, and my high school physics teacher, Dr. Jacobs, who allowed me *exactly* five minutes at the beginning of the class to tell jokes and do my antics to make the class laugh, and then, as agreed by our handshake, I was to sit down and keep my big mouth shut for the rest of the hour. He would actually time my five minutes with a stopwatch and yell "cut!" even in the middle of a punch line. Neither of us ever broke the bargain and I'm still grateful to him.

However, there was only one teacher who truly liked me, my homeroom teacher, biology teacher and our graduating class sponsor, Miss Bessie Abromowitz. The best way to describe this lovable human being is to tell you that she bore an uncanny resemblance to Golda Meir, the former prime minister of Israel. She was a special person not because she liked me, but because, like Golda Meir, everyone loved her. She was a great teacher, too. Whenever my antics got a little wild or my kidding around a little out of hand, she would always say to me after class, quietly so no one else could hear, "David, if only one day you channel all that energy and talent, you could be *somebody.*"

Well, it took me a very long time to channel it, but I did, and a couple of years ago, during an engagement outside Philadelphia, I drove into the city and went to my old high school. I got a "Hall Pass," permitting me to walk in the halls where adult guards were posted, where you could see the wire protective coverings on the windows, where you could read the graffiti, where you could feel the danger and anger and hopelessness, as it all existed when I was there, only now it was so much more obvious and intense.

I stopped at the door which read Biology Lab and peeked through the small rectangle of clear glass. Miss Abromowitz, much, much older, was in front of the classroom. She was pointing out the parts of the leaf, explaining, as she did for us, the miracle of osmosis. Time almost stood still. I was going to walk away, satisfied that I had just seen her one more time, when she turned and saw me. It had been a long time, graduation night, but her face brightened. She said something to the students and came into the hall.

"David Brenner, my, my, my, but it's good to see you!"

Even though I had grown up, I still couldn't kiss a teacher, so I just smiled and told her how glad I was to see her and that she looked well. We filled each other in on the achievements, failures, happy tidings and tragedies of my fellow classmates and then she commented on my career, adding: "I'm so proud of you, David, and I'm so happy for you, too, because you were always one of my favorite students, you know."

"Yes, I know. Thank you. Isn't it ironic, Miss Abromowitz, that you were the only teacher I ever had who truly liked me and you're the only one who is still alive!"

"You're still bad, David," she laughed.

She invited me to say a few words to her students. After telling stories that made the students laugh for ten or fifteen minutes, I stopped to "really look" at each of them. Into faces that a few years ago were mine and my friends. It was time to stop joking. It was time to say something, something important, something I had wished someone had said to me when I sat there searching aimlessly for a way out and up. Something, but what? I just started talking—from my heart.

"What's more important than the fact that I can stand up here and make you laugh or stand in front of a Las Vegas audience or on TV and do the same, or that I know some of your favorite Hollywood and TV stars—what's more important is that I used to be in this classroom. My seat was that one. The answers to the osmosis test are probably still taped inside. I guess what I'm trying to tell you is that I went to your school, lived in your houses, played in your streets, wore your clothes and felt inside what you feel; I dreamed your dreams; I'm one of you! And I made it. Now, I'm going to tell you the secret of how to do it. How to get out of the neighborhood. It's not easy, but you can do it. If I did, you can. All you got to do—this is the big secret—all you got to do—is channel all that energy and talent you got and you'll make it. You'll be somebody. A very wise person taught me that and she was right."

I looked at Miss Abromowitz. She was smiling but there were tears in her eyes.

I left the school and drove out of the city. It had been a strange day for me—happy and sad. I was happy I had gone back to my old school, but I did have one regret—I was sorry that I had not kissed Miss Abromowitz.

# GETTING OUT

# MY MAIN GOAL IN LIFE

I DON'T REMEMBER THE exact moment I realized that I was poor. Maybe it was seeing a movie in which people drove fancy cars, lived in fancy houses and ate fancy food, or maybe I saw a difference between the world I lived in and what I saw in magazine advertisements, or maybe it was in elementary school, when I noticed that a few of the other kids wore store-bought clothes that were in style, or perhaps it came to me when I couldn't afford to buy a candy bar or go to a movie or ride on a trolley, or maybe it was at home when I overheard my parents talking about not being able to buy something or another. One thing is for certain —whenever it was, it was too early in my life and it hurt!

No, I might not remember when I found out I was poor, but I can remember everything about being poor and what it felt like to be poor. It was as though it had all happened a few days or weeks ago, and, maybe for me, it'll always be that close. Poverty was a week ago this coming Friday. But it will never be next week, or the week after, or the week after that, or any week, ever again! I have a nine-year-old boy to thank for this, too—me.

Yes, at an age when most children daydream about being a fireman, policeman or baseball player, I used to lie in bed at night, daydreaming about my escape from the sweltering heat of my non-air-conditioned room, ignoring the noises of the streets, forgetting all the empty pockets in the house and the bare shelves in the refrigerator; I would lie in bed, arms folded behind my head, eyes staring up at the cracked ceiling. I saw pictures from the future, my future, wonderful pictures I had played over and over in my mind with one central character, an adult me, all grown up, successful and wealthy, sharing my achievements and money with my family in a hundred different, joyful situations. These pictures took me far from the ghetto, far from where I lay, far from my present reality. When I had nothing, I knew that someday I was going to have everything; when I couldn't afford to go anywhere, I knew that someday I would be able to go everywhere. Climbing into a bathtub of lukewarm water already used by my parents, sister and brother, I knew I would one day swim in the warm waters of the Caribbean; when I never owned a store-bought toy, I knew someday I would play on the deck of my own boat; when I watched my mother "turn the collar" of my one shirt to make it last another year, I knew someday I would own a suit for every day of the week; when everyone in my family did without so much, I knew that I would see to it that someday they would not do without anything!

These weren't just childhood dreams, they were future realities temporarily wrapped up in dreams. I was going to be "somebody" someday! It wasn't a thought, it was a fact! I wasn't going to be just another guy from the neighborhood. I didn't have any idea of how I was going to do it, but I knew that I would. I started planning on it when I was nine. I counted on it! I knew it was going to be as surely as I knew who I was. Nothing and no one would stop me! Only if life itself stopped would I fail to do it. I had decided on my main goal in life—to get out!

## EARLY IDEALISM

WHEN I WAS A real little boy, age five at the most, Atlantic City was in the last throes of its pregambling greatness, skeletal shades of what had been the "vacation showplace of the world." The touches of splendor were fading quickly. Men and women still dressed in their finest to walk the boards at night. Matter of fact, you weren't allowed on the boardwalk without a jacket. Even though I enjoy the casual, dress-as-you-may-care world of today, there was something special about the elegance of the past. I'm glad I saw some of it and remember.

One night, as I was sitting in a boardwalk pavilion, a section attached to the boardwalk which juts out over the beach and is filled with wooden benches for the weary, my mother and I were enjoying our favorite pastime game—watching people. We would make fun of the people, their shapes, their walks and their idiosyncracies, and we had a secret way of signaling each other to look at someone—by squeezing each other's hand. Well, as always, I was enjoying the game when I saw an old black man slowly walking by. He was dressed in a very shabby, torn pair of pants and nonmatching sport jacket. His shoes were scuffed. I lived in a poor neighborhood but had never seen a man this poorly dressed. I'll never forget it. The image is still clear in my mind.

"Mom, why is that man dressed that way?"

"Sometimes, David, life is much more difficult for black people than for white people."

"That's not fair, mom. Someday, I'm going to do something to change that."

I still believe it's unfair and I still wish there was a way to change it.


# ALCOHOL AND PHILOSOPHY

BEB, BLAINE, EDDIE METELITS and I were working our way through high school with jobs in the toys, novelties and sundry item wholesale houses in the downtown Market Street area. We delivered orders, kept stock, sold, cleaned up, got coffee and sandwiches, parked customers' cars, etc. Whatever the bosses decided you should do is what you did. One day the four of us happened to meet up with one another on our way delivering packages.

We were cutting through a parking lot at Second and Market Streets when up ahead we spotted a drunk. Often stores hired unemployed or "beached" Merchant Marines as extra help. Many of them had drinking problems. This one obviously did. He was holding a rather large box in his arms, which he never dropped as he careened from one car to another. He'd stagger a few steps, crash into the hood of a parked car, spin off it, bang into another car's fender, bounce back into the trunk of another car, juggle the package, stagger, bump, crash, spin.

We were laughing at him. Hearing us, he picked himself up and looked in our direction. He started staggering toward us. We laughed harder. His staggering lessened as he walked. We laughed a little less. He kept his eyes on us as he came closer, swaying just a little unsteadily as he walked now. He stopped about six feet in front of us and stared at each of us. We stopped laughing. His bloodshot eyes focused on me. He shifted his box so he could hold it with one arm. He pointed a finger at me and spoke in a hoarse, quiet, clear, steady voice.

"Everyone has a weakness. Everyone. Mine is alcohol. You should pray to God, son, that someday you'll discover yours."

He gripped the package in both hands and staggered away as drunk as ever. We watched until he turned the corner, then walked away without saying a word.


# NEW YORK, NEW YORK!

THE FIRST TIME I saw New York was in a revival John Garfield movie when I was about ten. I don't remember what movie it was, but I remember the scene. Garfield, who was and still is my favorite actor, is standing in a dinner jacket on the balcony of some penthouse apartment overlooking the New York skyline. He's with a beautiful lady and he says something to her from a good B-movie script, like "Someday, I'm gonna wrap up this town and put it in my vest pocket!" I loved the line and I loved the city. I remember the tremendous impact the shots of the city had on my young mind. I thought, "Now that's a city," and I knew I was going to spend most of my adult life living there.

When I was fourteen I made my first trip to New York City. It was even greater than in the movies or in my imagination. What an exciting, ever changing, dynamic place! I loved it!

My friend, Big Micky, reminded me of a story about New York I had forgotten. To me what happened was just a simple statement of fact, although to him it was a special revelation.

As we often did when we were sixteen, a whole gang of us, two or three carloads, drove up to New York and rented one hotel room in Times Square that we all snuck into. After spending a fantastic weekend there we would return to Philadelphia late Sunday night.

As Micky related it to me, he said that during one of these weekends he had awakened at the very first light of dawn. He saw me standing at the window overlooking Times Square. My back was to him—it was the same position I had been in when he had fallen asleep three hours before. My hands were in the pockets of my black suit pants. I was wearing a white shirt with a black velvet vest. I stood as still as a statue.

"Hey, Dave, how long you been standing there?"

"All night," I answered quietly, without turning around. Micky said I spoke as though I were talking in my sleep.

"Why?"

"Because someday I'm going to live here. This is where I'm going to become 'somebody', so I just want to see my city wake up."

He told me that he had gotten goosebumps when I spoke because he had never heard such determination in anyone's voice before. He fell back asleep watching his friend at the window, silhouetted by the rising morning sun.

I used to think I was having a love affair with New York City, but now I know it even goes beyond that. I am *addicted* to New York. As I once told a friend, "There are only two things in my life that have never, never, ever let me down—my parents and New York City!"

## FLYING AWAY

AS A SMALL CHILD lying in bed at night, I used to listen to the planes flying over my house. I'd often wonder about where they were going, and thought of how I'd like to be up there in them. Now there are times during my travels when I'll fly over a solitary house resting peacefully in a valley or on the side of a mountain. Sometimes I'll see a light burning in the window. I often wonder about whether the people living there are happy and what they do, and sometimes I think of how I'd like to be down there with them.

# STEAK

MY MOTHER MADE SOMETHING she called "fake steak." What it was was a hamburger patty flattened out into the shape of a steak, with a steak bone imbedded in it and some steak fat carefully placed around the outside of it. I always used to wonder what a "real steak" tasted like, but it was impossible for me to find out, so I just kept enjoying mom's creation.

A few years ago, I was in Philadelphia, performing at Palumbo's nightclub. My friend, Joe, and I went to Arthur's Steak House on Walnut Street and were enjoying filet mignon lunches. The maître d' asked if I would sign their guestbook and, of course, I agreed.

I wrote: "To Arthur's Steak House, where I ate my first steak."

The maître d' read it and laughed. Then he showed it to some waiters and bartenders and they laughed too. Joe and I didn't laugh, because we knew it was true and nothing to laugh about.


# J. B. VAN SCIVER'S WINDOW

J. B. VAN SCIVER'S was a furniture store located on City Line Avenue, one of the most affluent areas of Philadelphia filled with stores that catered to the wealthy. All of their merchandise was top-notch. Whenever we drove past the store as teenagers I'd look into the windows featuring displays of complete rooms of furniture, from kitchen to bedroom, and I used to think that I'd like to live in the store windows of Van Sciver's. A few weeks ago, I happened to be driving down City Line Avenue and saw that J. B. Van Sciver's had closed their store there. I just sat back in the limo. It really doesn't matter anymore, anyway.


# CAREER CHOICE

LOOKING BACK AT MY childhood friends, I've realized that most of them are now working in the field or trade they had first started in as teenagers or younger. The stockboy in the tobacco and

186

sundry wholesale house is a partner in the same business today; the fellow who ran errands for an engineering firm today works for an engineering company, the clean-up boy in the beauty shop became a hairdresser. And so it seems to go. We innocently spin our futures by the things we do, and our destiny is sometimes determined by insignificant events—the chance answering of a newspaper ad, walking into a place the moment a position happens to open up, falling into our futures by chance. One must be careful of those temporary jobs one takes as a youth. If it's too late for you, keep an eye on your children.

Maybe I avoided this invisible trap because of a mental game I played in every job I ever had. I would look at my boss or the owner and ask myself if I wanted to end up like him. I never have worked for anyone whom I wanted to look like, dress like, or be like in any manner or form. This is probably why I've ended up not working for anyone. However, when I step outside of myself and look at how I am today, I know I would like to be like me. Therefore, I know I'm doing what I truly enjoy, and that I am who I'd like to be.

## OVERSIMPLIFICATION?

STANDING ON THE CORNER of Moe's one night, I told my friends I knew how we could get out of the neighborhood: Everyone goes home, puts on his sneakers, meets back at the corner, and we just walk out and keep going until we find a nice place to live. They laughed, but I was serious.

## HOW TO GET OUT

I DIDN'T KNOW HOW to get out of the neighborhood. I couldn't figure out what I wanted to do with my life after high school. I was lost, like so many other teenagers. Maybe I needed time to think, time away from home. The draft answered the question for me.

It doesn't take long in the army for one to realize he hates it and wants to get out. I was in basic training about three weeks, surviving on three hours sleep per night, twenty-mile fast hikes with full sixty-pound backpacks, KP duty, guard duty, calisthenic punishments, saying "sir," saluting and a lot of other horrors life in green can offer. Not only was I still lost and confused, I was now miserable, too! One day a career soldier who had twenty some odd years in uniform called to me from behind my barracks.

"Psssst. Over here."

"What's up, pop?"

"You want to know how to get out of the army, Brenner?"

"Are you kidding? Who wouldn't? What's it going to cost me?"

"Come here and I'll tell you the secret for free."

"Nothing's free, pop. What's your angle?"

"No angle. Come over here so no one can hear us."

"All right, we're here. Now, what's the big secret? How do I get out of the army?"

"Do your time!"

"Do your . . . ? Lunatic!"

After a few more months in the service I realized that old soldier wasn't crazy. His advice was good. If you're going to have to do your time, just make the best of it until that time is up. I guess that also applies to living in the neighborhood and just about anything else in life—you've got to do your time.


## THE LAST OFFICER

I HAD RECEIVED MY mustering-out pay. My discharge papers were in my hands. I had done my time, all two years of it—a private first class.

First I was in the 101st Airborne, then I was in cryptography; now I was walking toward the front gate of Fort Dix, New Jersey, to the bus that would take me to Philly, my family, my friends, my freedom. The army did give me time to think, to sort out some of the pieces, to get to know myself better, to see the world, to grow up. I was still uncertain about what to do but I was better off than when I went in. Now don't misunderstand one thing— even though all this was true—I still hated being in the army— the regimentation, the harsh discipline, the wastefulness, the silly rules and regulations and especially the officers!

On this last day as the officer approached me, I snapped off a salute. He returned it.

"Good morning, sir!"

"Good morning, troop."

"Sir, I wish you'd do me the favor of accepting this one dollar bill which I've had in my wallet for the past two years just for this special occasion. Thank you, sir!"

I saluted again, the snappiest salute of my military career. The officer snapped his salute, I showed my discharge papers to the MP, walked through the gate and did an about-face to see the officer to whom I had given the dollar. He was holding it in his hand. He stared at me with a look of total bewilderment on his face.

After basic training I had written these words on the bill: "You are the last asshole I'm ever going to have to salute or call sir. Civilian, David Brenner."

I gave the officer the finger, ripped off my khaki uniform shirt, threw it over the fence, screamed as loud as I could and bounced away to get my bus. I was going back to the same ghetto I had left, but I was free, full of old ambitions and new hope.


# SILVERFISH

THEY'RE A SMALL INSECT, something like a thinned-down cockroach and their backs glisten silver—thus the name silverfish. Just like their counterparts, they are found in the kitchen and bathroom, around waterpipes and, eventually, around everything else. They're as disgusting as anything else that crawls.

My usual philosophy, even when it comes to bugs, is live and let live. I have found, however, that my liberal attitude towards crawling life is greatly influenced by numbers. Up to nine bugs, I'm still pretty liberal. When you get into double figures, my liberalism diminishes in direct proportion to the number.

It was my third and final year at Temple University in Philadelphia and I was still stuck in my old neighborhood. I was living on Market Street in West Philadelphia, and in addition to the horrendously noisy elevated train running directly across from my bedroom window, I had to endure the onslaught of all kinds of verminous armies because I lived above a laundromat and the heat of the dryers sent the crawling world a-crawling, upstairs, to me.

It was a very hot and humid July night. I had no air conditioning and the windows couldn't be opened because the elevated train would blow its filthy dust and soot right into my bedroom. There were no other windows in the apartment. The laundromat dryers added another twenty degrees to the already record-breaking temperatures. I had already taken a walk, as dangerous as it was in that area at night, and didn't have enough money to go to an air-conditioned movie or to buy a drink in an air-conditioned bar.

I could do only one thing—lie as still as possible and try to take my mind off the heat. Lying on my bed, a wet washcloth on my forehead, I entertained very few positive thoughts. My life, at that time, was not exactly going well. I had finished my time in the army; I had even finished college, getting a B.S. in Mass Communications, but I couldn't get a job. So here I was in my early twenties, still unable to pull myself up by my bootstraps and get the hell out of the damn neighborhood and start building a future. I was still lost.

I got out of bed and went into the kitchen to see if the semibroke refrigerator had made some more ice cubes for my head soaking. As soon as the light went on, I saw them. Not the usual twenty or thirty silverfish—but thousands! They were crawling over everything. The walls were shining with them. It was just too much to bear. I had reached the low point of my life at the time I had expected to begin the climb to the top.

I rolled up two magazines, placing one in each hand, and like a true madman, I attacked! I slammed the magazines against the table, chairs, refrigerator, cabinets, the sink. Leaping on top of anything that could support my weight, I launched the offensive drive against the walls. My arms spun like the blades of a windmill turned on high speed, lashing out at these silver menaces, these crawling pieces of proof of my failure in life. I killed, killed, killed, killed, killed! Not one would live, no wounded, no prisoners. Only death!

I didn't stop until all I held in my clenched fists were two stumps of rolled paper. I was standing on the washboard of the sink. My body was dripping with sweat and spotted with the blood of insects. I was breathing heavily, my arms ached. I sat down on the drainboard and looked at the carnage around me. Everything was dotted red and silver, pieces of insects were all over the place.

At age eighteen home on leave
from basic training in the 101st
Airborne—taking time out to
"find myself."

A nineteen-year-old slum kid on leave from the army in Paris, discovering that the world is larger than a street corner.

Before finding this place in London, at age nineteen, I thought all the Jews in the world only lived in Philadelphia, Brooklyn and Israel. A nice surprise!

After graduating first in my class at Temple University, I thanked everyone for coming and then took the El train back to my apartment in the same neighborhood in which I grew up. Still poor and unemployed.

Yes, that's *the* Tom Snyder (left). He was the narrator on many documentaries I wrote, produced and directed for Westinghouse Broadcasting. On sound is C.J. and Larry Bossone is on camera.

A two-part documentary I wrote, produced and directed, won awards, got me invited to Puerto Rico as the guest of Reverend Anjel Luis Jaime and Felicia Rincon, Mayoress of San Juan, and got me my own documentary series. I was on my way out of the neighborhood.

A successful documentary writer/producer/film director visits California for the first time. I loved San Francisco but thought L.A. needed a lot of work. I still do.

This is me talking with Merv Griffin and my director, Art Fisher, about a script I was producing, never dreaming that someday I'd be a performer on Merv's show.

My documentary career took me to Sweden where I worked with Ingmar Bergman, Liv Ullman (pictured) and Max von Sydow— a young filmmaker's dream! When I was a starving standup comedian, I saw part of my film on the Academy Awards.

Sometimes a documentary film
director has to be innovative. In
the supermarket basket is my last
cameraman, Arnie Baskin.

When I was doing this documentary on the misconceptions and inequities in the welfare system, I knew this would be my last film. The career had gotten me out of the neighborhood, but it was time to move on.

My head slowly dropped to my chest, my arms hung in dead weight next to my legs, beads of salty sweat stung my eyes.

Quietly I made a firm resolution to myself. "I've got to get out of here! I've got to get away from Sixtieth Street! I've got to start becoming somebody—NOW!"


## EIGHTY CENTS

MY OPPORTUNITY CAME A few weeks later.

Bill Seibel, a former Mass Communications professor of mine at Temple University, called me. There was a job audition being held at the network-owned and -operated TV station for a documentary writer. They were going to produce an eight-part series on crime and the criminal process and were looking to hire a writer. It would mean eleven weeks of employment and, more importantly, a professional writing credit.

My major had been Dramatic Writing, a dying if not dead TV art form; therefore, a stupid major. Nevertheless, I decided to go for the interview. I needed a job desperately. I called the executive who was conducting the interviews, Jack Reilly, and asked if I could see him after the weekend. We set an appointment for Monday in the early afternoon. The reason I wanted a few days before the interview was so I could write some documentaries and rewrite my college papers. I had from Friday afternoon to Monday morning to make the transition from unemployed dramatist to unemployed documentarian.

I got out the typewriter and started immediately. I stopped typing only long enough to grab something to eat or go to the bathroom. I worked straight through to Sunday morning. I borrowed my friend Bob's car and drove over to Bill Seibel's. He read what I had written and suggested certain changes. I got back into Bob's car and headed home.

While waiting for a traffic light to turn green I looked in my rearview mirror in time to see a car barreling down on me. The road divider was on my left, and there were cars to my right and straight ahead. I braced myself for the impact. It came. Bob's trunk was bent in. It was my first (and last) accident. The driver was an old, drunk, obviously poor (or wealthy eccentric) black man. I heard the police siren in the distance and knew they'd throw the book at him, especially after he told me he had no insurance. I convinced him to get in his car and get the hell out of there. He did. I filled out a phony hit-and-run accident report and returned Bob's car with apologies. Luckily his insurance covered the damage. (I've never borrowed anyone's car since that day.)

When I was back in my apartment my neck had become stiff and I had pains in my arms and shoulders. I kept typing. I stayed at it until eleven Monday morning. I hadn't slept since nine Friday morning—seventy-four hours. I showered, shaved, put on my best and only suit and hopped on the subway with my writing under my arm.

Mr. Reilly had asked me what I knew about directing a film and film editing and I had answered truthfully, "Nothing." Then he inquired about my knowledge of writing for films.

"Mr. Reilly, the answer to that question is the same as to the others. 'Nothing'. Look, this interview is embarrassing to me and a waste of time for you. If you're looking for 'experience', I'm not your man. Hire someone out of New York. But, if you're looking for 'potential', no one you bring in here is going to learn faster or better or work harder than I will! So, your decision is between experience and potential. Thank you for your time. I wish you luck with your project. Here are some examples of my writing."

I got up and left the office. When I returned to my apartment I called Bill Seibel, told him what happened, how I had blown the interview. I then thanked him for helping me give it the ol' college try, hung up, took off my suit and got back into my ghetto jeans and sneakers. Life goes on.

Like a lot of guys with whom I grew up, I had gotten married at a young age. It was the thing to do. The girl, who was wonderful, had a great deal of fortitude to live as we lived. She was a medical technician and could find only part-time work at that time. We were living off of her seventy-five dollars a week. "Living"? That was our best joke. We were "clinging," unlike my second marriage. That's right—I was married and divorced twice in my twenties, so you could say I'm not "husband material" and be 100 percent right. See, I'm more interesting than you had probably imagined, aren't I?

Anyway, back to the story. The following Friday afternoon, after my disastrous interview, I had gone down to Temple University to give Bill a hand with setting up a new studio. I returned to my apartment and was sitting in the bedroom reading one of the three paperback books I had purchased on my way home. Money or no money, you always need books. They are essentials.

"Okay, David, you want a financial report?"

"What are you talking about?"

"I think it's time for this corporation to give its stockholders a detailed and precise financial report."

I laughed. "Look, things are bad enough without discussing them. Call the stockholders' meeting for next month. In the Bahamas."

"No, let's do it now. How much you got?"

"Well, I bought these books, took the subway to Temple and back. So, whatever is on the dresser is how much I have."

"Let's see, three quarters and a nickle. Eighty cents. Okay, including our checking account, savings account, the contents of my wallet and the cookie jar, we have a grand total of . . . eighty cents."

"Eighty cents? What the hell are you talking about?"

"Well, our checking account is zero; we never had a savings account; there aren't even any cookies in the cookie jar, since I ate the last stale Lorna Doone this morning, and I just spent my last twenty-five cents to take the subway home."

"Goddamn! Look, don't worry about this. I'll sell my tape recorder, my clothes, everything before we ever touch one thing of yours. We'll make it. I promise you. I'll work it out. You'll see. Let me sleep on it."

That's just what we both did—took an escaping nap. The phone awakened me.

"Hello."

"Hello. May I speak with David Brenner? Mr. Jack Reilly calling.

"Speaking." I sat up and lit a cigarette.

"Hi, David? Jack Reilly here."

"Hi, Mr. Reilly, what can I do for you?"

"Well, I'll see you Monday morning at nine."

Great! A second interview. This time I wouldn't blow it like the first. Now, you've got to understand something about me. I'm not lazy at all and can work as hard and as long as anyone, but I've never been a morning person. I've been nocturnal since childhood. I figured that even though this could be the most important moment in my life, I'd like to do it in the afternoon.

"That's great, Mr. Reilly, only I wonder if we could make it in the afternoon sometime?"

"Well, David, we begin work here at nine."

"Yes, I understand that, but I made some appointments in the morning, so it would be much more convenient for me if I came to talk to you in the afternoon."

"I don't think you understand, David. You got the job. You begin working as the writer of the series beginning at nine Monday morning. At the top salary you asked for, by the way. I read your stuff and decided to go with potential."

"Thank you, Mr. Reilly. I'll see you at nine."

I hung up and sat there stunned. After a couple of minutes, I shook my wife's shoulder gently. "Wake up, wake up."

"What's up, David?"

"I've slept on it and decided what to do. Monday morning at nine, I'm going to begin writing television documentaries."

"What are you . . ."

"I got the job! I start Monday! Now put on your best. I'm going to borrow some money in the street and we're going to celebrate!"

I jumped off the bed and went to the dresser to put the keys and things in my pants pocket. I picked up the eighty cents.

"Someday I'm going to put this eighty cents on black velvet in a silver frame with a little placard that reads 'Lest We Forget', so I'll always remember how broke I really was once."

Today the frame is on a shelf in my den, but I don't ever have to look at it—I remember all too well.


# PROVING IT

YOU DON'T WANT TO show up too early the first day on a new job. It makes you look overanxious. Even though this was more than a job for me—I knew it could be the start of a career, an opportunity to bust out of the neighborhood, the possible beginning of my whole future, the first step in the answer to all my boyhood dreams. Still, I didn't want to walk into the TV studio a half hour early.

There was a little coffee shop around the corner from the studio called The Little Spot. That's exactly what it was, physically. A counter with eight stools. I sat down and ordered a cup of coffee. Halfway through the cup, I got an attack of stomach cramps, nearly doubling me up.

"Hey, buddy, your coffee is bad!" I exclaimed.

"What are you talking about? This is freshly brewed!"

"I'm telling you there's something wrong with it! I'm all cramped."

"I don't care what you are, it can't be the coffee! Look! See, a new brew!"

Then it hit me. All of my life—well, since age nine anyway—I had been telling everyone that someday I was going to be "somebody" and today someone was saying back to me, "Okay, David, the door is open. Let's see you prove it!" It wasn't the coffee—it was me. I was scared.

"Sorry, pal, the coffee is fine."

At one minute to nine I walked into the studio. Six months later I was the writer/producer/director of my own documentary television series. I had proven it . . . to myself, anyway.

*Whenever I start to get overly anxious or impatient about anything, I think of how New York City was built—by putting one brick on top of another brick on top of another brick on top of . . .*

## TOM SNYDER: ON ASSIGNMENT

YES, THE VERY SAME Tom Snyder. Before becoming a star of late night network TV, Tom was an ace reporter and newscaster for Westinghouse Broadcasting in Philadelphia. I was the head of their documentary department and chose Tom to be the narrator of my documentary films. Oh, he was the same loud-mouthed, arrogant, know-it-all, controversial, laughing Tom Snyder America came to love and hate, but he was full of talent even back then. Tom was the best. He could memorize a script faster and deliver it better than anyone. Besides, I really liked him. We had some great laughs together.

We were up in New England working on a documentary entitled "They All Discovered America," a study of the evidence suggesting the whole array of possible discoverers who might have come to our shores before Christopher Columbus. Of course, as with any study dealing with this subject, the American Indian was excluded, written off once again as just some people who happened to be here when the *real discoverers* arrived. I asked my boss how he would feel if someone drove off in his Mercedes that he had owned for years with the simple explanation that he was "discovering it." He didn't understand the analogy so we went ahead without the Indians.

We began filming during a bitter cold spell in November, and most of the filming was done outdoors. One night we were filming on top of and inside of a massive series of underground caves known as Pattee Caves, so named after the farmer who, with his sons, is said to have built them for reasons unknown. However, some research turned up the fact that Farmer Pattee had only one child—a daughter. Our anthropologist expert was suggesting that the farmer and daughter could not have possibly built so large and complex a cave system, and that possibly the Vikings had constructed and lived in these wondrous underground caverns.

We were in the deepest of all the caves, maybe sixty or seventy feet below the surface. It was cold and damp; stalactites hung from the cracks in the ceiling. We had hung our lights, running the wires up to generators on the surface. Tom and I both had to crouch, since I am six feet two inches tall and he's about six feet five. There were seven of us jammed into this small area, including Larry Bassone, the cameraman, CJ on sound, Dave Csik on lights, Diane Ackman, the script consultant and our cave expert. It was about four in the morning; we had been working since seven the previous morning. We were cold and tired, the place was real spooky but none of this is a good excuse for what one of us did . . .

Now, Tom is a big guy. He looks big on TV and he is big! Come on, six feet five inches is a big guy. And he talks big—in person, on TV and in his sleep, I'm sure. Tom is a big walking, big talking, big kind of guy. Most of us equate big with brave. So, you'd have to say that Tom is also a brave guy, too, right? Well, I casually walked over to the side of the cave Tom was going to lean against to do his narration.

"Tom," I said very nonchalantly, "I think it's very important that you stress the point that this entire cave complex is supported by just this one little rock here—oops!"

When I "accidentally" dislodged the rock from the ceiling above my head, Tom screamed, a big man's kind of scream, and tore ass out of that cave!

Of course, when he sheepishly came back to rejoin his hysterical friends and coworkers, he had a typical Tom Snyder line:

"Ha! Ha! You got to admit that was a funny routine I did! Fooled all of you, didn't I? Ha! Ha!"

He fooled no one, which was one of the main reasons we liked him so much.

While filming "They All Discovered America" we stayed at the Viking Inn, ironically enough. The whole motif, of course, was Viking, or a motel decorator's conception of Viking—lots of horns, shields, swords and fur. You get the ugly picture, don't you?

We had Viking costumes with us, because we were doing some "reenactment scenes" with actors on the beaches and in a Viking boat. When you work hard, and, regardless of what you may imagine about the world of TV and filmmaking, while it is a glamorous and rewarding business, it is a lot of hard work. Well, well, well worth it—but hard! Anyway, when you work hard, it is good to play hard. At least that's the way I look at it and the way I live. Fun and laughter can make the hardest of a day's work pass quicker and easier.

We had been filming out in the cold for about eleven hours. I called it quits and Tom and I helped the crew "wrap up" (union, schmunion, we were a team and worked as a team). Then he and I got into our station wagon and headed back to the motel. We had reached the stage of exhausted silliness.

"Tom, let's have some fun," I suggested.

And we did! Tom and I dressed up like Vikings. The whole bit, including the steel helmets with the horns sticking out of them. With my nose it looked like three horns. We stood opposite each other at the front entrance of the Viking Inn, and, as people came up the path and reached us we slammed our huge swords together, blocking the entrance and demanded that the people identify themselves, show their room keys and state the nature of their visit.

"The name's Bickford. Tom Bickford. This here's my wife, Agnes. We're from Dayton, Ohio. This is my room key, 407, and we're staying here on our way up to Maine to visit our daughter,

Beth, her husband, Bill, and our two grandchildren, Steve and Betty, seven and nine. I sell automotive parts."

"Okay, you may pass! Have a nice stay among us Vikings."

"Thank you and your people for treating us just fine."

"Let's move it, Mack!"

"Yes, of course. Thank you. Thank you, Vikings!"

Not one of the more than fifty or sixty people we stopped questioned us, and they all did exactly what we asked them to. Sometimes the Discoverers of America can be such schmucks!

We had filmed from sunrise to sunset on the beach. The wind blowing in across the ocean brought cold sea water spray with it. At the day's end, we were all freezing. Tom decided it was the perfect time to enjoy a hot Turkish bath. I passed it up for just a simple soak in my motel bathtub. I dropped Tom off at the local Turkish bath, promising to send someone to pick him up in an hour. As he entered I pulled away, circled the block and parked across the street. After waiting outside ten minutes, I entered the Turkish bath.

The man wearing the turban, whom I tipped twenty dollars, led me upstairs to the steam room. I looked through the little glass window in the door. Through the steam I could see Tom stretched out on his stomach on a large table. His body was covered with soapy water and a heavyset man wearing a towel and a turban was gently stroking and smacking Tom with large, soapy leaves. I nodded to my man, who entered the room and whispered in the ear of Tom's man who nodded, looked at me and nodded again. I entered and he handed me the leaves. I dipped them in the large bucket containing the soapy water and started whipping the hell out of Tom's naked body. Whack! Whack! Whack!

"Now, are you going to tell us the names of your commanding officers?" I screamed in a foreign accent, continuing to beat Tom. WHACK! WHACK!

"What the fuck?" Tom screamed and tried to turn over, but the table was slippery from the soap and the leaves whipping him made it even more difficult to maneuver.

"How many tanks do you have?" WHACK! "Do you know General Patton?" WHACK WHACK WHACK!

Finally, he managed to sit up and defend himself with his arms raised in front of his face and chest.

198

"Death to the Yankee spy," I screamed and emptied the bucket of soapy water over his head. "We don't need you anyway. Your friend, Brenner, has told us everything!"

I ran out of the room with Tom bellowing like a wounded bull.

"Brenner, you son-of-a-bitch! When I catch you, I'm going to kill ya!"

When he finally did catch me all he did was laugh, and you know how annoying Tom Snyder's laugh can be. I was sorry he didn't just kill me.

*Someone once asked me what I would ask for if I had one wish. I answered that "I'd wish that God had a sense of humor."*

*Many times you hear people explain why they can be happy on a vacation and not at home, simply because they are on a vacation. What they fail to realize, I think, is that everyone is on a vacation every day of his or her life —a vacation from death. So be happy—celebrate!*

# THE BIG GAMBLE

IN MAY OF 1969, I was a writer/producer/film director for the Public Broadcasting Laboratory, which produced on the Educational Network a weekly ninety-minute program, a magazine format, very similar to the soon-to-follow "Ninety Minutes." I started out in Cultural Programming, then switched to Political Satire and then came back to roost in my most natural environment, documentaries.

I had just completed a documentary segment for the show entitled "Nobody's Business," in which we cleared up a lot of the misinformation concerning welfare. We were in the farm migratory town of Laneer, California. This was used as our microcosm of the welfare world and its recipients. To me, it was *another* poverty show. I had done a lot of them. The same shots in each —poor family in their home, children sitting on dirty floors, unemployed men loitering, ad infinitum. I just knew that the family who waved good-bye to us as we left their shack would be the same family waving hellos to us if we were to return at any given time in the future. Documentaries are aired, studies are done, congressional investigations are held, public outcries are heard and then everything goes back to normal. Stroke-yourself time. I don't believe that the problem with the world is that we are looking for answers and solutions. We have all the answers —we simply don't want to implement them. It's a matter of priorities and self-interest. I was feeling fed up by the system.

"We're going to sell all the equipment, take the money we get for it, plus the expense money we're carrying, and give every dime to the poor people of Laneer. That way we'll know our TV show did some good," I said.

"Very funny, Brenner. Okay, let's go over tomorrow's interviews. We have the woman who . . ."

"I'm serious. I figure with the rented station wagon and the Avis car we can get about $150,000. That'll really help these people."

Arnie Baskin, my cameraman, stared at me. "You aren't serious, are you?"

"Completely!"

"They'll arrest you."

"Exactly. They'll cover it on network news—'Documentary producer sells film equipment and gives money to the poor.' That's when I'll tell them that I've been making documentary films about the poor and needy and the way the system deals with them for years and nothing's ever been done to change anything. This time I'll know I've done some good."

It took my associates three days to talk me out of my plan. We made the documentary, with all the usual scenes, it aired and was forgotten and the people of Laneer continued having their problems (Probably still do) and I decided to get out of documentaries and television. I put in for a two-week vacation.

The day I was leaving I was offered a job doing short film subjects on any subject, anywhere in the world, my choice, for one of the network news programs. It was the job I had been looking for my whole career. The base pay would be $30,000— very good for a bachelor in 1969—plus an open expense account. In other words, as I traveled around the world making short films, my paychecks would go right into the bank. What a deal—what a temptation. I said I would make my decision within two weeks.

I rented a little house on the obscure West Indian island of Nevis. It was just me, an island woman who cooked and cleaned for me, the beautiful beach and clear water. I had never been by myself one day let alone fifteen, but I was determined to search my soul and select a new road for the future. It was a difficult task. As the days passed I felt wonderful but was no closer to a decision than when I arrived.

I thought about a scene in a feature film I had seen a few years back. A protestor was walking back and forth outside a governor's mansion. He carried a placard denouncing the state for its plan to electrocute a man who was believed to be innocent. It was a bitterly cold night and the protestor asked the cop standing outside the mansion's front gate for a match. As the cop lit the man's cigarette he said, "What are you trying to do, buddy? You can't change the world." The protestor answered, "You don't understand. I'm not trying to change the world. I'm just trying to keep the world from changing me." I decided that this would be my new philosophy in life. But what to do?

Then the rains came. Three days and nights of torrential tropical rains. No sun, no beach, no ocean. Alone in this little house with only a transoceanic radio and my thoughts. I turned on the radio for company as I sat on a rattan chair on the covered porch, watching and listening to the torrid rain beating down. The news came on, the horrible news of 1969—war, destruction, death, poverty, murders . . . as I listened I thought to myself how people have got to laugh at life and at themselves a little more. Laughter can help people make it through these times. Then I thought of how I had always made people laugh, since I was practically a baby. It was then that I decided to put my new career decision off for one year, take the nine thousand dollars I had saved, use it for survival and just get up on the stages in New York and make people laugh. During that year, without the pressure on me, I could take my time to decide what to do for a new career and then go for it.

When I returned to the States I quit my job and then called the network executive who had made me that marvelous job offer.

". . . so thank you anyway."

"Is it a matter of money? I'll see if I can get you more, David. What do you need? What's your bottom line? Let's talk green."

"Thanks, but it's not money. I'm quitting television."

"What do you mean 'quitting'? You're a documentarian. You've made dozens of fine films."

"One hundred and fifteen."

"Right. And what about all the awards and citations?"

"Twenty-six. They're hanging on the office walls of executives."

"Well, doesn't all that mean something to you?"

"A lot. It's been a great career, but it's over. I've done it all. Now I want to do something else."

"Like what?"

"Well, I'm not sure yet, but, for right now, I'm going to hang around Greenwich Village and do stand-up comedy."

He laughed loudly.

"Thanks. That's my first laugh."

On June 9, 1969, I stood on a stage for the first time in my life and joked around. The rest may not be history but it certainly has been a rewarding career.

I wrote about this because I thought that maybe some of you may be standing at career or job crossroads. All I can tell you is that it's a very big gamble, but do it! The only failure, I believe, is not trying. What the hell—take a shot!

# SHOW BUSINESS

# THE GREATEST SOUND IN THE WORLD

WHEN I PASSED MY ninth birthday, my good friend, Dee-Dee, who worked in the fish department of Gollub's Supermarket since he was seven years old, got me my first job working for Mr. Sobel, the store's butcher. It was the beginning of a long, never ending, never even pausing series of rotten jobs. I did a lot of things, none of which I would have done had I had a choice, but I didn't. Poor kids rarely do. When my friends asked me how come I was never late even once for any of my jobs, why I showed up at work unless I was so sick I couldn't stand and why I worked so damn hard once I got there, I always answered like this:

"If I can do all this on a job I hate, imagine how good I'll be the day I start doing work I love."

Well, that day finally came. I love my job. I can't think of any position in any field that could be more rewarding, more fun, more personally satisfying, more challenging, more of everything wonderful than standing up onstage, all alone, in front of an audience of strangers and making them laugh. Different people will tell you different sounds are the greatest. To me, the greatest sound in the whole world is laughter!

# MY FIRST JOKE

THIS IS THE FIRST joke I ever told. I was about two years old when my father taught it to me.

A man is walking by a tailor shop and he sees a sign in the window. "My name is Fink and what do you think, I press suits for nothing." So the man runs home and gets all his suits out of his closet and rushes back to the tailor's, leaving them to be pressed. A few days later he goes into the tailor's, hands him his receipt ticket. The tailor gives him his suits and a bill for twenty-four dollars. The man looks at the bill and then at the tailor.

"What is this bill for? Your sign reads 'My name is Fink and what do you think, I press suits for nothing'!"

"Mister, you read the sign wrong. My sign reads 'My name is Fink and what do you think, I press suits for *nothing*?'"

## "HOOTENANNIES"

THEY ARE CALLED HOOTENANNY Nights, or "Hoots." You could call them auditions or practice sessions. Many small clubs in Manhattan, such as the African Room, the Champagne Gallery, the Wha, the Village Gate, Folk City, Hilly's, Trudy Heller's, the Upstairs at The Downstairs, Pips, the Apartment, the Bitter End and many fly-by-night joints would hold a hoot night during which one amateur act after another, all trying but not necessarily talented, would get up on the stage for five to ten minutes and do their "thing," whatever the hell that was, and it could be anything from the normal impressionist, magician, puppeteer, juggler, singer, dancer, comedian to the bizarre—Man Who Walks and Talks, Gay Man Making Love to a Piano. You would see it all.

The year was 1969. It was Friday night at the Gaslight Club on MacDougal Street in the Village. Steve Landesberg and I went there together to do the hoot. Protesting was still very big then and, therefore, so was folk singing. Most of the time on the hoots was taken by folk singers with their original songs about stopping the war, feeding the hungry, saving the minorities, helping the elderly, banning the bomb, saving the salmon, stopping the sale of retread tires, eliminating Sears & Roebuck, preventing the construction of Levittowns, stopping the illegal flow of wooden matches into Korea, and all the other important and unimportant issues of that era.

As I listened and watched one folk singer after another go up on the stage and perform I was mesmerized by their style and motif. When it was finally my turn, I mentioned this to the audience about how I had watched each folk singer as he tuned his guitar, explained in detail how he wrote the song, where it was written, why it was written, what it meant to him, what it should mean to you, and, finally, how it would help cure some evil in the world. Five minutes of introduction and two and a half minutes of music. A peace sign and then another introduction/tuning/singing. Amazing!

I went on to wonder what it would be like if a comedian adapted the same motif and style. So, while making believe I was tuning an imaginary guitar, turning the frets and making guitar string sounds, I tried out my new idea.

"I was living in Haight Ashbury with a girl named Esther . . . (TUNE) . . . we had an argument . . . (TUNE) . . . I said I was leaving . . . (TUNE) . . . Esther tried to stop me from going . . . (TUNE) . . . she was in the bathtub at the time . . . (TUNE) . . . she slipped trying to get out . . . (TUNE) . . . fell . . . (TUNE) . . . and broke the big toe on her right foot . . . (TUNE) . . . it was at that very moment . . . (TUNE) . . . that I write the following joke . . . (TUNE) . . . which I call The Broken Big Toe on Esther's Right Foot. I'd like to do it for you now. If you know it, please say the punch line along with me. (Exaggerated comedian's stance) Hey, folks, I was living in Haight Ashbury with this chick, Esther . . ."

They didn't laugh. Not one person! Let's be honest—they hated me! They glowered at me! Every single one of them. It was so bad that my good pal, Steve, poked his head around a pillar, smiled, waved and left the club. I had forgotten that everyone in the audience was either a folk singer or with a folk singer. I had also forgotten that in spite of the "peace and love and right on, brother, ban the bomb, end the war, and freedom for all, etc.," most of them were all there for the same purpose which, incidentally, was never mentioned in any of the songs—to get a gig that would pay a few dollars and be heard by someone so that maybe they'd get on the "Tonight Show" or Ed Sullivan or Merv Griffin or Mike Douglas or Dick Cavett or David Frost or Virginia Graham, so that they could then get big recording contracts and sell-out concerts and buy that gorgeous home with a swimming pool in Beverly Hills where they could sit and smoke cigars and drink Dom Perignon and forget about the war, and the bomb and the whales and the hungry and the mistreated minorities and all the acts that didn't make it as big as they. So please, accept my apology, dear *Artist!* Peace!

## A WEEKEND AT PIPS

"YOU CAN'T MAKE IT as a comedian until you've worked a weekend at Pips."

This was a fact! A rule! A goal for every young comedian in New York. Pips. A weekend at Pips. What is Pips? It's the first comedy workshop established in this country. It is a small coffee house/winery/snackery/nightclub located right on Sheepshead Bay in Brooklyn at 2005 Emmons Avenue, next door to Joe's Clam Bar. It is owned by a former comedian whose stage name was Georgie Starr and whose real name is George Schultz, friend of such comedy greats as Lenny Bruce and Buddy Hackett, reportedly the originator of Rodney Dangerfield's hook, "No Respect," a comedy maven who possesses an uncanny ability to know instantly if a joke will work. He also decided whether you were good enough to play "his Pips" for a weekend, seven or eight shows in three days, thirty dollars and all the hamburgers and sodas you wanted. This crucial career decision was made at open auditions held after the regularly scheduled late shows on Friday nights. It was the bottom rung on the ladder of Big Apple quasi-success.

In early August of 1969, when I was a comedian all of eight weeks, I called Pips and put my name on the audition list. Act after act got up on the stage. Most were horrible and Brooklynites let you know it. I was getting more nervous by the minute. Finally, about two in the morning, in front of no more than forty people, the act before me went on. He was a folk singer. Now, I don't have the best musical ear in the world, but even I can tell when someone stinks, and this guy stank. He was capable of putting an end to both audition nights and folk singing in one fell swoop. When he finished his one audition song, I was too scared to go on, so I yelled "Encore! Encore!" applauding loudly. A couple people in the audience picked it up from me. The kid did a second song and again I repeated my call of "encore" with even more people joining in this time. By the time he finished his fourth encore, I was no longer nervous. The folk singer floated off the stage thinking he was the greatest thing to ever hit Sheepshead Bay, New York City, the United States, the world, the universe—never to understand why he "bombed" the next few auditions and why he is not in show business today.

Oh, yes, I passed the audition, but George, or Mr. Schultz as I called him then, drove me crazy. As soon as I walked offstage after my set, during which I did make the people laugh, he walked up to me.

"You got it all, kid. You're going to be a big star!"

"Thanks, Mr. Schultz. What about the weekend?"

"The personality, likability, everything."

"Thanks. What about the weekend?"

"Good face. Got to use it more."

"I will. What about the weekend?"

"And gestures. Gesture more. Hands, moves."

"Right. What about the weekend?"

"Big star. Just stay with it. Big star!"

"The weekend. What about the weekend?"

He walked away, slouched over and mumbling something about my subhosting the "Tonight Show" someday.

Finally, after weeks of daily phone calls to George Schultz, it happened.

"Hi, Mr. Schultz? This is David Brenner. Remember, I auditioned two weeks ago? I was wondering . . . yeah, right a 'big star!' You told me . . . but what about . . . yes, I'll smile more . . . right, now about the weekend . . . great . . . yeah, I take the D train . . . see you Friday, and thanks."

Like most things in life, no matter how important they might have been in the beginning, after you've had them a while, you no longer have the same enthusiasm that you once did. This was certainly true of Pips. Sure, the thirty dollars (George says he pays 1932 wages) were needed and so were those moments on stage necessary for growth as a comedian, but those long rides to and from the city on the D train with carloads of "dementoes" and "disturboes," were grueling. By late 1970, I had played Pips probably thirty-five weekends. As Thanksgiving approached, George called me several times about working Pips on New Year's Eve. God, who wants to go all the way out to Sheepshead Bay and entertain a bunch of drunks? Not I. George pleaded, asked, begged and finally conned me, the clever bastard.

"Listen, David, there's one thing I didn't tell you about Pips."

"It was featured in the movie *Brigadoon.*"

"Funny. Boy's a real comic. No, there's something strange, mystical about Pips."

"Okay, I'll go for it—like what?"

"Everyone who has played a New Year's at Pips has gone on to become a star."

"What the hell you talking about, George?"

"Rodney, Robert Klein, David Frye all played it on New Year's and look at them today—stars."

"Really?"

"Sure, ask them. So how about it?"

"Hmmmm. Okay. George, but I want your word there'll be no noisemakers on the tables. The stupid hats are okay but no noise-makers."

"You got my word, man."

Of course there were noisemakers.

"Come on, man, Jews and Italians like to make noise on New Year's. I had to give it to them or they would make their own noises, by throwing bottles through the front window, or tossing chairs at the chandelier or heaving a Jew comic into the cappuccino machine."

"Okay, forget it George."

"*Boychic*, this job is going to make you a star. Trust me."

I had never stopped to think that Pips had been opened about ten years at that time and George had only mentioned three comedians who had played New Year's and went on to stardom. So, what happened to the other seven guys who played Pips New Year's Eve? They faded into obscurity. As it turned out, eight days after I played Pips that New Year's Eve, I made my debut on the "Tonight Show" and started my climb to becoming a star. The following year, George talked to my comedian friend Steve Landesberg.

". . . Rodney, Klein, Frye and Brenner all played on New Year's at Pips . . ."

Another sucker bit the dust.

The biggest con of all was a couple years ago when I was playing a concert at Brooklyn College. George called me the day of the concert.

"So, man, you're going to be at Brooklyn College tonight.

That's only a few minutes from Pips. Maybe you'd like to stop by."

"George, I'm not doing a set at Pips."

"Of course not, man, I mean just to visit your pal, Georgie."

"Well, maybe George. So, how are . . ."

"You got to let me know, man."

"Why, George?" I asked suspiciously.

"Because I gotta give Joe time to prepare some special foods for you."

It was true that the owner of Joe's Clam Bar always did whip up some fantastic seafood and Italian dishes for me whenever I visited.

"George, I'm really beat from the road and by the time the concert ends, and we get to . . ."

"Come on, it's five minutes out of your way. I haven't seen you in a long time. We can talk, have some laughs. What time should I expect you?"

"Well, the concert should end around ten, so until I change, speak to a few people and get out of there . . . about eleven."

"Great! See you then. I'll meet you in Joe's. Tell your driver to pull in the back by the kitchen so you don't get hassled walking through the restaurant."

As always, the meal in Joe's was sensational! And, as usual, we did have a lot of laughs.

"Great meal, huh, David? Well, what do you say you just poke your head into Pips. Say hello to the people?"

"Oh, no, George, you're not conning me into going up on the stage."

"Come on, man, you know me better than that. Marty and Seth want to say hello to you, that's all."

"Why can't your sons pop in here to say hi?"

"They're busy in Pips. Come on, man, two minutes, no big deal. After you talk to the boys, you can just wave to the audience and leave. You're already here."

"Okay, George, but two minutes. That's all. No con jobs!"

George looked at me with that expression that reads, "How could you ever think such nasty things of me, your friend?" As soon as we got near the front door of Joe's, it was obvious that the con was on. Several small clues like the police barriers blocking off the entire length of Emmons Avenue, the dozens of police holding back the hundreds of people, the flashbulbs going off, the wild cheering and applauding, the outstretched arms holding autograph books and, the biggest clue of all—the two-foot-high banner stretched across the entire front of Pips which read "DAVID BRENNER LIVE AT PIPS—TONIGHT ONLY!" As the police formed a protective circle around me and led me into Pips I cranked my neck to see George, who was directly behind me.

"When did you order the banner, George?"

"The day I heard you were playing Brooklyn College, sucker!"

"Thank you. Thanks a lot. Okay, thanks a lot. Well, it certainly is great to be back on the stage at Pips! I can remember my first weekend at Pips and I'll never forget this, my last appearance here. No, George knows I'm kidding. Right, George?"

George looked worried and stayed that way until the next time I got up at Pips and the next time and the next time and . . .

On August 13, 1982, Steve Landesberg and I performed at Pips in celebration of its twentieth anniversary. This time, George didn't have to con us—we both wanted to do it. However, I've already made plans for August 13, 1987, and August 13, 1992, and August 13, 1997, and . . .


## BREAKING THE HABIT

GEORGE SCHULTZ IS A buffalo, one of the few surviving 1940s-hip Jews. One September morning in 1979, he called me.

"I've had it, man. It's all over. Hello, how are you?"

"Fine, George. What's over?"

"Doctor, man. The smoking. Got emphysema. So when you doing Carson?"

"Beginning of October. You've got to quit smoking!"

"Can't, man. Love the shit. Booze, broads, drugs, smoke and Dannon Yogurt. Life, man. Did I ever tell you about the time I had to soak my dick in yogurt to get rid of a rash?"

"No, but listen, George, I'll give up smoking if you will. I read about an acupuncturist in New York magazine. Very high success rate."

"No needles, man. Can they just glue them to your skin?"

"I'll pay for it, George. Go with you. I'll make the appointment and call you back. Don't leave until I call."

"Can't. There's a great war movie on at ten. I saw it. About two thousand Nazis get it. One in the back with a bazooka, man. Need help on the Carson shot?"

"No, I'm fine, thanks. Call you back."

I found the article in the magazine. I called and made appointments for George and me every morning at nine-thirty for a week. It would be good for me, too. I started smoking when I was nine years old. I had quit twice for two years each time but now I was back to my daily three-and-a-half packs a day. I didn't know if I could quit, but I wanted to try for my sake and for George's. I called him back. I'm not certain what it is about me, but regardless of how serious the situation, I always think of the funny side or a way to make it funny.

"Hi ya doin', George?"

"Hi ya doin'? Hi ya doin'? Thank you. Thank you very much. Hi ya doin'?"

George always makes fun of my Philadelphia way of saying hello and thanking audiences at the start of my show. It's a real lousy impression, but it's always funny.

"I made appointments for us, George, starting Monday morning. Get a paper and pen."

I gave George the address of the doctor and told him I'd meet him there. Then my madness took over.

"Now write this down, George. Ming. M-i-n-g. Ying. Y-i-n-g. Wang. W-a-n-g. Got it?"

"Yeah, man, but what the hell is Ming Ying Wang?"

"It's the name of the acupuncturist. It's mister, too, not doctor."

"Are you putting me on, man? Ming Ying Wang? You gotta be kidding. Sounds like I should bring my dirty shirts."

"He's Chinese, George. Now, all the appointments are at nine-thirty except the one on Monday, that's at nine-fifteen. Guess for filling out forms. I'll meet you there."

"Come on, man, you pulling my limbs? I can tell you're laughing. I hear it in your voice, man. I'm Charlie Chan when it comes to Ying Ming Wong."

"Ming Ying *Wang*. All right, you're right. I am laughing and I'll tell you why. Mr. Wang shares an office with a doctor Corcos. He's a proctologist. I was laughing because I thought of how funny it would be if you went to him by mistake. Largest acupuncture in history."

"Funny, man, but don't do it on Carson. So, this is on the level?"

"Would I mess around with you at a time like this? With emphysema?"

"Yes. But I'll see you nine-fifteen Monday. Wow, a Nazi just got it with his own grenade. Die, you Nazi bastard! Channel five."

When I got to the doctor's office at nine-thirty, right on time, George jumped out of his seat the minute I walked in.

"Something's screwy here, man," he whispered, although no one else was in the waiting room and the receptionist's window was closed and the shade was drawn.

"What do you mean, George?"

"I got here ten after. The receptionist comes out. The regular kind, man. You know—white dress, bun in back, waitress's shoes. I tell her I want to see Ming Ying Wang, got it written right here, see? She says 'You mean Dr. Corcos.' I say, 'No, my ass is fine.' I then say very slowly Mi-ng . . . Yi-ng . . . Wang.' You know what she did, man? She looked at me for a moment, walked away quickly, shut her window, pulled down the shade and then I heard her lock her door. That was like fifteen minutes ago, man. No one else has been here. Queer, isn't it, man? I think we'd better split. Could be a heavy drug scene, cops, raid, jail, my sons coming to bail out their old Jew father, headlines, Pips closes, ruined."

I cracked up. The receptionist's shade went up and the nurse opened the window.

"Oh, Mr. Brenner. I'm glad to meet you. See you on TV all the time."

"Thank you. My friend George Schultz and I are here for our appointment with Dr. Corcos."

"You bastard! I should've figured you'd pull off some of your jerk-off humor!"

"You'll have to pardon Mr. Schultz. He's very nervous. Not himself. Tortured by Japanese in World War Two. By General . . ."

"Ming Ying Wang," George said in unison with me.

We both laughed and entered for our first treatment.

Let me tell you what finally helped me quit smoking. The acupuncture itself did decrease my urge for a cigarette for about two hours right after the treatment, but then the craving returned. Better than the acupuncture was what Dr. Corcos said to me, in reply to my telling him about how the craving for cigarettes was driving me mad. His advice helped me to break the habit.

"Don't let it drive you crazy. Have a cigarette anytime you want. But take only one drag and then put it out."

I tried it. Psychologically, I knew I could have a cigarette if I wanted one, and once in a while I'd have one, but only one drag, plus it was a lot of bother to get up and walk into another room for just one drag. Before I knew it, the "one drags" grew further and further apart, until they ended altogether—on September 26, 1979. One of the most difficult and smartest things I've ever done.

What about George? Well, he called me just today while I was getting ready to host the "Tonight Show."

"Well, man, a common cold almost did me in. Good-byseville. Couldn't breathe. Felt like I was drowning. They were going to rush me to the hospital but I responded to the medication. Had X-rays. Doctor told me my lungs couldn't handle even a common cold, man. Said he was making a fortune off of cigarette-smoking related diseases. Then he told me some good news—my emphysema can still be curbed. My lungs can make the big comeback if I quit smoking now. Otherwise he said I'm a goner. I haven't had a drink or a cigarette in five days! I swear, man! It's a motha but I'm trying. A common cold, man. What a stupid ass way to go, right, man? I mean, blowing apart some PLO terrorist hideout and going up with the blast is one thing, but a common cold? Man, this time I'm quitting for good!"

I sure hope so. I really love the guy.


# THE ELECTRIC HANDKERCHIEFS

"TWENTY-FIVE HUNDRED DOLLARS FOR one night? You've got to be kidding!"

My agent wasn't kidding. If I would act as the master of ceremonies at an all-night, twenty-four-hour rock marathon concert at a college in upstate New York, that's what I would be paid. The most I had ever made for a one-nighter up to that time was $250, so of course I took it.

My job was to "fill in" during the time one rock band got off the stage and the next one got on. Each musical set was to be forty-five minutes. The breaks could run anywhere from one minute to ten minutes, depending on the number and kind of instruments the band was using and how fast they could set up and tear down. The one thousand or so students sat on the floor of the large hall, I guess to make it different or hip.

When I first walked on stage, I tested the waters, so to speak, doing about fifteen minutes of potpourri material in order to gauge where the audience was in respect to their intelligence, urban or rural leaning, hipness, appreciation of first-person stories, patience for long stories, etc. They scored high in all areas. My job would be easy.

After the first band finished and the second was setting up, I got into it—delivering about twenty minutes of sure-fire humorous missiles, each of which hit the target dead center. I was a big smash! I introduced the next rock and roll band, the music began and I walked offstage, feeling real good! It was going to be a fun night and oh, so financially rewarding.

I sat backstage with my file of jokes, going over what I should do in the next set, thinking how this would probably turn out to be the best gig I had had in my little-over-one-year career as a stand-up comedian.

The second band finished, I walked out on stage applauding, calling out their band name for additional audience applause. I started my routine. It wasn't going as well as the previous set. Oh, they were laughing but not as much, not as enthusiastically. I "punched it up" a little more, getting somewhat better response, but not what I should have been getting. Luckily, the next group was ready rather quickly, so I read their names off the three-by-five index card that was prepared for me by the college's entertainment director and disappeared backstage.

I decided to go with my best material for the next set. Hit them with the triple-A stuff, the killers, the never-miss, the dynamite! Forty-five minutes of music passed and I moved out to stage center briskly and confidently and immediately exploded with the crème de la crème of my act. Some mild laughter, mostly indifference, some hostility. What the hell?? As I worked I ducked down a little, in order to get below the spotlight and see the audience better. Audience? Human dribble and wash rags would be more like it! Bodies were stretched out, heads on top of stomachs and legs and other heads; faces turned skyward with glassy eyes staring into space; faces flattened against the floor with arms stretched out like fallen skydivers; leaning back to back and not knowing it; joints being passed from slow-moving hand to slow-moving hand; pills being popped into loosely hanging jaws; tiny spoons shakily being placed below flaring nostrils. Everyone was stoned out of his or her mind, except for the very few who were laughing at what I said. I had to think of how to make balls of putty and pickled mushrooms laugh. At last the next group was ready and I introduced them.

Offstage I talked about my problem to some of the musicians. Well, I talked to them until I noticed that they too were gone, looking off into space as though they were waiting for secret instructions from Mars. I was in the middle of a Federico Fellini movie and the only one without a script. I studied my remaining material, trying desperately to figure out what could be said in no more than three words, none of which could be more than two syllables and that related to drugs. I had nothing to offer.

The next time I walked out onstage, no one even noticed I was there. Whoever had laughed forty-five minutes previously had left the premises—either physically or mentally. I couldn't remember the name of the group that had played and figured that no one within earshot, or cannon shot for that matter, remembered either, so I sent them on their way as "The Electric Handkerchiefs." Then I ducked and looked at the crowd, which now looked like a still life from a Mathew Brady collection of Civil War photographs, The Battle of Gettysburg Aftermath. I was standing on a stage looking at carnage without bloodshed, the conquest of outer space without having to travel, physical exercise without movement. If these were representatives of America's future, we were in for some very laid-back, strung-out times ahead. There was no sense in trying to perform, so I stood on stage just looking around and thinking. No one noticed; no one cared. When the next band was ready, I said, "And now, let's have a real warm welcome, and try to applaud with both hands this time—it's somewhat easier to hear that way—The Electric Handkerchiefs!" Nothing! I walked off.

Forty-five minutes later, I walked back out onstage.

"Let's hear it for The Electric Handkerchiefs."

Then ten minutes or so later.

"Now, straight from Canada, a big Stateside welcome for The Electric Handkerchiefs!"

That's what I did for the next two sets. Just walked up to the mike, "That was The Electric Handkerchiefs and now let's say hello to—The Electric Handkerchiefs . . . Okay, a round of applause for The Electric Handkerchiefs and a really big, big round of applause for the next group—The Electric Handkerchiefs!" No one in the audience noticed and no one in any band noticed. If they weren't noticing the oxygen around them, how could anyone expect to notice what I was saying? However, when I announced the last Electric Handkerchiefs off and the new Electric Handkerchiefs on, one person did notice—the professor who was the entertainment director, the man who had hired me. He came backstage to talk to me.

"What is it with you and The Electric Handkerchiefs?"

"Great group. Do you like them?"

"Seriously."

"Seriously. You want me to be 'serious' in an environment in which the exploding of an H-bomb would be noticed by less than two percent of the population in this hall and only because it would be a somewhat rude interruption to their spacial trip up the anal passage of Walt Disney's Pluto? What you have out there, professor, in case you didn't notice, through the misty green haze that is suspended above what can loosely be referred to as their heads, is the world of the nonliving. They will unanimously elect anyone their leader who can count up to one backwards. In my old neighborhood in Philly, we called this kind of situation 'FUBAR'—Fucked Up Beyond All Recognition. Look around you. See that 'musician' over there? He's been blowing into the wrong end of his saxophone for thirty minutes now, and his buddy, the one with the fluorescent green earring in his nose, has been keeping time to it. See that statue over there by the curtains. That's one of your usherettes. The last person she led out to his seat on the floor tried to pick it up. And you 'seriously' want to know what's going on around here? And you 'seriously' want me to do material? Let me tell you what I am going to do. All night, between each group, I am going to walk out on that stage and say, 'Let's hear it for The Electric Handkerchiefs, and now let's welcome The Electric Handkerchiefs,' because nothing else makes sense. What you could do is have anyone else in the world do the same or not say anything more than 'Hey, you! You with the rolled-up dollar bill hanging out your nose, and you without eyelids—you're on,' and give me my check and let me get the hell out of here. What do you say, professor?"

Ten minutes later, my check in my pocket, I was in my rented car heading back to New York City with the radio OFF! Don't get me wrong. I don't care what people do for kicks as long as they don't hurt someone. They can sniff glue or suck a glue factory; they can sniff cocaine or Dr. Scholl's foot powder; they can swallow a downer or down an upper or eat a swallow; they can pop pills or pull their puds. *I* don't care—as long as they're not in one of my audiences or in my bathtub. Of course, if they want to "get off" on life by just living it, that's fine with me, too. Whatever makes you happy—and no one else unhappy.

## KARATE MOUTH

"DON'T EVEN BOTHER GOING into the room, Brenner. There are four guys without necks at a front table who have heckled every act off the stage. It isn't worth your time. Better off going down to the Village. I'll go with you."

"I've spent the whole day listening to my tapes and I'm going to work out tonight! Show me the guys."

"Okay, but it's like trying to make Al Capone laugh."

He was right. Twelve hundred pounds of stupidity evenly divided into four bodies. They were semidrunk and very loud, intimidating everyone else so much that none of the other customers were talking above a whisper. No one was onstage and some people were starting to leave. I wanted to do a set. I never missed a night of practice. I was preparing for my audition for the "Tonight Show," so every workout was vital. I told the MC-owner to announce me, which he loved because he never liked me and was going to enjoy watching my comic demise.

I was announced and no one applauded. They were afraid. The four gorillas kept talking and laughing. I took the mike stand and moved it right in front of the Planet of the Apes table and yelled, "Hello." It startled them just long enough to get their attention for a split second.

"I want to apologize to all of you for being late but one of my students in my karate school is competing in the world Karate Olympics next month and he needed me to work out some of his weaker points. I know what a thrill it was when I won the title,

219

so I *had* to do it. Anyway, how are you four guys doing? Any problems?"

The blobs just shook their heads and I went on with my show. No heckles, just a lot of laughs. Sometimes the muscle in my head works real good.

# AN AMERICAN COMEDIAN IN CANADA

IT WAS 1970. I had played the Troubador on Santa Monica in Los Angeles ($250), Mister Kelly's on Rush Street in Chicago ($500) and now had a gig at a famous jazz room, The Colonial Inn on Yonge Street in Toronto, Canada ($500). In three weeks I would have earned $1,250 which, after deducting agency commissions, airfares, hotel rooms, food, cigarettes, tips, cleaning, magazines, buses, taxis, phone calls, federal, state and city taxes, would leave me about $650 in debt. My career was rolling! Actually, the whole exercise was called "experience," learning how to do whatever you do, the best you can do it. After that, it'll all happen. Right then it wasn't, but I was having fun anyhow.

The opening act in front of me was a self-contained, all-female rock and roll band who called themselves The Enchanted Forrest. They were a good act and very nice ladies. We got along fine. The only problem was that there was no MC so I had to readjust the stage for my act. After the band would go off, I would walk on, reset the lights, strike their microphones, set up mine, walk off and then walk back to not exactly the biggest welcoming applause ever registered in show business. Needless to say, the first ten minutes of my half-hour act were extremely rough and the last twenty minutes were excruciatingly painful. I was bombing beyond bombing!

One night as I was "working," I heard a voice from the back of the room near the bar call out some nicety like "Get the fuck off the stage!" I continued working until the next interruption, "I told you to shut the fuck up!" It was the same voice, only it sounded closer. I knew, probably from one of my high school science classes, that a human voice doesn't get closer unless the body that goes with it is also getting closer. I bent down under the bright spotlight I had set to shine into my own eyes, so I could see into the audience. The "voice" easily weighed two hundred and fifty pounds. I couldn't make out the tattoos that partially showed above the collar of his T-shirt, but I think one was a depiction of the St. Valentine's Day Massacre in Chicago and the other was The Last Supper with all the Apostles as weightlifters. Pleading in Yiddish was a definite out. I thought of limping around the stage as I spoke of "Nam," but Canada wasn't exactly enjoying her involuntary involvement in our draft problems. I just continued telling jokes. Not that I wasn't upset but, I'm not certain, I think I was speaking Sanskrit.

The tattooed ape was now at the edge of the stage. He was about to step up. I stopped being the comedian and became the kid from the streets. I said something on the mike to make the people laugh.

"Excuse me while I talk with my baby brother."

Then holding the mike stand in my right hand I leaned over to Mr. Ape and said quietly, off mike, with a smile on my face, "If you put one finger on this stage I'll crush in your fuckin' head, you ugly mothahfucker!" I stood up. He backed off into the darkness.

Pretty brave, huh? Didn't expect that of me, did you? I thought the same thing as I later climbed out the back window of the club, and, with my coat collar pulled way up over my head, limped out of the alley and down the street to my hotel.

Anyway, the gig was going terribly. The owner said he liked me, the girls from the band laughed backstage, but it wasn't enough. I wanted to make the audience laugh. I wanted to be a hit.

One night after a particularly bad night onstage, hardly one person laughed, I walked into the bathroom in my hotel room, pulled the chain to turn on the bare bulb above the sink and stood looking at myself in the medicine cabinet mirror. It was time for a pep talk.

"Come on, Brenner, what's the big deal? So, you're bombing. So what! You're doing well in other places. It's going well overall. You're performing better and better all the time. The material is getting better, too. Hell, the main thing is that you're having fun —traveling around the country, having no boss, doing whatever you want, whenever you want, with whomever you want. God, who wouldn't want to take your place? Damn, it's a good life and the main thing is and always will be your health. You got your health, you putz! What more do you want? You're young, not bad looking, having fun, and you got your health. Life is great, you putz! Putz! Putz! Putz! But why aren't they laughing?" The pep talk failed.

They weren't laughing and it really bothered me. I had to do something. Find out what was wrong and correct it. One night, after setting my stage, I blew into the mike real loud, getting people's attention.

"Testing! One, two, three! Testing! Testing! Harry had a hankering for hungry Hungarian harlots! Testing! Okay, folks, it seems to be on. Ladies and gentlemen! It is my pleasure to introduce tonight's main attraction. We are honored to have him with us. He is the U.S.A.'s fastest rising young comedian. Please give a warm Canadian welcome, as only we Canadians can do, to a very funny man and a real nice guy—Mr. David Brenner!"

I led the applause as I looked offstage. Then, still applauding and still smiling, I left the stage as though walking toward the approaching performer. The audience kept applauding. As I got to the wings I spun around and walked out to the mike.

"Thank you very much, my Canadian friends, and my deepest thanks to the MC, a wonderful human being and a damn good-looking man. My name is David Brenner and . . ."

It worked. I was a hit from that night on. It is true that little things do mean a lot.

A little postscript. A few years after my gig at the Colonial Inn, I appeared in concert at the Canadian National Exposition and for one hour heard the audience of 24,900 people laugh with me. I guess you can say that Canada has always been good to me—after a couple of introductory nights, anyway.


## THE NIGHT OF NIGHTS

AS I MENTIONED, I had given myself one year to play around as a stand-up comedian. However, at the end of the year, I thought I should at least make one appearance on television before giving it up. That way, when I would tell people that I had once been a stand-up comedian and they doubted me, I could pull out the old kinescope, put it on a projector, turn out the lights and "roll it"—"Now making his debut on the 'Tonight Show' is a new, young comedian—David Brenner!"

The very first time my name was
in lights. What a thrill!

I made my television debut on
The Tonight Show on January 8,
1971—one day short of nineteen
months since I first stepped on a
stage as a standup comedian.

One appearance on The Tonight
Show and a whole wonderful
world welcomed me! Buddy
Hackett got me into the main
showroom at the Sahara. I was
on my way!

My parents made *their* TV debut on the Mike Douglas Show one time when I co-hosted. They were adorable, lovable and funny—naturally.

Vaudeville Time. Left to right: Pinky Lee, former vaudevillian song and dance man and comedian, Lou "Murphy" Brenner, pie-covered Mike Douglas, Lou Brenner's comedian son, David, Ann Corio and Jerry Lester.

When I co-hosted the Mike Douglas show for the first time, my good pal and fellow stand-up comedian Mike Preminger came on to "break it up." Notice he copied my dress style.

When I co-hosted Mike Douglas for the first time, my good pal and fellow stand-up comedian Richard Lewis also came on to "break it up." Notice he, too, copied my dress style.

In November, 1977, I surprised
Mom and Lou with the first
brand new car any Brenner had
ever owned.

In 1980 my parents flew out to
L.A. to make another appearance
on the Mike Douglas show. I
surprised them with a private
Lear Jet ride to Las Vegas for my
opening night.

My father always wanted to drive
a Rolls Royce. Here he is driving
mine in the Nevada desert. After
this, he was happy so I put the
car up for sale. It had served its
purpose.

Enjoying my favorite pastime aboard my little sailboat, WAWCO, on Lake Mead, Nevada. Show business has made it all possible.

When Joan Rivers sent me this photo, she wrote "This is my favorite picture of the two of us."

With George Burns. To meet this
fine man was one of the great
thrills and pleasures of my life—a
lot of fun, too.

The man who once said, "There are those who like to read books; those who like to write books; and, persons such as myself, who like to live lives about which books are written," going back on his words to write *Soft Pretzels with Mustard.*

My personal manager, Steve Reidman, doing what he always does while I'm working my ass off on stage.

The next six months were the most difficult. Oh, I was becoming a better performer and gathering somewhat of a following in sections of Manhattan, but I was really hurting for cash. Another big setback was that Craig Tennis, chief talent coordinator for the "Tonight Show," had seen me work at the Bitter End where, on that particular night, I did a lot of politically oriented material to appeal to that select crowd, not knowing Craig was in the audience. Craig told my agent, Rick Bernstein, after seeing my performance that night that I did "vomit material" and there's "no way he'll ever be on the 'Tonight Show.' " I'd say that's a mild rejection, at least, wouldn't you?

Nevertheless, I forged ahead, or sideways anyway, continuing to work on stages every night with the same goal—the "Tonight Show." In November of 1970, I sold my entire wardrobe, probably worth $7,000, for $250, out of which $220 went for December's rent. The change from that transaction plus the $30 I made for a weekend at Pips were keeping me alive. I felt, and George Schultz concurred, that I was ready for the "Tonight Show." Rick Bernstein set up an audition a few days before Christmas.

Like a fighter training for the championship, I selected the eight minutes of material I would do at the audition—none of it political, of course—and every night, as many times a night as I could find any stage anywhere, I practiced the same eight minutes, over and over and over again, changing a word here, taking a longer pause there, switching this joke with that joke, deleting this line and adding that line, making it better all the time, until I had it the best I could. Every night I did the routine it worked, no matter what stage, what kind of audience, how late the hour I performed, what act preceded me. I was confident of the material and myself.

The "Tonight Show" auditions were held at the Victor Jay Theater on West Forty-fourth Street across from the NBC studios. I had been there on several occasions, acting like the manager of an auditioning act, just to get the free finger sandwiches and soda which were provided. Now it was my turn. When they announced my name, I walked up on that little stage and just did what I had been doing every night for the past couple weeks all around New York and it worked like it had been working. As we say, "I killed 'em!"

The next day, Rick Bernstein got a phone call from Craig Tennis, who admitted he was wrong about me and that I would get a date on the show but he couldn't say when. It could be months. I started thinking about a new career. On January 7, 1971, in the early evening, Rick Bernstein called me.

"Tomorrow night."

"I'm ready. Thanks!"

On January 8, 1971, at 12:50 A.M., one day short of nineteen months since my debut as a stand-up comedian, I walked out on the "Tonight Show" stage. I wasn't nervous. While I was standing behind the curtain in those last few seconds before going on I just thought how I had put a chunk of my life into preparing for these next six minutes and I wasn't going to blow it! No way!

It was one of those magical nights during which everything worked better than I had even fantasized it would. Into everyone's life "the night of nights" may never come, but if it does, it's always remembered. I was lucky. The audience went crazy. After my stand-up I walked back through the curtain and into the Green Room. I heard the audience applauding and thought Johnny had come up with one of his great ad libs. Then someone came in and told me to "go out again." I thought the video tape machine had broken and I'd have to do another stand-up, so, as I was hurrying back, I was thinking of other material I could do, because you can't do the same thing twice for the same audience. I came through the curtain and was heading for the mark on the floor where I was to stand during my monologue, when Johnny called me over and shook my hand. They were still applauding *for me!* On the air, Johnny told the audience how he had said to me, "We were looking for you," and my reply, "I did well. Why should I come back?"

Once again I was in the Green Room, still stunned, when the door flew open and in stormed Jerry Lewis.

"You're the greatest! I ran over here just to tell you that! I called the show and told them not to let you out of the building until I got here! You're so good, I think I'm going to hate you!"

He shook my hand and ran out to surprise Johnny on the air. I had always been a big fan of Jerry's. I couldn't believe what was happening to me. And this was just the beginning. Within twenty-four hours of that first appearance, I was offered $10,000 worth of jobs, including opening for Robert Goulet at the Monticello Club in Framingham, Massachusetts, a second appearance on the "Tonight Show"; an invitation to appear on what turned out to be the last "live" Ed Sullivan Show, and, because Buddy Hackett saw me that night and called the entertainment director at the Sahara Hotel in Las Vegas, I got an offer to play the main showroom. Within a week, the "Tonight Show" informed my agent that I had received the second largest mail response for a newcomer in the history of the show.

I had borrowed money to buy a suit to wear that night. It was a damn good investment. So was the $9,000 I had spent, so was the time, and the hard work. Whatever I have and my family has today has come from jokes and all the jokes started that special night on the "Tonight Show," and that can be traced back to that white sand beach on the island of Nevis when I decided to take a chance, to start at the bottom again, to at least try to reach my dreams. I truly believe there's a Nevis beach waiting for everyone. You've just got to take the chance to go there. If you do, I wish you the best. At worst you'll have tried, which is pretty damn good in itself. Do it!


## THE BOSTON SHUTTLE

WITH MY ONE SUIT, two dress shirts, necessities and what I had on my back, along with my pal and mentor, George Schultz, I sat in a taxi heading for La Guardia Airport all excited about my first "major showroom" job. The Monticello Theater nightclub in Framingham, Massachusetts, held about fifteen hundred people. The largest nightclub I had worked up to that time was Mister Kelly's in Chicago, which sat about three hundred.

When we approached the Boston shuttle gate, I wanted to be sure I was heading in the right direction, so I asked the airport attendant standing there, "Is this the shuttle to Boston?" He, in his typical New York friendliness, answered, "Where the hell you think it's going?" I didn't bother to answer back. George and I hurried through the gate, across the runway and into the plane.

We hung up our garment bags and took our seats. This was going to be a great day. As the plane taxied out to its take-off runway the pilot came on with his usual boring announcements, concerning the local time, the flying altitude, our take-off position, the names of our flight attendants and, finally, the weather—

"... and right now it is eighteen degrees with rain mixed with snow in our nation's capital. Enjoy the flight."

I thought, "What a putz. He thinks Boston is our capital. Even if he knew Washington was, why would anyone flying to Boston care about the weather in Washington? I would . . . oh, no. It can't be!" I said out loud, "Stewardess! Stewardess!"

"Yes, sir."

"Call me David. Stewardess, I'm going to Boston."

"That's wonderful, David, but the plane is going to Washington."

"You've got to turn around and go back!"

"We can't do that for two reasons. One, there's a very important VIP on board, Vice-President Hubert Humphrey, two seats in front of you, and, besides that, we're too far out on the runway."

"I don't care who's on board! Besides, the Vice-President does nothing anyway. You've got to go back!"

"We can't and that's that, David."

"Call me sir! You've got to because I'm opening tonight in Boston!"

I don't think she knew what "opening" meant and it must have rattled her a little, maybe making her think that I'm some sort of sicko who is going to open his body or something. All I know is that it made her hurry into the cockpit. A moment later, she came out and with a disgusted look on her face, gave me the okay sign. I smiled at George and settled back in my seat as the plane began to pivot around. Then the captain made an announcement.

"Ladies and gentlemen, we're going back to the gate. It seems that one of our passengers got on the wrong plane. There'll be about a forty-five-minute delay. I'm sorry."

Well, it turned into a scene out of a Western in which the townspeople get all worked up and turn into an ugly mob. They were yelling things like "Let's get him!" and "Hang 'im!" I guess I got caught up in it, and, the next thing I knew I was on my feet in the aisle facing the lynch mob.

"Okay," I yelled, "who's the stupid bastard?"

Well, this really fired up the crowd. Now they got real ugly. Men were on their feet, yelling all kinds of obscenities. I'm sure the Secret Service men were panicking. Anyway, as soon as I sat down, George turned to me.

"What are you, crazy or what, man? How the hell are we going to get off the plane? They'll know it was us. They'll beat us to

226

death, man! There's not a Jewish face in the whole plane."

George is one of the most paranoid Jews in the world. To him everyone over age fifty is a potential ex-Nazi. He's always avoiding crowds made up of too many men with blond hair and blue eyes. However, in this particular case, excluding the ethnic aspect of it, he was correct. They'd know it was us who had delayed the flight. I tried the windows. They didn't open. The plane came to a stop at the gate.

"We're trapped, man! Surrounded by hostile gentiles, thirsting for Jew blood! Butchered like pigs, pardon the expression, and all because of you, you comic putz!"

I stood up. George cowered in his seat.

"I'm not going, man. You're on your own. Good luck in Boston —if you make it."

I turned in the aisle, staring at all those angry faces, the burning rays from those hundreds of icy blue eyes, Cossacks without horses. I raised my arms, pointing up the aisle.

"I don't know about the rest of you folks," my voice boomed, "but, personally, I refuse to fly on any airline that screws up things this badly!"

George and I stormed off the plane with five other guys! The gig with Robert Goulet in *Monticello* was fabulous!

*I was guest on the "Tonight Show" one night when Joan Rivers was filling in for Johnny Carson and she suddenly asked everyone how they would like to die if they had a choice. I replied, "I don't know how I'd prefer to die, but I'd like my obituary to start off 'Yesterday the world's richest and only nine-hundred-year-old man passed away.'"*

# RICHARD LEWIS

I'M NOT GOING TO go into a whole psychological profile on Richard Lewis, a comedian/actor/writer and long-time friend. Suffice it to say that he is highly, most highly, most Mount Everest highly neurotic, paranoid, insecure and an all-around nervous wreck. These may be the reasons why he is so talented and funny. In all humbleness, I must say that I have been Richard's comedy hero since he first began his career. When he was a comedian maybe a month, and I was fairly well established at the time, he invited me to see him work out at a crummy club I had once played for nothing, too, called the Champagne Gallery on MacDougal Street in Greenwich Village. I showed up that Saturday night although he didn't expect it and never forgot it. Showing up made me an instant and eternal hero in his eyes. I had nothing better to do and was in the neighborhood anyway, but why argue?

Throughout the years, Richard has been the butt of many of my practical jokes because he's such an easy subject and because I love him. One of the best, or worst according to whose side you're on, was during one of Richard's low points in life. Perfect time for an attack.

It was a blistering cold winter night in Manhattan. Richard called from his one-room quasi-shack in New Jersey and asked if he could come over to my apartment and talk. I said of course.

With a glass of red wine in his hand, which he had brought from home, not a bottle, just a glass, he spoke for a few hours about how depressed he was concerning the recent breakup with his live-in love of five years and the seemingly dead end of his young career. I listened most of the time, adding a word of encouragement here and there. Talking it out was the real therapy. About four in the morning, he thanked me and said he'd better be starting home. I suggested that he not return to his depressing Abe Lincoln, one-room log cabin in the bitter cold. I once told him that the only saving grace about the tiny dwelling he occupied was that should he die there, he won't have to pay for a coffin—they'll just lower the house into the ground. Anyway he decided to accept my invitation to crash on my living room couch for the night. He thanked me and I got him bedding. We said good-night and I had started into the hallway leading to my bedroom when I turned to Richard.

"You know, Richard, no matter how bleak life may look, the only thing of real importance is that when you get up in the morning, you can put your shoes on. If you can do that, you've got it made."

"Wow! You know, I never thought of it that way. Damn, you're right, David! What am I getting so crazy about? I'll find another girl friend. My career will happen one day. I got my health, right? I can put my shoes on in the morning. I'll never forget what you just taught me. Thanks a million, David."

"Forget it, Richard. Good night."

228

"Good night."

The next morning, Richard had to get up early to drive back to Jersey and take care of a few matters. I had left him an alarm clock. When he awoke, he sat on the sofa and slid his feet into his loafers—well, partially, because he couldn't get them all the way on due to the bottle caps I had stuffed in the toes. He wasn't able to put his shoes on in the morning. He left depressed. But if you knew Richard, you would know that he would have left that way, anyway.

Well, Richard did find another girl friend, of course. Matter of fact, he's constantly finding them and leaving them and getting depressed until the next one. And his career has happened, mainly in the field of comedy writing, although he is doing very funny stand-up work on TV today.

Like most of us, it began with the "Tonight Show." Richard had gotten a date for his first appearance. Besides honing the comedy material, the material one wears is important, too. Richard asked me to help him pick out an outfit for his TV debut, because I had been voted to the Ten Best Dressed Men in America list twice and supposedly knew what worked and didn't work on the tube.

I took Richard to a store on Lexington Avenue called House of Cromwell. It was there I was buying a lot of my clothes and had helped two other friends select their TV debut outfits, Freddie Prinze and Michael Preminger. I did it to be helpful and because it gave me a golden opportunity to have some laughs, at the expense of my friends, naturally.

Freddie's was a good one. He didn't have the money for the suit he wanted, so I loaned him a hundred dollars. He wore it on his first appearance on the "Tonight Show." Afterwards I sent him a threatening letter, written à la the Godfather, telling him he'd better pay back the money he owed or he'd find himself swimming in the Hudson River and the Manhattan River and the Harlem River—simultaneously. The threats got worse with each letter. All were signed "Tony, Guido and Alphonse." It was a joke until his mother happened to see one of the letters lying open on his bed, read it and waited until the wee hours one morning for him to come home and explain what was going on. Freddie laughingly explained who I was and that it was a joke, but his mother, Mary, didn't believe him. She was ready to hide him out in her native Puerto Rico. Finally, Freddie came to one of my gigs, stole the life-size lobby billboard advertising me and showed it to his mother. Mary looked at it and said, "If this boy is so famous a comedian, why is he getting the Mafia after you?"

Helping out Mike Preminger was even better. While he was looking for a good TV suit, I showed him the lightweight two-piece summer outfits—a shirt and matching pants—I had bought. He saw me wearing a couple of them and liked them. They came in all colors and weren't expensive. I took him to the House of Cromwell. Mike tried on a blue one and then a tan one. I handed him the fire-engine red one to try on.

"Aw, come on, Brenner, I couldn't wear that."

"Why not? I have it."

"Well, you're different. You can wear anything because you don't care what people think."

"Right. Dress for yourself."

"Well, for myself, I couldn't walk around in that. It's too . . . too . . ."

"Too what?"

Prem looked around and then whispered,

"Feminine. Gay."

"What're you telling me? I look feminine in mine?"

"Shhhh. No, but, I'm . . . well, you know, I'm . . ."

"Look, at least try it on. You might like it." I handed it to Prem and he went into the dressing room. A couple minutes later he came out. He looked ridiculous. First of all, he's about five feet six inches tall so there was a lot of extra material rolled up around his ankles. Secondly, he looked as uncomfortably as he felt. I resisted the big laugh rolling inside my stomach and winked at the salesman so he wouldn't laugh either.

"Not bad, Prem. Look in the mirror."

"Not bad? I look like a bonfire searching for a place to happen."

"I like it."

"I look like one of Santa's disturbed helpers. Forget it."

"Look, I've got an idea. Why don't you just casually walk around the store. There are a lot of people there. Make believe you're browsing. That way you'll be able to find out if you feel funny wearing it in public."

He reluctantly agreed and left the curtained dressing area. I waited until he was in the center of the store, in an open aisle,

230

surrounded by sixty men and women, and then I extended my arm, pointing my finger at Prem and yelled, "Hey, look at that gay guy in the funny red suit!"

Gales of laughter rose above the clothing racks. Prem's face was so red you couldn't tell where the suit left off and he began.

Now it was Richard's turn. We picked out a nice suit, shirt and belt. I bought a few items myself. While Richard was waiting for the alterations to be done I paid for my things. I walked through the shoplifting screen and waited for him by the door. Richard paid and started through the screening arch when the alarms went off. A solidly built Latino asked Richard to show him his shopping bag.

"This is ridiculous. I just bought a suit and things. Maybe your salesman forgot to clip off the sensor tags."

The bodyguard took Richard's shopping bag and asked him to walk through the arch again. People had gathered. The alarm was extra loud. Again the alarms went off. This time the guard got a little nervous as did Richard when he held him a little too tightly.

"Hey, let go, little King Kong. I didn't steal anything!"

More people gathered. The guard started to physically lead Richard back through the arch.

"Listen, you're holding me a little too tight. I have a black belt. Matter of fact, I just bought it here. Don't get it, huh? Wait just a minute!"

Richard broke loose of the guard's grip. Other guards and the two store owners were now approaching the scene. Tension mounted.

"I don't like being treated like a common thief. I happen to be with my friend, David Brenner."

Eyes turned toward me.

"Is that true, David?" one of the owners asked.

A hush came over everyone. Richard was smiling.

"Never saw the crook."

I turned and left the store. It took the guards about an hour to discover the sensor tag I had slipped into the ripped lining of Richard's leather jacket. My friends no longer ask me to go shopping with them and it's a shame because I would just love to!

Not everyone does well his or her first time on the "Tonight Show," even those with great talent. Sometimes the performer is a little off because of nervousness, and for a comedian, who is so dependent on absolutely perfect timing and control of delivery, this can destroy his presentation. It's a real bad break, because it means maybe a full year before the opportunity will arise again, and, worse than that, great expectations and dreams also must be postponed.

Such an unfortunate thing happened to Richard Lewis. He didn't live up to his talent on his "Tonight Show" debut. I was working in Las Vegas at the time, saw his shot, and invited him to be my guest for a few days in Vegas to take his mind off things before he returned to New York.

The day after he arrived Richard and I took a ride around Vegas. On the way back to our rooms, we stopped at a red light near a small shopping center close to our hotel. In it was a store that sold knickknacks, souvenirs like a plastic toilet seat with gambling chips in it, or a crucifix with Jesus holding a pair of dice with the number seven on them—typical, classy Vegas stuff. The name of the store was Ramseys.

"That's unbelievable, isn't it, Richard? Only in Vegas could there be a store like that?"

"What store?"

"That one—Ramseys."

"What is it?"

"The name tells you what it is."

"Ramseys? What's Ramseys?"

"Think, man. Didn't you use them as a teenager?"

"You mean rubbers? I thought it was spelled r-a-m-s-e-s."

"You thought wrong. Anyway, everything in that store is made from rubbers. Ashtrays, lamps, tables, footstools. They even have a TV made from rubbers. Of course, they have protective covering."

"Let's go in."

"You must be kidding."

The light changed and I pulled away. Richard almost strained his neck watching the store.

"Look, a guy just came out. Wonder what he bought? Looked real seedy. Probably a rubber hardhat."

A couple days later, we were driving past the store again.

"Hey, David, let's go in the rubber store."

"Richard, I've got an image to protect. Suppose some straight-laced fan sees me walking into that kind of place. Got to think of the career first."

"Well, after the other night, I don't have a career, so let me go in."

"We're already a block away and I want to eat something. Maybe another time, before you leave."

I avoided the small shopping center for the next two days. On the day Richard was leaving for New York, I purposely led us by the shopping center. Richard had to be the one to bring it up, so it wouldn't arouse suspicion. The store was now behind us. Damn, it hadn't worked.

"Wait, David, I'm going in."

"What?"

"The store."

"What store?"

"With the rubbers."

"Forget it! Let's go."

"Come on, who knows when I'll be in Vegas again. Just for a few minutes."

"I don't believe you're really interested in seeing that crap."

"For laughs."

"All right, you go in. I'll wait around here. Now, when you enter, the front part is a regular souvenir store. The rubber stuff is in the back room, so ask to go in there. I'll wait here, maybe get an ice cream. Have a good time, you pervert."

"Maybe I can have my girl friend's name spelled out in condoms."

He left.

"May I help you, young man?" asked the sweet-faced, little old lady behind the counter in Ramseys.

"Ehh . . . well . . . yes. I . . . I . . . rubbers."

"What?"

"Rubbers . . . ehh . . . tables and lamps."

"Oh. I'm sorry, we only carry small items. You want Macy's."

"No, I want to go in your back room . . . please."

"What back room?"

"Where you have all the things made from rubb . . . prophylactics."

"Young man, there is no back room and you'd better leave before I call the police. Don't let my age fool you, I can deal with a pervert like you quite well. Now get!"

You would never believe that Richard still considers me one of his best friends, would you?

# JIMMIE WALKER

I WAS A COMEDIAN all of six months and had just walked into the African Room on West Forty-fourth Street, one of the many hootenanny type clubs. I often worked out there. On stage was a skinny black kid. He looked like a burnt lollipop. He was talking about pitching quarters on the streets in Harlem and he was very funny, getting big laughs. As usual, the audience was mostly black. After his set, he came offstage and I introduced myself. Ironically, we stood talking under the giant gorilla that decorated the back part of the club. He told me his name was Jimmie Walker, he was twenty years old, worked at night as a radio engineer, lived in Harlem and did comedy in his spare time.

"Did you ever work in front of a white audience?"

"No."

"Well, if you want to make it so-called 'big' you've got to get the whites behind you, like Flip Wilson, Redd Foxx, Richie Pryor and Cosby did. After my set, I'm going over to the Improvisation where a bunch of new guys like ourselves work out all the time. If you'd like, you can hang out with me."

That's how Jimmie Walker and I met and he became part of the 1969 group of show business hopefuls, which included in alphabetical order Nicky Arnold, Peter Boyle, David Brenner, Al Jarreau, Steve Landesberg, Jimmy Martinez, Bette Midler, Marty Nadler, Mike Preminger, Lenny Schultz, Alan Uger, Jimmie Walker and many others who are still trying, or never made it and just faded away.

Before Jimmie became J.J. on "Good Times" and became a star, we had our own private laughs in those early days in New York. He telephoned early one evening saying that he was nearby and wanted to drop by my apartment. We could get a bite to eat and talk. I told him Steve Landesberg was with me, so the three of us could hang out and hit the clubs in the Village together.

At that time, I lived in a one-room apartment on East Sixty-ninth Street. The doormen knew all my friends and would usually just buzz as a courtesy to let me know someone was coming up. This particular night, a new doorman was filling in for one of the regulars who was on vacation. He rang my buzzer.

"Mr. Brenner, there's a young man here to see you."

"What's his name?"

"Wait, I'll find out. What's your name?"

"He says he's the Imperial Black Prince."

"Oh, it must be the delivery boy from the deli. Tell him to use the service elevator. Thank you."

I hung up the intercom phone. A moment later, it buzzed again.

"Hello, Mr. Brenner? I'm sorry to bother you but that young man refused to use the service elevator. Matter of fact, he cursed at me. He's on his way up."

"You're kidding! How big is he?"

"Oh, he's not big at all. Tall, but the skinniest person I think I've ever seen. He . . ."

"Did he have a gun or a knife?"

"No, I didn't see any, but, if you want I'll call the police and have . . ."

"No, but thanks anyway. I've got my pal Landesberg with me, so I think we can handle this guy. Next time, though, make sure all minority group members use the service elevator."

"Yes, sir."

"That includes Swedes!"

"I understand."

The doorbell rang. I let in a fuming, ranting, raving, cursing, skinny black militant from Harlem who, when the three of us left the building, refused to walk ahead of us with his hands tied behind his back. Damn, Steve and I were willing to wear sheets.

Most of the time, in those early days, all of us aspiring young comedians would take the bus or subway to and from gigs. Once in a great while, if the hour were late, or the mood was just right, or someone had a couple spare shillings from one of the all-too-rare paying jobs, or there were enough of us to split the fare, we'd take a cab. Most often, the sharing taxi riders would be Jimmie Walker, Steve Landesberg, Jimmy Martinez, Mike Preminger and me. Mike always would complain throughout the entire ride that he needed the money for rent and was doing it only because he didn't feel like riding on the subway alone. Sometimes, after the whole gang of us would grab a late snack at the Camelot Coffee House at Forty-ninth and Eighth, I would share a cab with Jimmie Walker, who would drop me off at Sixty-ninth and Third Avenue, on the posh, upper East Side of Manhattan, where I occupied my cigar-box-sized one-room apartment, and then he would continue up to his place in Harlem.

After midnight, especially in that neighborhood around Eighth Avenue, most cab drivers were reluctant to pick up blacks because of their prejudicial fear of muggings. In order to avoid the anger and frustration over seeing an empty cab whip by us, Jimmy would stand in the entranceway of the coffee house and I would stand in the street to hail a cab. Once the cab stopped, I would hold open the door, and Jimmy would come racing out and jump inside with me right behind. Some of the cab drivers really would be pissed off but could do nothing but drive us both home.

We always told the driver "First stop is Sixty-ninth and Third and then One Hundred Twenty-fifth and Lenox." Once in a while, when we knew the driver was especially angry and bigoted, when we got to Sixty-ninth Street, Jimmy would get out of the cab and I'd say to the driver, "Now, mothah, take me to One Hundred Twenty-fifth and Lenox." We always got a good belly laugh pulling off this joke.

*I have toyed with the idea of putting the following epitaph on my gravestone: "If this is a joke—I don't get it." What do you think?*

## THE ROAD MANAGER

IN THE SPRING OF 1976, my career was starting to move up to a higher plateau, thank goodness, and this caused me to be inundated with more to do in more areas. It became impossible for me to travel on the road by myself, making hotel reservations, airline reservations, changing same, conducting rehearsals, getting around securely, handling the phone, arranging press interviews and media appearances, and the myriad of chores and details that go into being a performer. I hired a road manager to take care of all of it, freeing me to spend my time being creative.

Chuck Besanty is a "laid-back" Los Angelino, mild, mellow, and mannerly. We hit it off right away, professionally and personally. He's the kind of guy you just can't help but like. He's also the kind of guy you just can't help but fool—and he's so "easy." My cup of tea.

236

We had been on the road several weeks in a row. It's fun, of course, but it's also very tiring, physically and mentally. I was really starting to feel the wear and tear. After all, I first went out on the road in the summer of sixty-nine, seven years before. We were in Lake Tahoe for a week, a respite of sorts. Chuck wrapped up his afternoons by having a massage in the men's club. He kept bugging me to have one. I'm not crazy about massages, but Chuck wouldn't lay off.

He was being such a nudge about the damn massages that I finally consented to have one. Besides, it was raining that day. As massages go, it was a good one. I did feel better. Chuck had an appointment right after me.

"How'd you like it?"

"It was good."

"Told you."

"Right. Okay, I'm going down to my room. See you about four-thirty for dinner."

"Okay."

Chuck climbed up on the table and I walked out, not all the way out, just far enough away that he couldn't see me. After five minutes, I sneaked back in and put my fingers to my lips, signaling the masseur that he shouldn't say anything. Chuck was lying on his back, his eyes covered with perfume-scented cotton patches. His body was oiled. A towel was draped over his midsection. The masseur was massaging his face.

I walked up to the masseur and got on one side of him. I hand-motioned for him to pick up one hand and I would replace it with mine. I hovered my hand above his, until I had the rhythm and motion just right and then nodded. The masseur lifted his hand and I quickly put mine in its place. I kept the rhythm with his other hand, then signaled him to remove his other hand, so now I was massaging Chuck's face. The transition was so smooth, Chuck didn't even notice.

I was giving Chuck a pretty good facial. I then slipped my finger up one of his nostrils, casually, as though I had made a mistake. Chuck didn't do a thing about it! He just lay there with someone else's finger up his nose. I took the finger out and massaged him for a moment and then shoved my finger up his nostril again. This time less casually and farther. Chuck only grunted a little. I then started stretching out his nostril, as I pressed my other hand against his cheek to hold his head down on the table. It was as though I were trying to rip open his nose. Only when his nostril was opened far enough that I could have stuck my fist into it did Chuck shake loose and sit up.

"What's going on, Al? Did you . . ."

I think it was from that time that Chuck developed the habit of keeping one eye open whenever he has a massage.

We were working the Holiday House in Monroeville, Pennsylvania. We had been there seven nights and had three to go. It's a nice town, but once you've seen the shopping center and the two movies, you've done the Chamber of Commerce's brochure from A to Z. Besides, it was my third time there, so I had really done it all twice before.

One day while going through the shopping center again, hoping that one of the stores may have changed its window display, we passed an electronic shop and a pair of walkie-talkies caught my eye. I bought them.

After the second show that night, Chuck and I went to my suite to discuss business matters. Afterward, I pulled out the walkie-talkies.

"Let's see how these work. It'll be fun."

We read the instructions and set up the system.

"Okay, Chuck, go into the other room and talk."

"Hello, David, do you hear me? . . . Do you hear me?"

"Chuck, the proper expression is 'do you read me?' and you must say 'over' when you're finished so I know when to speak. Over."

"Got you. Uh, over."

"Not 'Got you,' Chuck, 'Roger.' Over."

"Yeah . . . huh . . . Roger. Over."

"Okay, Chuck, take it into the hall and see if it works from there. Over."

"Okay, over."

"Not 'okay,' putz, 'Roger.' Over."

"I'm now in the hall. Can you hear . . . uh, read me? Over."

"I read you loud and clear. Can you read me? Over."

"Yes, Roger, I do. Over."

" 'Roger' means 'yes' and 'I do.' Now go down the hall a way and see if it comes in. Over."

"Okay . . . I mean, Roger, I'm going down the hall. I'm now

passing Room 304. A tray is on the floor outside. They had a club sandwich and hamburger and two cokes for dinner. Then again, from the look of the remains it couldn't have been last night. I'm now passing 300 and am at the end of . . . hi . . . no, I'm talking to a friend . . . no, my phone works. We're just having some fun . . . you, too. Good night. Hello, David? Over."

During his monologue, I went into the bathroom, brushed my teeth and washed my face and hands. I returned to the bedroom and took off my shoes and socks.

"Not, 'hello'—'come in', over."

"Jesus. Okay. Come in, David, come in . . . come in, David, come in . . . do you read me? . . . David, come in . . . Damn . . ."

"I'm still waiting for your 'over.' "

"I don't believe . . ."

"Excuse me, Chuck, I didn't say 'over.' I just said I was waiting for *your* 'over.' Now I'll give you *my* over—over."

"Fine. I'm coming back. Over."

"Just take it to the dressing room, Chuck. Thanks. Over."

"Okay. But I'm getting tired. Over."

"Thanks, Chuck. Over."

"Okay. Well, I'm now walking to the back stairs and starting down them. The rugs are frayed . . . ah, there's a chicken wing that must've dropped off the waiter's tray. I am now on the first floor landing and heading . . ."

"Chuck? Sorry to interrupt before you say 'over,' but you needn't give me a blow-by-blow description of the staircase. Just contact me when you get to the dressing room. Over."

"Roger, over."

I got undressed while Chuck walked to the dressing room.

"Come in, David. This is Control Center. Do you read me? Over."

"Yes, I read you loud and clear. It's amazing. Let's see if these'll work from the disco. Over."

"The disco? Over."

"Yes, the disco. If they work there, they'll work anywhere. Over."

"Yes, but the disco is packed. It's Saturday night. Besides, I've got to go outside to get to it and it's freezing. I want to come back. Over."

"Come on, Control Center, don't be an L.A. pansy all your life! Over."

"All right, but this is the last test. After this, I'm coming back upstairs! Over."

"Roger. I read you loud and clear. That's an A-okay. Over."

"Whatever all that meant. Okay, I'm heading out into the blizzard and the disco. Central Control saying 'you'll be hearing from me.' Over."

"Godspeed, Central Control. All systems 'go.' Over."

I got into bed and turned out the light.

"Hello, this is Control Center from the disco. Do you read me? Over."

"You're breaking up. Go closer to the dance floor. Do you read me? Over."

"Okay. I'm now walking through . . . oh, excuse me . . . no, I don't dance, but thank you . . . I'm listening to the ballgame . . . yes, but it's from L.A., the Dodgers . . . you, too. Okay, I'm now on the lip of the dance floor, and . . . no, I'm not into coke, but thanks . . . no, ludes either . . . I don't smoke . . . no, I'm not. I'm a mainliner, the big H. You want to shoot up? How about shooting it into your ankle or . . . knew that would shake him . . . okay, my foot is now on the dance floor! I'm shouting because of the blaring music! People are staring at me! Can you read me? I want to get out of here! I want . . . no, I'm not dancing with your girl . . . I'm not alone! My girl friend is a midget . . . come in, *please* . . . do you read me? Over!"

"I'VE BEEN READING YOU ALL ALONG! GOOD NIGHT, PUTZ! OVER AND OUT!"

I went to sleep. The next day I sent the walkie-talkies to Chuck's kids so all was forgiven.

Chuck left his job with me after six months. It had nothing to do with this or other incidents. He wanted to spend more time at home with his family. Today, he and Barbara, his wife, own a store called Penny Arcade in Aspen, Colorado, and are very happy. Chuck and I have remained friends, although every time we talk on the phone, I hang up on him in the middle of the conversation.

About a year after Chuck left as my road manager, I was working in Las Vegas. I had some friends visiting me and Chuck and his wife came up for the night to say hello and gamble. I usually eat a few hours before my shows because I feel better working on an empty stomach, but, once in a while, I'll go to dinner between shows. We went to the seafood restaurant, Dome of the Sea, in the Dunes Hotel. It is a beautiful restaurant that seats about a hundred people. In the center of the room is a manmade mini-lake, measuring about sixty feet by twenty feet. The tables surround the lake. In the middle of it is a large, swan-shaped boat in which a woman sits in formal gown playing the harp. She floats slowly from one end of the water to the other. The atmosphere is sedate and sophisticated. It is one of the quieter places in Las Vegas, but is also one of its strongest attractions. The eight of us finished dinner and had ordered dessert and after-dinner drinks.

"Chuck, I'll give you $750 if you stand at one end of the lake, scream at the top of your lungs, 'I'll save you, Veronica,' and then dive in and swim to the other end to where the swan will be."

Everyone laughed. Chuck looked at the water and the harpist.

"Can I check out the water first?"

"Sure."

Chuck called over one of the maître d's.

"What's in the water?"

"Oh, there's lights, electrical wires, some prongs."

"In other words, a man could get killed maybe if he fell in, say?"

"Possible." The maître d' left.

"Eight hundred, Chuck."

"I could get killed so you push it up fifty bucks?"

"Only because your wife is here. It'd be $752 if she weren't."

"Can I take off my sport jacket and shoes?"

"Of course."

Chuck took them off. All of us were laughing, knowing he was only pretending. He stood up.

"Remember, Chuck, the harpist must be all the way at the other end of the lake."

"Got it," he said, pulling his pants up like a scene from an old thirties movie.

We all watched as he walked to the far end of the water. He made believe he was looking at the dessert tray. He glanced at us. He was smiling and we were laughing. He then looked into the water, like a tourist just passing the time. He looked at us again, smiling. We looked at him again, laughing.

"I'll save you, Veronica!" he roared, and dove headfirst into the water.

When he surfaced, his head was covered with green slime. The water probably hadn't been cleaned in years. And then, afraid he didn't yell it loud enough the first time, he screamed at the top of his lungs, "I'll save you, Veronica!" and began swimming quickly toward the harpist, splashing water all over the diners. After reaching the swan, he walked to the edge and climbed out, looking like the Creature From the Green Slime Lagoon.

I've got to admit that I, as well as the others, never thought Chuck would do it. I'll tell you what's even more amazing. First, the harpist never batted an eye nor lost a stroke on her harp; "Stardust" continued throughout the entire swim. Secondly, you know what all the customers did? The entire room gave Chuck a standing ovation. I did, too, plus eight one hundred dollar bills.

There's some aftermath to this story. Chuck had forgotten that he was in Las Vegas for only the night and didn't have a change of clothes. He and Barbara had to get in a cab and find an all-night laundromat. Barbara stood guard while a naked Chuck hid behind the machines that washed and dried his clothes. Another result was the rumors that were started. The next night some man walked up to me.

"I hear you gave some guy $800,000 to jump in the Dome of the Sea pool."

"For eight hundred thousand, I could've bought the restaurant. The guy who did it is Chuck Besanty from L.A. and he did it for eight dollars!"

# FAST MOVES

STEVE REIDMAN FOLLOWED CHUCK BESANTY as my road manager in October of 1976 and is now my personal manager. The big difference between the two positions is money. The big similarity is that we still travel on the road together. My job is the jokes. His is everything else, soup to nuts—ordering soup, getting rid of the nuts. He does his job excellently, but once in a great while he goofs.

When Steve first came to work with me, I told him that I never had to put anyone out of a showroom because I can usually control them verbally. However, there was always the possibility, and maybe even the danger, of an uncontrollable lunatic or drunk. If that should ever happen, I would use a code signaling Steve to get Security to remove the person. The code was that I would say to the heckler or person disturbing the show, "Sir (or madam), you are bad news!"

The first week on the road with Steve, I was working a thousand-seat nightclub in the Midwest. The audience was drinking, laughing and having a good time. I had to work hard but I was happy with the responses. A man started to call out drunken nonsequiturs, as the drunks usually do.

"David, make call in the woods, Alabama."

These are difficult statements with which to deal. I usually say something like, "Well, only if blue cordless pajamas and Tennessee."

After a few verbal exchanges such as these, the drunk is usually satisfied with the conversation and will sit down in his seat or on the floor and behave. Well, on this particular night, the drunk was just a little louder than most and a little larger, too! However, I knew he could be controlled eventually and I kept working toward that inevitable goal.

As I was making the audience laugh over my rapport with the wasted heckler I noticed uniformed security guards hurrying along the walls of the nightclub, closing in on the area of the drunk. I saw Steve leading some of the guards, moving quicker than I had ever seen him move. I figured that he had gotten a threatening call or a tip about a lunatic in the audience. I kept working and eventually the drunk was satiated. I went on with the remainder of the show.

When I came offstage, I asked Steve what the commotion was all about. Because of his inexperience he thought that the drunk was out of control and beyond redemption. He went into more of a state of panic when he couldn't remember the code.

"What is the code by the way?"

"I say to the drunk or whatever, 'Sir, you are bad news.' "
Steve laughed.

"Why, what's so funny?"

"I told the cops to get ready to move as soon as they heard you say, 'Sir, you are an asshole!' "

Security is always a prime concern of mine, and of everyone in show business. Normally our security systems are excellent and are in effect at all times. However, there's always the exception . . .

I was playing a summer theater tent in New England. After the show Steve and I spent time in the dressing room trailer behind the theater, changing out of stage clothes and into jeans, answering fan mail, signing autographs, discussing the show and other business and just generally relaxing. The audience had been long gone by the time we came out and walked to our car that was parked behind the trailer. We got in and headed for our hotel. Steve was driving and I was relaxing. We were discussing that night's show and the material I was working on for my upcoming hosting of the "Tonight Show."

There was a little haze on the dark back road. We always prefer the scenic routes even at night. From the corner of my eye, I saw the top of someone's head slowly rising in the backseat. I immediately turned in my seat, placing my back against the dashboard for support and raised my arm to throw a punch as soon as the guy's face appeared. There were now two heads coming up! Steve saw me moving and looked in the rearview mirror where he could see the two silhouetted forms.

Steve then did what any man would do in such a tight and dangerous situation—he screamed, blew the horn and turned the car into the oncoming traffic lane. The swerving car threw me off balance and the two guys in the backseat popped up.

"Did we scare you *that much*?"

Two teenage girls. Now this is an embarrassing situation. Here we are, two men and one of us goes into a full state of panic over what turns out to be two harmless groupies who hid in the car hoping to meet me, never thinking we would drive away so fast. I had to explain Steve's reaction. I couldn't tell them what I knew to be the truth. You see, Steve was raised in Los Angeles where the only real danger is getting accidently hit on the head with an old pair of Gucci loafers being thrown out of a window, or running into someone so mean he doesn't even say, "Have a nice day." The men in that part of the country are not exactly our most streetwise, fast-to-jump-into-action men. As a matter of fact, in my old neighborhood, we had a name for guys like that —we called them "girls." Actually, it's the right way to grow up, only the world isn't always that peaceful. Anyway, this is what I told the two stowaways:

"You're very lucky you're still alive. Steve here has a black belt in Rodeo Drive Karate. His normal reaction would have been to throw one of his "Siamese" punches, but when he saw you were girls, in order to control his natural instinct to kill, he expended his anger by screaming and blowing the horn."

"But why did he cross the road divider?"

"Good question. It was a muscle spasm. So strong it turned the wheel."

"Why are we still driving on the wrong side of the road?"

"Steve's originally from England."

Steve slowly maneuvered the car back to the right side of the road, made a U-turn and drove back to the theater where we deposited the two fans. He never said a word. I didn't either—I was laughing too hard. I wonder if anyone raised in Los Angeles ever has been accepted in the Marine Corps?

Las Vegas truly is the mecca of show business. It's a lot of fun to work there. However, the routine of two shows nightly, seven nights a week, along with the late night gambling, the crowds, etc. can start to get to you. In the beginning of 1978, I did something no other coheadliner comedian had ever done in Las Vegas—I worked seven weeks and two nights in a row, two shows per night, no nights off. By the fifth week I was heading for the banana cage. I needed a diversion, something to do to take me away from the action, something that would help me relax, let the juice stop boiling, bring me down to the sanity level. I had always enjoyed the beauty and tranquility of Lake Mead, a mere forty-minute drive from the strip through magnificently beautiful desert, so I decided to buy a boat—a thirty-foot cabin cruiser. It was a beauty. White with blue racing stripes, a head, galley, cabin, stereo, air conditioning and lots of power!

The day my boat was launched, the dealer sent someone to take us out on the lake to familiarize us with the boat and the waters. Steve and I took turns at the wheel since we both like to water-ski and could take turns doing it once we both learned how to drive the boat. After about two hours all was going well except my friend, Rick Bernstein, who's always one day away from starting a diet, was below deck when we made a turn and, instead of grabbing onto something solid, he decided to stop his fall with the dining table. Not only didn't the table stop his fall, it became part of it, crashing in splinters to the floor. Okay, the table can be fixed.

We pulled the boat into a marina for gasoline. The instructor then told Steve to start the boat and pull it back from the dock a little. Steve kicked over the engines, powerful 350s, and by mistake put it into forward. It slowly started to inch forward, out of the water and onto the cement-covered ground. When the instructor yelled "Reverse!" Steve realized what he was doing. Well, that good Gucci-loafer-have-a-nice-day panic took over and instead of putting the throttle into reverse, he threw it forward —all the way. We would've been inside the restaurant had I not simultaneously whipped the gears into neutral.

Hey, anyone can make a little mistake, especially the first day you have a boat, right? Right. The scratches in the hull were sanded out and the hull was repainted. The boat looked brand new instead of three hours old.

Five months later, I was boating us around the lake, taking Steve water-skiing for the empteenth time. I had never been on water skis because Steve wanted to practice driving the boat some more. So, Steve, his future wife, Kim, and my friends were all having a wonderful summer water-skiing. I was having a wonderful summer driving them around the lake.

Steve tossed the water skis into the boat and climbed aboard.

"Boy, it's really great out there today! Calm as glass. I'm a little chilly. Let me get a towel. Be right up."

I'm drenched in sweat from maneuvering the boat for his hour of skiing and he's chilly. They say the lake is 1,600 feet deep and a body never surfaces, and . . . "Listen, David, I'll take the wheel. Why don't you stretch out back there and relax."

He saved his young life. I stretched out in the back and enjoyed the fast ride across the wide lake. It was so relaxing. We crossed the large stretch of open water and were heading into the channel that would take us back to the marina when Steve saw some water skiers a few hundred yards ahead. The rule is to slow down so as not to cause a wake for the skiers. Steve meant to do that but pushed the throttle forward, instead of backward, increasing our speed. There was still plenty of time to correct the situation, but —well, need I say any more about Gucci and having nice day? He threw it into reverse, blowing the transmissions! We limped back into the marina, me sweating at the wheel, Steve remorseful but cool in the bow seat.

Lake Mead has not seen Steve Reidman since that day in '78 and it hasn't asked for him either. I sold the power boat and am now into sailing but won't go into my experience with Steve and the sailboat. Enough is enough. Besides, he's liable to read this book and he's the best manager a guy could want. However, there is one more story about which I'm certain he'll have no objections.

Regardless of what I've written about Steve so far, he is fast of mind if not of body. It is tough to put one over on him and I consider myself to be among the best. I did get him once.

Steve is a vegetarian. No meat, no chicken, no fish. He is also a health nut of sorts, especially concerning sugar. If anything was even on the shelf next to a package of sugar, Steve wouldn't eat it. I respect this. I think it's stupid, but I respect it.

While we were working in Green Bay, Wisconsin, Steve wasn't feeling well. He had a fever and the sniffles. It looked like a flu or a bad cold to me, but Steve insisted that vegetarians and health food addicts do not get colds, so it was something that "only looked like one." Anyway, we were staying in a motel just a short drive from the theater where I was working. Steve had no appetite, so I went down to the restaurant alone for dinner. After eating, I asked the man in charge of the restaurant to do me a favor.

"My manager, Steve Reidman, is in room 907. He isn't feeling well. The doctor told him to eat but he won't. Would you please deliver an order to his room? Remember, no matter what he says or does, see that he takes the tray of food into the room."

"Of course, Mr. Brenner. What would you like us to take Mr. Reidman?"

"The doctor gave me a list of what he's supposed to eat. Ah, here it is. A full roasted chicken, mashed potatoes with gravy, a big glass of Coke, a chocolate cake and a large sundae with vanilla ice cream and lots of whipped cream and a cherry and, if you have them, a little paper umbrella. It'll cheer him up, poor guy."

"We'll get it up to him right away and don't worry about him accepting it, I'll send my biggest waiter."

"Perfect. Thanks."

I ate my ice cream and apple pie quickly and hurried upstairs.

I opened my door ever so slightly. I had a room a couple rooms down from Steve. The waiter arrived. He pounded on Steve's door.

"Who is it?"

"Room service."

"I didn't order anything. Wrong room."

"Mr. Reidman?"

"Yes, but I . . ."

"Open the door!"

"What?"

"I said open the goddamn door before I knock it down! You've got to eat."

I heard the door open and then close and then the chain slipped on.

I laughed throughout my shower and while getting dressed. I waited for Steve to pick me up to go to the theater. He knocked and I opened the door.

"Hi, you look much better. Did you eat?"

"No. I wasn't hungry."

"You should have something in your stomach. You know about feeding a fever and starving a cold, don't you?"

"I have both."

"So don't eat between meals. Anything new?"

"No, why?"

We passed his room. There was no tray of food in the hall waiting to be picked up. Steve had done exactly what I thought he might do—hid the tray in his room, so I wouldn't have the satisfaction of knowing he had gotten the food delivered. We continued down the hall and into our car. Steve was driving.

"So, nothing's new, huh? What did you do, Steve, sleep or watch TV?"

"TV. Dodgers."

"Win?"

"Of course."

"No interruptions?"

"Like what?"

"Phone or anything?"

"No."

"Room service?"

"No."

"That's strange, Steve, I could've sworn I heard someone calling out 'room service' about two hours ago."

"Must've been someone else's room."

"Sounded like yours."

"I didn't hear anything. But I might've been in the shower."

"So, you didn't get any room service?"

"No."

I didn't say anything for a couple of minutes, then I pressed the "Play" button on my tape recorder which I had hidden in the hall and put it on high volume . . .

KNOCK! KNOCK!

"Who is it?"

"Room service."

"I didn't order anything. Wrong room."

"Mr. Reidman?"

"Yes, but I . . ."

"Open the door!"

Steve and I laughed about that all the way to the nightclub and then all the way across the country.

All of these stories about Steve are the truth, regardless of what you may read in the book he might write about me someday. Of course, if he writes anything about me I'm not crazy about, I have this other tape recording from a night in San Antonio when Steve, dressed as a large female duck and . . .


# PEANUT BUTTER

FROM THE TIME I was a small child up until this very moment, I've played a lot of pranks and practical jokes on a lot of people. As I mentioned, it is my way of having fun and expressing my feelings for someone. I never kid with someone I don't like. Anyway, of all the many practical jokes, I consider the following to be my best.

Buddy Hackett saw me on my first appearance on the "Tonight Show" on January 8, 1971, and that same night called the Sahara Hotel in Las Vegas to ask the entertainment director to put me into the main showroom as soon as possible. A few weeks later I was walking out on that stage. Frankie Avalon, a fellow Philadelphian, opened the show and Sonny and Cher closed it. I was a fifteen-minute serving in the middle.

During that engagement, we all became friends. After it, Sonny and Cher and I toured as a "package." Then, when Sonny and Cher's career took off, I took off with them as their opening act right up until the last time they performed together. It was a thrilling time!

Sonny and I had several things in common. Height wasn't one of them, but a love for practical jokes was and we pulled off some beauties on each other.

One time in Las Vegas, Sonny and Denis Pregnolato, his manager, stole all my clothes. I didn't say anything but retaliated by having all the furniture removed from their suite. Sonny's best one against me was based on a bit I used to do about telling how tough someone was just by hearing his name. No one is afraid of Sheldon Horowitz, but Tony Belafookio . . . One night the entire entranceway to the stage was blocked by what I thought must have been a newly constructed wall or a piano. It turned out to be a man, well, half man, half ape who said he was the *real* Tony Belafookio. The guy hung around me for days, costing me lunches which I paid for in order to appease the beast and a lot of nervous moments. Later on, while I was a houseguest at Sonny and Cher's house in L.A., the very same Tony Belafookio walked in. He was their bodyguard, Walter. Good one!

Well, the practical joke rivalry went on for years and was pretty evened up. One day, sitting around some hotel room somewhere, we started discussing who was better at pulling off practical jokes. Finally, I decided how to settle the debate once and for all.

"Tell you what, Sonny, there's one way to settle this. Rather than go after each other, would you agree that I am the King of Practical Jokes if I were to get someone, a normal person, a straight kind of person, to put peanut butter up his own ass?"

"Yes," Sonny laughed. "I'd call you the king, but how the hell could you do that?"

"I have no idea," I smiled, "but I'll figure it out."

"I have to be an eyewitness to it," Sonny stipulated.

I agreed.

Now I have to give you some background on my bad back in order to continue this story. I have a pinched sciatic nerve in my lower back. I got it helping a friend move himself in to a new apartment. I told him Jews don't move furniture, but he didn't believe me and as a result I was crippled with pain for six months on the road. I went to every kind of doctor you can name, the best, but nothing worked. It was so bad sometimes that I was

250

unable to walk onto the stage. They had to put me on the stage in the dark and then turn on the spotlights. Sonny told me about his bad back and how a doctor Steve Lawrence told him about had cured him. Sonny explained how Dr. Milton Reder of New York, one of America's foremost ear, nose and throat specialists, puts wires with cotton on the end of them into a solution and then inserts them painlessly up your nostrils, anesthetizing the ganglia nerve that transmits messages of pain to the brain and the pain goes away and eventually stays away. It sounded like a setup if I ever heard one, so I sent Steve Landesberg, who also suffers from a bad back, in to see the doctor first. Ain't I a nice guy? Steve lived, so I went. It worked! Today I am on Dr. Reder's long list of people he has helped and today he's not only at the top of my list of medical saviors, he's also near the top of my very very short and select list of favorite human beings.

Now we can continue. A month or so after Sonny and I had the conversation about the undisputed king of practical jokes, we were in the middle of one of our five-week-long one-nighter tours, bouncing every night from one town to another, very often in a different state as well. Tiring but fun! Sonny and Cher had leased a private jet for the tour. Including their band, secretaries, baby nurse, etc., there were about fourteen of us. One was Sonny and Cher's road manager, whom we will call Jerry, mainly because his real name is Jerry.

As we were airborne, heading for the next town, Jerry stood up in the aisle of the plane and stretched.

"Damn, my back is killing me! Must've pulled a muscle."

"If we were going to New York," Sonny said, "you could go see Dr. Reder. He'd have you fixed in no time. Right, David?"

"Right, and if we were going to be in South Carolina, Jerry, Major Rodriguez would fix you up."

"Who's that?"

"Oh, they had big write-ups about him in Newsweek and Time a few months ago. Didn't you read it?"

"No. What's he do?"

"Well, I knew him when I was in basic training with the 101st Airborne in Fort Jackson, South Carolina. Fixed a lot of guys' backs then. You can imagine how many men get hurt jumping out of planes. Anyway, like Dr. Reder, it's a very unorthodox method. That's what the hullabaloo was all about. Seems the AMA wouldn't accept his methods, the army asked him to stop using them, he refused, the army pressed for a court-martial and the major just retired. Quit on principle. Quite a guy! Well, doesn't matter, anyway, 'cause we're not going to be in South Carolina."

About ten minutes later, Jerry came up to me.

"We are going to be in South Carolina. Four days from now."

"You're mistaken, Jerry. We're going to North Carolina."

"No, here, look at the routing sheet. See, night after Baltimore, Maryland—Greenville, South Carolina."

'I'll be damned. Home of the Screaming Eagles. Well, look, I don't know if the major is still living there, or what, but I'll try to track him down for you. How's that?"

"Oh, that would be great, David. I really want to get rid of the pain."

"I understand."

When we landed and checked into our hotel, I called Greenville information and got the phone number of an acting school. I called the school, told them I was looking for someone who could play the role of a doctor for a practical joke. I'd pay well. They said they had just the person, middle-aged, handlebar moustache, very sophisticated, good actor—perfect. I told them where I'd be staying and to have the actor meet me there a few hours after I arrived in town that morning. I then called Jerry and told him the good news. He was excited. Then I sat down and started plotting a detailed plan.

When we arrived in Greenville, I went off on a shopping spree by myself. Then I returned to the hotel to meet the "doctor." The school was right. He was perfect. We spent several hours going over every detail and forming bits and pieces of a scenario to follow. We would ask each other about soldiers who were in my company; we'd make references to incidents that happened; whenever, or if, I started to laugh, he would tell me he would do to me what he used to do to me in the army—put me out of the room! We created and rehearsed a script which validated his profession and our knowing each other from my army days. I shook hands with the "doctor" and he left to return at a designated time. I then called Jerry and told him the time the doctor would be in his room. I then called Sonny and Denis and told them when to meet me in Jerry's room.

A few hours later, the four of us were all standing in Jerry's room when there was a knock on the door. Jerry let the doctor in, who was carrying the small black shaving kit filled with the items I had purchased and concocted.

"Major, it's so good to . . ."

"Colonel, Brenner. I retired a colonel. How have you been?"

"Fine, sir. I'd like to introduce you to Sonny Bono."

"Yes, of course, my wife and I are big fans of yours and Cher's."

"Thank you, sir."

"This is Denis Pregnolato, Sonny's manager and Jerry, his road manager and the one with the bad back."

"Well, let's get started, shall we? Got lots of patients just like when I was taking care of your old company, Brenner. Say, what ever happened to Anderson?"

"Bucky?"

"Right, Bucky Anderson. He really was a strange one."

"He made it through all two years, Maj . . . Colonel."

"Good. Well, Jerry, did you read about my methods in Time magazine or Newsweek?"

"No, sir, I didn't. I'm sorry, sir."

"Well, they said I was unorthodox and I am, but I'll cure you! All you got to do is believe in me and do exactly as I say. Understand?"

"Yes, sir."

"Okay, take off all your clothes and lie down on the floor on your stomach."

Jerry started taking off his clothes. I was holding back a burst of laughter. Sonny and Denis were looking at me. Finally, they caught on. They smiled. I smiled back and winked.

"So, Brenner, you really made something of yourself in civilian life. You never were much of a soldier. You and that Italian kid from Cleveland.

We both said the name together in perfect sync.

"Ralph Silvestro."

Jerry was now naked and lying on his stomach. The doctor ran his knuckles down Jerry's spine.

"Okay, Jerry, now get up and let me see you walk away from me toward the door."

Jerry did it.

"Okay. Jerry, did anyone ever tell you that you walked more on one side than on the other?"

One of my jokes. Sonny and Denis almost exploded. Jerry was so mesmerized and concerned, he only said, "No."

"Okay, Jerry, sit on the bed so your legs extend over the edge."

Jerry obeyed and the doctor opened his black shaving kit bag and began to go through our rehearsed procedure.

"Jerry, there are five sets of nerve endings in your body. One at the bottom of each foot, one in each armpit and the last at the base of your spine. My entire treatment is based on stimulating those nerve endings, thereby eliminating the pain in the small nerves of the back. Understand so far?"

"Yes, sir."

"Good. First I want you to take this."

He handed Jerry the miniature putting golf club I had bought.

"This is specially treated and is to be rubbed up and down your spine about twenty times each day, preferably when you first get out of bed, and before you go to the toilet. Let me see you do it."

Jerry did it. Sonny stuffed his fist in his mouth. Denis turned his back to us. I looked out of the window. The fuses on our explosive laughter had been lit, but we were holding back as best we could.

"Very good, Jerry."

"Thank you, sir."

"Okay, now take this medicine. This is to be put on the bottom of your feet before you get out of bed. Put it on."

It was a combination of Pepto Bismol and Johnson's Baby Oil. Sonny, Denis and I turned to watch Jerry put it on his feet.

"Then you have to have someone tickle your feet with this chicken feather for five minutes. Do you have someone who can do it?"

"My girl friend is traveling with me."

"Fine. For now, we'll let Denis do it. Denis."

Denis tickled Jerry's feet for five minutes and it was a godsend, because it gave all of us a chance to let out all the bottled-up laughter.

"That's enough, Denis. Thank you. How do you feel Jerry, better?"

"A little bit, sir, except my stomach hurts from laughing."

"Laughter's good medicine in itself, isn't that so, Brenner?"

I nodded.

"Now, could I trouble you, Sonny, to get me a glass of water? Thank you. Here, Jerry, these are sort of painkillers, but they won't make you drowsy and you can operate heavy machinery after taking them, even if you never operated it before, which is one of the amazing side effects [another one of my jokes]. You take two of these [TUMS with the name scratched off carefully by me] in the middle of breakfast. Take two now."

Tums are huge and Jerry could just about swallow them.

"Look here, Jerry. Know what this is?"

"Swimming nose guards."

"Very good, son. Okay, you have to wear these, but only indoors to keep out the impure air which affects nerves almost as badly as nerve gas. Someday the whole world's population will be wearing them. Put them on."

Jerry put them on. His voice became very nasal.

"Sir, I work indoors. I do rehearsals with orchestras and work with stagehands and ushers and all kinds of people. I can't walk around like this!"

"Forget it then!" the doctor said angrily, reaching up and pulling the nose guard off Jerry's nose and then letting it go so it snapped back into his face. I had to go into a coughing fit to keep from cracking up.

"I shouldn't have even bothered to come here!" he yelled as he started repacking his kit. Jerry put on the nose guard.

"I'm sorry, doctor. It just seemed a little strange. Please continue."

"Okay," the doctor smiled. "Here, son, look at this. This is the underarm nerve solidifier and tranquilizing agent. I call it BF-21. [I called it Man Tan Artificial Tanning Cream.] Every morning and right before you go to bed, you rub this into both armpits. Do it now."

Jerry complied.

"Now comes the main ingredient of my treatment. Le tour de force, as it were. See this. Smell it and tell me what it smells like."

Jerry opened the lid of the cocktail shaker and sniffed its contents.

"Smells like peanut butter."

"Perfect! Yes, it does have a very slight peanut oil base, but its true value is that it completely seals the nerve box, allowing its powerful medical aroma, which is my own secret formula, to penetrate every single muscle fiber and nerve ending in your spine, leading to complete and permanent recovery! Stand up, Jerry! Good! You did that well. Now, I want you to take four fingers of this secret formula and place it gently at the base of your spine, avoiding your rectum, if possible. Do it!"

Jerry did it and I looked straight into Sonny's eyes. Slight smiles crossed both our faces and Sonny nodded to me and I to him.

"I'd suggest, Jerry, that you wear a rolled-up T-shirt in your underwear shorts so you don't stain your outer fatigues, I mean, pants. Sorry. Old habits are hard to die. Remember to put this on your spine first thing in the morning and right before you go to sleep. And, that, my friend, is it! Let me know how it works, although I know you'll be perfect in two weeks, max. No charge. Good luck to all of your troops."

That night, as I stood behind the curtain in the concert hall, I heard a nasal voice behind me.

"Brenner, I've got peanut butter in my ass."

"For crying out loud, Jerry. I'm about to go out there in a few seconds and make thirty-five thousand people laugh. You think I've got time to listen to your problems?"

Four days later, as we were getting into our limo to go to the airport, Jerry turned to Cher, whom we made swear she wouldn't tell him it was a joke.

"Cher, do you think I'm being put on?"

"All I can tell you, Jerry, is that if someone told me to put peanut butter up my ass, I'd really check into it."

That night on the plane Jerry smelled normal, but it didn't matter by that time, because I had already been declared the King of Practical Jokes. I'm sure George Washington Carver never thought his discovery of the uses of the peanut would ever come to this.

*I believe that a better way of judging how much an audience likes and enjoys you is not to just listen to the laughter but to listen to how quiet they are when you speak in between the laughter. I have always listened to the silence. It is a beautiful sound to a performer.*

## STORIES I'VE LIKED

THERE ARE A FEW stories told to me by family, friends or persons unknown. Some of them date as far back as childhood. Not only are these stories and jokes that I have enjoyed hearing and think-

256

ing about, but they may have even influenced my thoughts and actions, too. I wish I knew the authors, for I'd like to give them credit, but, unfortunately I don't. Anyway, I pass them on to you—

*The Fish Bowl*—Two fish are swimming around in a fish bowl. One fish asks the other, "Is there a God?" The second fish answers, "Of course there's a God!" to which the first fish says, "What makes you so certain there's a God?" The second fish replies, "Someone changes the water."

*The Indian Chief*—An Indian chief is sleeping under a tree when a white man wearing a suit and carrying an attaché case wakens him.

"Chief, I'm sorry to wake you but I am from the American Oil Company and we'd like to lease your land to drill for oil."

"What will that mean for me?"

"Well, chief, if we find oil on your reservation land, we'll make a lot of money together."

"What will that mean for me?"

"Chief, you will be rich, very rich."

"What will that mean for me?"

"Chief, if you're very rich, you can do anything you want!"

"I was doing that before you woke me up."

*The Blindman and the Elephant*—Three blind men were wondering what an elephant looked like. One day they heard that the circus was in town so they went to find out once and for all exactly what an elephant looked like. The circus manager led them into a tent where the elephant was chained to the middle of the floor. The three blindmen walked up to the elephant. The first blindman reached out and grabbed the elephant's tail.

"Oh, an elephant is short and thin like a small snake."

The second blindman took the elephant's leg.

"No, an elephant is round and firm like a tree trunk."

The third blindman felt the elephant's side.

"You are both wrong. An elephant is wide and flat like a wall."

*Profit*—An old Jewish man owned the largest department store in town. He had not taken one day off in forty years. Finally, his son, a Harvard Business School graduate, talked his father into

257

taking a two-week vacation. After four days at home, the old man was going crazy, so he took the bus to his store. When he arrived at his store, he found all the doors locked and a note on each saying "CLOSED FOR INVENTORY." The old man banged on the door until a workman came. He told the man that he wanted to see his son in his office. When the son walked in, the father turned to him.

"In forty years, this store has never been closed one single day, not one minute. So, why is it closed now?"

"I'm taking inventory, pop."

"What's inventory?"

"Well, pop, inventory is when you look up how many of a certain product you bought, how much you paid for it, how many you sold, what you sold it for and how many are left in stock. That's how you can tell your profit."

"I see. Okay, son, please hand me that cigar box over there. Thank you."

The old man removed the cigars and put something inside the box, returning it to his son.

"Here. Open this box and tell me what you see."

"Three one-dollar bills, pop."

"Right. That's what I had when I got off the boat from Europe. Three dollars. Everything else is profit. Now, open the store!"

*Nothing*—A rabbi was delivering his holiday sermon to his congregation. He ended it with a plea for giving funds to the synagogue.

"We are born nothing. We die nothing. If, in between, we can do something for our fellow man, that is what we should do. Each of us is nothing!"

A man in the front row stood.

"Rabbi. My name is Finkelstein. I own the bank in town and I am nothing. I'll give $10,000!"

The man seated to him stood.

"Rabbi. My name is Goldstein. I own the haberdashery and the drugstore in town. I, too, am nothing. I'll also give $10,000!"

From up in the back of the last balcony an old man wearing a worn and shabby suit stood.

"Rabbi. My name is Bernstein. I own the vegetable pushcart in town. I am nothing. I'll give $25!"

Finkelstein turned to Goldstein and whispered, "Look who's trying to be a nothing!"

## MY MOST EMBARRASSING MOMENT ON TV

THERE WAS A TELEVISION game show a few years back called "The Magnificent Marble Machine." I really liked the show. I thought it was a lot of fun. It lasted only a couple of seasons. Figures.

The name came from what was truly a "magnificent" pinball machine. Its dimensions were about thirty feet long by twelve feet wide. I was really good at pinball. Why not? I had spent most of my free hours between eight and eighteen shaking ("goofing" as it was called by true aficionados of the sport) every pinball machine from Market Street to Chester Avenue, from Sixty-third to Fifty-second Streets. When I played them "legit," I won lots of free games. Of course, people, especially poor people, try to beat any system, and pinball machines were no exception.

One trick called for the assistance of two strong friends. As I stood playing the machine they would stand on either side of the machine and gently and slowly lift it. I would slide my feet forward and then they would lay the two front, metal legs of the machine back down on the toes of my shoes. This way the ball didn't roll down as quickly, so one could rack up higher scores and win more free games. When the maximum number of free games that could be won was reached, the machine was taken off the shoes. Yes, it hurt the toes, and, yes, it was difficult explaining to my mother how the tops of my shoes sometimes wore out before the bottoms, but it was well worth it!

Another trick was to drill a tiny hole in the side of the machine through which you could slip a thin piece of metal that would hit a "bumper" and rack up points. The hole would be filled in with a little chewing gum of a matching color.

Another method of beating the system was my very own creation. It was a new twist to an old scam. The day after the man invented the vending machine, some kid invented the "slug," a fake coin. They were usually made out of metal, sometimes certain plumbing washers would work. My brainstorm was LP records! With a stylus, I traced the shape of a nickle on the record, placing the nickle-sized circles as closely together as possible. Then I heated the LP over an open fire. When it became pliable, I would cut out the circle from the soft record with my father's linoleum cutter. Then it was a simple matter of filing down the circles to the exact size of a nickle and smoothing them with sandpaper. I could get up to about one hundred and twenty nickles per LP. That's six dollars worth. Now the LPs didn't cost me anything because they were my sister's. As often happens when one is enjoying a walk on the wild side, I got caught by a store owner and was arrested. It was my fault—getting caught, that is—because I had heard they were looking for the guys using the "record slugs" and when one of my homemade slugs became jammed in the money slot of a pinball machine, instead of just leaving the store, I was anxious to play the machine, so I kept trying to dislodge the slug with a tooth I had broken off my comb. Eventually the owner saw what I was doing and grabbed me. I told the police that some "older guy" sold me the slugs for two cents apiece, and, since I was a believable bullshitter even at the age of twelve, they let me go. My sister wasn't as lenient. When she discovered what I was doing with her LP collection, she ended my manufacturing career. You could say I was slugged out of the slug business.

The years off the playing field had not dulled my talent. I was so good at playing "The Magnificent Marble Machine" and telling the contestant who was my playing partner what to do that one time I won doubles and triples of every possible prize a contestant could win—two cars, three trips to Hawaii and Europe, two mobile homes, etc. This motivated the producers to change the rules.

So you see I was a super pinball machine player. Modesty aside for a moment—I was probably the best player of all my fellow celebrities, but I had one major problem. In order to play the machine for the prizes, you had to answer questions, which I was as capable of doing as anyone. That wasn't my problem. In order to answer the questions, you had to know how to spell. *That* was my problem! I could never spell and I still can't. In a test given in my senior year in college, I scored the lowest of 26,000 students. Truth. To this day I spell words phonetically, the way they sound. Like the word "laugh," I spell "laff." Why not? It looks like laugh and it sounds like laugh and, if you want more laughs, you just add "f's"—laff-f-f-f-f. I'm serious about the phonetic spelling and my inability to truly spell. Okay, I've asked the publishers of this book to allow the previous sentence to be printed again without the proofreader's corrections as I wrote it—"I'm searius about the fonetic speling and my inahbility to truley spel." Now, you believe me? Good.

Of course I knew I had this problem as a child. When I'd get my written essay examinations back with red circles whipped around words all over the place and "SP's" next to the circles and low grades with a handwritten note by the teacher that "spelling is important, David," I knew something was wrong. I did try to do something about it, but the teachers didn't help. Let's say I'd get a test paper back with a circle around the word "laff." I would raise my hand.

"Excuse me, Miss McConnell, I got two points taken off the exam because I misspelled the word 'laff.' Could you please tell me how to spell it so I can memorize it and never get it wrong again? Thank you very much."

Now, instead of just telling me how to spell it, the teachers would always say, angrily, too, "Don't be lazy, David Brenner! Look the word up in the dictionary!"

Teachers are really stupid! In order to look a word up in a dictionary you have to know how to spell it! I'd go to the front of the room, open the dictionary that was on the stand there and look up "l-a-f-f" and it wasn't there. Then I'd look through every "l"—let's see . . . lap . . . lag . . . "l-a-u-g-h" . . . what's a "luggah"? So I never learned to spell, which is what led to my most embarrassing moment on TV.

I'll explain a little bit about the "game" to you, so you can better visualize what happened. Bert Convey, the MC of "The Magnificent Marble Machine" would tell you how many words were in the answer you were looking for and how many letters were in each of those words. Then the clue to the answer would come out on a large bulletin board one letter at a time until it formed complete words. This was similar to the news bulletin that moves across Times Square or like the words that sometimes flash across the bottom of your TV screen announcing a breaking news bulletin. THE GUINNESS BOOK OF RECORDS CLAIMED TODAY THAT IT HAS FOUND AN HONEST POLITICIAN. THIS HASN'T BEEN CONFIRMED. WE'LL KEEP YOU POSTED. Get it?

Now, let's use an example of a clue and answer from the show. Let's say the MC tells you that the answer has three words in it and the first word has three letters, the second has five letters and the third has ten letters. So that's 3-5-10. Then the clue starts coming out across the board, one letter at a time . . . F-A-M-O-U-S . . . (something or someone famous) . . . S-W-O-R-D . . . (famous sword? Excalibur! No wrong number of letters) . . . S-M-A-N . . . ("Famous swordsman??? Famous—got it!").

Now when you think you have the answer you press down on a buzzer on the top of the desk you're sitting at, next to your contestant. Hopefully you did this before the opposing celebrity and his or her contestant push their buzzer. The MC then calls on you and you give your answer.

"The Three Musketeers!"

"Right!"

Bells go off, lights light up, audience applauds, the contestant thanks you, your fellow celebrity shakes his or her finger at you indicating you're going to get yours, etc. More clues, more answers, until one team gets a certain number of points, winning the game and a chance to play the Magnificent Marble Machine.

Okay, now here's what happened that fateful day. My contestant and I were in a tie-breaker with the other team. The next answer would determine the winner. The MC read from the index card very slowly so we'd all understand.

"Okay, contestants and celebrities, the answer we are looking for, the one that will determine who will get the chance to play our Magnificent Marble Machine and win up to fifty thousand dollars worth of prizes has only one word, three letters."

"One word, three letters," I thought. "Even I know twenty-six letters, so I got a chance."

"Now," the MC continued, "here comes the clue."

On the screen, the letters began to appear. I had my hand on the buzzer, ready to press down. "A-T-H-L-E-T-I-C . . ." "Come on! I know my sports figures pretty good," I thought to myself. ". . . S-U-P-P-O-R-T-E-R." "Athletic supporter? Athletic . . ." I hit the buzzer hard, jumping to my feet.

"Yes, David Brenner, what is the answer?"

"Jok!" I yelled.

The MC stared. The audience went ape—laughing, screaming, squealing, applauding! I stood there with a stupid smile on my face as the camera zoomed in for a close-up for all of America to see. It was so out of hand they had to take a commercial break to calm down the audience. I had to sit there through the break. The answer was "fan," F-A-N, "fan." Athletic supporter—fan?

Shit! After the two-minute commercial break, the audience was still laughing. The MC had to do something to stop them so the show could continue. He didn't mean to be malicious, but I could not believe what he asked me in front of millions of people.

"David Brenner, how did you ever get the word jock with only three letters?"

The audience went crazy all over again and they moved in for an even closer shot. But I answered him, street-corner style.

"I don't know, Bert. All I know is I never went to gym class wearing a fan."

The laughter and applause was so great we had to take another commercial break. We did continue the game. My team won, but you could hear giggling throughout the rest of the show. Some of it was mine.

Well, I took and still take a lot of ribbing from both the public and the celebrities who heard about what I had done. However, I think this will stop for all time when I tell you about a star who topped my "jok" answer.

I'm going to use her name, because we all love her and she is a good sport and an intelligent lady. Then again, maybe she'll kill me for this? No, she won't. Okay, here goes . . .

The celebrity was singer/actress Leslie Uggams. The answer she was looking for was one word, seven letters, 1-7. The clue was "Airplane part most appealing to a stripteaser?" The answer was TAKEOFF. Leslie's answer was—are you ready?—COCKPIT!

Case closed!


# THE BRAVEST MAN WHO EVER LIVED

I HAD DONE MY stand-up monologue and panel conversation on the "Tonight Show." It went very well. Johnny Carson brought out his next guest, an author who had written a book entitled something like *Leadership in America.* This was just after we had been bombarded day and night for an entire year with the Watergate scandal. I, like most Americans I think, had had enough of politics and leadership. I didn't feel like listening. Now there is very little you can do on the "Tonight Show" when you don't feel like listening to a guest. You can try to count the number of people in the audience who are wearing eyeglasses by the number of shiny glass disks you can see, or you can daydream. I decided on the latter. First, I've got to tell you something about Johnny Carson. He loves to catch people who are not watching the "Tonight Show," especially when they are *on* the "Tonight Show"! Johnny knew I was daydreaming because I was smiling.

"Who do you think would make a good leader for the country, David?" Johnny asked, suddenly and unexpectedly.

Do you remember how in school when you were daydreaming and you didn't really hear the question the teacher asked, but you did hear your name at the end of it? And you put your memory bank tape into reverse, spun it back to the question, hopefully before it was erased?

I figured that the best thing to do was to say something that maybe was a little strange, but sounded intelligent, to which the audience would just say, "Hmmmm," and figure it out later. That, by the way, is what I say to people when I don't know what to say—"Hmmmmmm." Let's say someone comes up to me, points to his new shoes and says, "See these shoes, Brenner, seventy-five dollars," and I don't know if that's a bargain or he got ripped off. I say, "Hmmmmm."

Anyway, I say to Johnny, "I don't think anyone in the political arena today is capable of leading this great nation of ours, so what we've got to do is reincarnate the bravest man who ever lived and let him lead our country." The audience said "Hmmmmm," and looked at me like RCA Victor dogs—His Master's Voice.

I thought I was off the hook, but you know Johnny Carson. He's so smart. He looks at me and says, "Well, David, who is the bravest man who ever lived?"

I saw my whole career passing before my eyes. Then I said something which I thought was pretty smart. I got a lot of mail about it—letters saying things like "you're crazy," and "what a weirdo." Well, I don't think it was weird at all. What I said, and remember this was on the spur of the moment, was the following:

"Johnny, I think the bravest man who ever lived in the history of mankind was the first man who drank milk. Now, wait a minute. Think about it. Make believe you're a caveman, or cavewoman, and you're sitting in a cave when one caveman stands up and says, "See that animal running over there? The ugly one with the balloon? Well, I'm going to run after that animal, squeeze that balloon and whatever comes out—I'm going to drink it!"

Now, if you happened to see the show that night, here's the part you didn't see. That the censors bleeped. Once I heard the audience and Johnny Carson laughing, I got on a roll and I said, "Wait a minute, Johnny, I'm wrong. The bravest man who ever lived was the first man who ate an egg. 'I'm going to take whatever falls out of that chicken's ass, put it in that pan over there, fry and eat it!' "

Of course, on TV it came out ". . . falls out of that chicken's BLEEP . . ." A few wrote me and asked, "What is a chicken's BLEEP?" I wrote back, "Write NBC and ask them. Then again, you'll probably just get back some form letter from one of their executive BLEEPholes."

## PERSONAL PERSPECTIVES

THE YEAR WAS 1974. Sonny and Cher, the mainstay of my income, had split. All jobs were cancelled. No future income on the books. I had broken off with a girl friend of four years. I was doing a lot of TV but the move to the next rung hadn't happened. While on the road a decorator had ripped me off for about $14,000 and I was suing. I owed the bank $10,000. I was really feeling sorry for myself. I left my apartment on Sixty-ninth Street between Second and Third Avenues, walked up Third and turned onto Seventieth Street. The man coming towards me was in his early fifties, very well dressed, a pleasant face. He grabbed his chest, let out a little cry of pain and collapsed to the pavement. I helped a passing doctor attend to him but it was too late. He died. I stood up and walked away. It was a lovely spring day and I had no major problems.

## BECAUSE YOU KEEP ASKING

HARDLY A DAY PASSES without a reporter or a fan asking me questions about the TV series I taped for NBC in 1976 called "Snip." So, I am going to answer the most frequently asked questions.

For those of you who don't remember "Snip," and actually I'm amazed that anyone does, it was to be a weekly situation comedy series in which I was to star, playing the role of a recently divorced hairdresser still in love with his ex-wife, played by Leslie Ann Warren, who left me because of my extramarital activities and then moved to New England and opened her own beauty shop. I go to visit her there and stay, working in the shop and sleeping on the downstairs sofa. We taped seven programs but not one was ever aired.

## Answers

1. Yes, it was funny. I thought so and, more importantly, the audience thought so, too, because we never once had to add a laugh track to "sweeten" the laughter from the studio audience.

2. Yes, it was the only show in the history of TV to be cancelled the week before it was to premier.

3. The only reason given me why NBC was cancelling the show was because "they" felt the show was "too offbeat." No further comment was ever made.

4. Yes, it is true that five of the shows were aired on Australian TV, on a Monday through Friday basis, and were the biggest hit in Australian television history, even though no one knew me or my costar, Leslie Ann Warren. They asked for more but there were no more to give them.

5. Yes, Leslie Ann Warren's career took off in spite of "Snip's" cancellation.

6. Yes, my career took off in spite of "Snip's" cancellation.

7. Yes, in a way, I was glad the show didn't go to series because I didn't like having to deal with TV executives and committee decisions, didn't like the regimented hours or living in Beverly Hills, and I missed performing my own act LIVE on stage —a lot!

8. Yes, I have one regret and that is that the network executives didn't allow the public to decide whether they liked or disliked "Snip."

9. Yes, I *would* do my own TV show, but it would have to be one of quality and would have to be done in New York City. Still, I'm very happy doing what I'm doing now—performing on-stage and making people laugh.

*I have a motto in life. You can believe something only "ten days after the check clears the bank." If this seems to be a rather cynical outlook, you tell me what your motto would be if the following happened to you: You did a performance to raise money for* crippled children *at a show sponsored by the* city's detectives *in memory of a* police officer killed *in the line of duty, and their check bounced! It happened to me—but only once!*


## THE PRIZE

IN 1977, I WAS nominated for Male Comedy Star of Las Vegas. I knew I wasn't going to beat out the likes of Bill Cosby, Don Rickles and Shecky Green, but I was happy to be considered and knew I'd enjoy participating in the television special taped in Las Vegas. In addition to being a nominee, I was also presenting the award for Best Variety Act. Giving out the Comedy Award was Chuck Mangione, not only a fantastic jazz artist but a fantastic laugher. When Chuck goes, everyone goes! His laugh isn't contagious—it's an epidemic! I've always been able to crack him up.

During the entire six hours we were around for rehearsals and taping, I kept coming up to Chuck and by either approaching him quietly to his face or sneaking up from behind him, I would threaten him in some of the following ways:

"I don't care whose name is in that envelope, Chuck. If you don't announce me as the winner, I'm going to pull your lips open so wide, you'll be able to play the wrong end of your trumpet!"

"Listen, you little Ginzo, if you don't want to be going home in cement shoes and a lake, you know who to announce!"

"How'd you like to be the first to play a trumpet with his ass?"

"Don't make your last album, your *last* album!"

"Okay, Spaghetti Breath, it's me or you. Play it smart or play it dead."

"How'd you like to be part of the New Jersey Turnpike?"

"You wanna see your family and friends again—or what?"

"No one can play trumpet without fingers!"

"How would you like to fit inside your hat—all of you?"

With every line, for the entire day, Chuck would scream his great laugh. I'd say something in his ear, he'd crack up, I'd fade into the shadows.

Finally, it was time for the presentation of the Comedy Award. I had already been on camera as a presenter. I decided to take off my makeup and tux, change back into my jeans and watch Chuck from the backstage monitor. I was certain I wouldn't win and I wanted to be comfortable. After removing the makeup, I decided it was more of a hassle to climb the two flights of stairs to my dressing room and change clothes than to stay in my tux for a few more minutes. I walked backstage and stood with Don Rickles and Shecky Green, watching Chuck Mangione on stage.

"Ladies and gentlemen, the winner of the Las Vegas Male Comedy Star of 1977 is . . . (opens envelope, pulls out card, looks at it) . . . Thank God . . . (cracks up) . . . David Brenner!"

I was shocked! Shecky shook my hand and Don told me I was "too young to win anything." I ran out onstage. Chuck handed me my trophy and I shook his hand, saying the following very quietly so the microphone couldn't pick it up:

"You just saved your fuckin' Ginzo ass!"

Chuck screamed with laughter and I made my *truly* unexpected acceptance speech.


## THE MAN FROM FREDONIA

I HAD MET A young radio disc jockey and reporter, Nick, at a press conference after a concert at Fredonia State College in upstate New York. Turns out that the guy is very funny and writes very good, hip material. I write 99.99 percent of my own material, but, at the time, I was working on a TV pilot in New York and couldn't devote the time I wanted to it, so I decided that Nick's sense of humor would be perfect for "punching up" my original script— that is, rewriting the existing jokes and creating new ones. I asked my manager to hire him for the job and fly him into New York. What Steve didn't tell me was that Nick had never been to the city before. In fact, the only "big city" experience he had ever had was a quick afternoon in and out of Buffalo at the age of nine. If you read his writings, though, you'd swear he was born and raised on the F train in New York City.

I picked Nick up at the hotel to go to our first meeting at CBS. When we got there, I got into the revolving door. Nick got in the partition with me and we took Chinese-size steps together to move the door. You can imagine how ridiculous we looked to everyone in the lobby as we came out. I'm six feet two inches tall and Nick is about six five and broad. I laughed. It was a very funny bit and quite nervy. After all, to Nick I'm a star and this was his first job in show business. You got to give him a lot of credit for having the nerve to do that and I did.

After the meeting at CBS, we had a second meeting at the William Morris Agency a couple blocks away. Back down in the CBS lobby, I got into the revolving door and once again Nick got in it with me. I laughed again but made a mental note to tell him later that you never repeat a joke, no matter how good. We walked to the agency.

This time I signaled Nick to go into the revolving door first. He did and I pushed it and got into the next partition. When I came out, Nick was nodding his head.

"I guess these are for one guy at a time, huh? I wondered when I was checking into the hotel why that old man looked at me so funny when I got in the revolving door with him."

I swear to you, this is the truth! Nick was not putting me on. You can imagine how that old man must have felt when this giant, with a suitcase, too, got into the revolving door with him and to move they had to take baby steps together. There are only a few incidents in life that, when they are recalled, elicit as much laughter as the first time you saw or heard about them. The Man from Fredonia has given me one.

*As I was lying on the floor in my Las Vegas hotel room one morning doing exhausting exercises to combat the middle-age abdominal "love handles," I thought about how, when you're seventeen, every muscle in your body is as tight as a rubber band, your stomach is flat and hard, all your moves and reactions are split-second fast, your eyes see perfect like a hawk's, your hearing is flawless and you're also an idiot! We never have it all, do we?*

# MEETING THE STARS

I MUST ADMIT THAT there have been a few stars I was actually thrilled to meet. I don't think anyone is completely immune to being starstruck.

Jack Benny to me and to my father was the greatest! My father played me tapes of old Jack Benny radio shows from the time I was in diapers. I grew up laughing to him. Second only, by the way, to laughing at my father. One day, I was standing near the Lake Tahoe showroom I was opening in that night, when I saw a group of men walk out. In the middle of them was Jack Benny. He had been working there the previous week. I tossed around the idea of going up to him and telling him how much I had admired him all my life and how my father idolized him, but then I thought it might seem silly, even if I were lucky enough that someone with him would recognize me and tell him I was a new comedian just starting out on TV. As I was thinking this I saw Jack Benny excuse himself from the others and start walking in my direction, smiling. He was going to say hello to someone he saw behind me. I thought maybe I could say a couple words as he passed. Then it hit me—he couldn't be coming this way to see anyone behind me. I was standing in front of a wall! He was coming to talk to me? Jack Benny? Impossible!

"David, I just wanted to come over here and tell you how much I have enjoyed all your appearances on television, from the very first one. You are the best young comedian to come along in a long time and I'm going to always be a big fan of yours!"

I won't forget that moment until I've forgotten the Alamo and my name! What a thrill!

I was running a little late getting to the Las Vegas Hotel for the taping of a Mike Douglas Show. I made it in plenty of time, but as I came into the temporary "green room," a voice behind me boomed out, "It's about time you got here, David. Everybody's been looking everywhere for you!" I turned to see who it was—John Wayne! Talk about bigger than life. I shook his hand.

"When I was a little kid, I decided when I grew up I was going to be a cowboy. All because of you. Of course it was an impossible thing to do, in this day and age . . . but . . . well, I just want to thank you for that wonderful dream."

When I came offstage, someone told me John Wayne really cracked up over my routines. I was very happy to hear that.

The "Tonight Show" was running late. I really didn't want to get "bumped" off the show because the next morning I was leaving on a long road tour and wanted to plug the dates. The talent coordinator came to my dressing room to tell me that George Raft had consented to come back the next night to do the show. George Raft was one of my boyhood idols, along with Bogie, Garfield and Robinson. I had never met him but felt I should thank him for being so magnanimous in allowing me to go on the show instead of himself. However, the "thank you" came out this way:

"Hi. I'm David Brenner and I can't wait to call my childhood friends and tell them I 'bumped off' George Raft."

He laughed heartily. He was a real nice man.

I was sitting in an outdoor café with Sonny Bono. We had already spent some minutes talking to the people at the next table, Buddy Hackett and Jack Lemmon, when I saw someone coming down the street toward us who made my heart jump. I had seen him kill and get killed in the darkness of my neighborhood theaters so many times as a kid. He was one of my favorite actors and one of my heroes—Richard Conte. I told Sonny about it and asked for suggestions of what to say, deciding finally to just say or nod a hello and let the man alone. Richard Conte stopped at our table, said hello to Sonny, then put his hand out to me.

"I just want to shake the hand of the man who makes me laugh more than anyone else."

Thank goodness Buddy Hackett didn't hear. Then again, if he did and tried to do anything about it, I know Richard Conte would've pulled a big gat out of his inside pocket and blasted him full of holes and then he and I would've jumped on the running board of the fast-moving, black Packard that would've spun around the corner on two wheels to pick us up and both of us, with our guns blazing, would've . . .

"Red Skelton is at the bar?"

"What?"

"Red Skelton is sitting at the bar. He came to see you."

"Red Skelton is here at Palumbo's in South Philly? You got to be kidding. Someone's ripping you off for free drinks."

"It's him! For sure! Says he's a big fan of yours. Honest."

"What's he doing at the bar? Get him a table for Christ sake!"

"We're completely sold out. We've even put the boss's office desk chair in the room!"

"Tell Red about it!"

Another very funny and very nice man I was thrilled to meet.

I came off the stage of the nightclub in New York where I was filling in for the comedian who owned the club but wasn't feeling well enough that night to go on. I was a novice and welcomed the chance to work the room. As I came offstage after a pretty good set I heard thunderous applause, screams and whistles. I turned in time to see the entire audience up on their feet. I couldn't see the stage from where I was standing, but I couldn't help recognize the voice as he said, "That young kid, David Brenner, was so damn good, I figured I'd better come up here so you don't forget an old-timer like me."

That's the night I first met Bob Hope. By the way, he killed them that night, as I was still only dreaming of doing someday.

My agent called to offer me a regional commercial to be shot in an old theater in Los Angeles. It would only take one full day of my time. The other principal in the commercial was George Burns, and . . .

"I'll take it!"

"Wait. I didn't tell you the money."

"You said enough. George Burns. I'll do it for nothing just to meet him. I love him!"

I do. Oh, yes, I did get paid, of course. And, by the way, it didn't take one full day to shoot the commercial. We were in and out in two hours. George is not only a true professional, he's pretty wonderful too.

Of course, I was thrilled to meet many other stars and personalities, like Milton Berle, John Lennon, Jackie Gleason, Dustin Hoffman, Al Pacino, Robert De Niro, Vincent Price, Joe Louis, Jack Dempsey, Hoyt Axton, George C. Scott . . . there are plenty of others, too, whom I'd better mention before I alienate someone, including the stars I would like to have met but haven't so far, like Barbra Streisand, Frank Sinatra, Anthony Quinn, Charles

Bronson, oh . . . okay, yes, I did meet Charlton Heston and . . . I don't believe I almost left out Steve Martin and Robin Williams . . . wait, I'd better mention as many as I can think of so I don't get anyone pissed off who could do something for my career someday, because you never know and, well, I like Frankie Avalon, Bobby Rydell, Dionne Warwick, Ann-Margret, Angie Dickinson, Diana Ross . . . God, Mike Douglas has a show on cable TV so mention him and Phil Donahue whose show I first did when it was only a local program in Chicago and there's also Broadway, so let's not forget Elizabeth Ashley and Raquel Welch and, damn, I almost left out one of the hottest box office draws, Dudley Moore and his ex-girl friend, Susan Anton, and the biggest of all, black or white—my ol' pal, Richard Pryor, and my truly old pal from Philly, Bill Cosby, and in case I need music, my friend Marvin Hamlisch and Barry Manilow and Neil Sedaka and Eddie Rabbitt and Charo . . . and let's not forget any of those fine directors and producers who may have power when this book is published to make it into a movie, such as Spiegelman and Spelling and Coppola, and my dear friend Sly Stallone who might use me in Rocky IX, and there are the up-and-comers who might be up and coming when I'm down and going like Joe Piscopo and Eddie Murphy from "Saturday Night Live," and who knows maybe even David Letterman might make it and there's always the comeback trail of such greats as Fred Silverman and . . . oh, yeah, John Travolta . . . why the hell did I even start this Meeting the Stars story? Somebody's bound to be left out and will get angry and hold it against me. Merv Griffin! I almost forgot Merv! Wait a minute! Let's settle down for a second. I'll just do what I've always done in handling people who could do something for me and my career—"If by any chance I have offended you, being me, I can only say that you can just take a flying dump on the moon! That's right, if you don't like me for me—T.S.! And I don't mean Eliot!"

Wow, now I feel so much better . . . did I mention that I know Brooke Shields personally and . . .

# AND THEN CAME JOAN

IT WAS 1978. NINE years on the road. A long time. I loved my work but was starting to feel the sharp edge of excitement and fun beginning to dull. It's only natural, that no matter how much you enjoy what you do, the years will begin to slowly erode the glitter. I wasn't even close to the point of giving up my career, but I knew that I needed some kind of "shot in the arm." My agent, Arthur Moskowitz at William Morris, suggested that Joan Rivers and I would be an interesting duo on stage. It was a unique idea—two comedians on the same stage. Traditionally, a comedian was in a show with a singer, a dancer, a juggler, a puppeteer, a flame eater—anything but another comedian. The idea was so different and so good that only two other people thought it would work —me and Joan Rivers. Not even her manager liked the idea. We talked to everyone—and I mean *everyone*—but no one would even consider it. We never stopped trying. In the meantime, we each had our own successful careers.

I wanted to work with Joan because I had been a fan of hers since before I was a comedian. When I was a TV producer in Chicago, I saw her perform at Mister Kelly's. I had never seen anyone better than she was onstage and I had seen a lot of comedians. I watched her on TV whenever she did the "Ed Sullivan Show" or the "Tonight Show." When I first appeared as a comedian on TV, Joan was quoted in the L.A. *Times* as saying that she felt there were two new comedians who would make it. She named me as one, though we had never even met. When we did meet it was when I appeared on the same "Tonight Show" as she. It was early in my career. After my stand-up, I came and sat down on the panel to talk with Johnny Carson. Joan, who had gone on before me, was highly complimentary. In subsequent years, we became friends.

Finally, in February 1981, almost two years after the birth of the idea, the Diplomat Hotel in Hollywood, Florida, booked Joan and me together. They got us for what is called *bubkas* in Show Business (Yiddish word meaning "nothing"). Not only did the chemistry between Joan and me work, but business was booming and I understand the reviews were sensational (I gave up reading reviews early in my career because I have my own opinion about myself). We were a hit! Since then, we have worked all the "circuits" and have broken attendance record after attendance record all over the country!

Of course there are side benefits to this success story for me. I have the fun of working with not only one of America's true humorists but one of America's real screwballs. This woman is functioning on one wheel, her oars are out of the water, her bulbs have blown out, her spark plugs are not sparking, her pistons are not pisting, her ball bearings are not balling. If life is a sundae, Joan is the sprinkling of nuts; if life is a bowling alley, Joan is the eleventh pin; if life is a merry-go-round, Joan is the fifth leg on the swan; if life is a department store, Joan is the "Going into Orbit Sale," if life is a complaint department, Joan is the handleless and spoutless kettle, and, if life is to have fun and enjoy, Joan is the one to give it to you—to me—to all of us. I've adored working with her—it's been a ball!

# TOP BILLING

ON SEPTEMBER 6, 1982, I checked into the Ambassador Club at JFK to await my flight to Los Angeles. As I was pouring myself a cup of Sanka I heard a voice from nearby.

"They shouldn't allow Philadelphians in here."

Another person trying to be amusing. Usually I can cope with public humor, but not early in the morning, so I ignored it, hoping it would just go away like a house fly sitting by an open window. It didn't.

"No, they certainly shouldn't allow people from Philadelphia to come in here!"

"Okay, I heard you," I said, without looking at the source.

Then I turned to return to my seat and there was the early ayem jokester—Danny Kaye! I have been a fan of his since I was a kid! We had never met. I walked over to shake hands.

"I thought it was just a lunatic calling out. I had no idea it was a professional one. It's a real pleasure meeting you, Danny. If I make the public laugh just one tenth as much as you've made me laugh, I'll be happy."

We talked a few moments and I returned to my seat in the other section of the club. No sooner had I sat down and opened the

New York *Times* to pass the time, than I heard another voice. This time the accent was British and familiar.

"How are you, David? So good to see you again."

Anthony Newley and I had worked together both on stage and on TV. When I was his opening act for the first time at the now defunct Latin Casino in Cherry Hill, New Jersey, in 1972, he sent a bottle of champagne to my dressing room with a note, "Wishing you a wonderful engagement. Looking forward to meeting you. Tony." Only a class act would treat an opening act so nicely.

"Good to see you, too, Tony. You know who's in the other room? Danny Kaye. You know what this means, don't you? If this plane goes down, we don't get top billing."

Tony laughed. Just then Red Buttons walked in and joined us. The billing was getting more confusing. The three of us were discussing the size of print that should be used for each of us in the report of the air crash, when Mariel Hemingway and Ingmar Bergman's cameraman, Sven Nykvist, popped into the room, followed closely behind by Bob Fosse. Things were now getting way out of hand. None of us could decide who was going to get top billing or the order of the billing or the size of the letters. Anthony Newley suggested alphabetical order, which sounded reasonable until he added it should be determined by first names and "proper" first names, at that. Red Buttons was happy to use last names but rejected "birth-given last names." His original name was "Schwad" or something like that. It was time to board the flight, so we all left (in random order but together).

As we all started taking our seats aboard the 747 in saunters a latecomer—Dick Van Patten! I flopped down in my seat depressed, because I was certain now that the newspapers would read ". . . also appearing at the crash was comedian David Brenner, a former opening act for Anthony Newley."

Luckily, we landed in L.A. safe and sound, luggage and egos intact.


## FREDDIE PRINZE

JACK ALBERTSON WAS GOING to read my telegram during his eulogy of Freddie Prinze, but he broke down before he could. I wasn't at the funeral because "they" said that unless I flew into L.A. a day before the funeral for a "rehearsal," I couldn't be a pall-bearer. I knew that meant it was going to be a "Hollywood" scene, so I didn't fly in for the rehearsal and waited to visit the grave after the tinsel had been swept away. Anyway, for the record, this is the telegram Jack was to read: "I regret that I cannot be among the many who are honoring Freddie today, but I am glad to have been among the very few who honored him in life. David Brenner." Freddie was a very special person. I'll always miss him.


## NO WOMAN BELIEVES IT

EVER SINCE I WAS a little kid I wanted to go on a trip with my older brother. He had been my hero as a child but was so much older that he moved out of the house before we got to do many of the things brothers do together. When I became a young man, we would talk about what he referred to as "The Brothers' Trip," but we never took it. Once in the late sixties I offered him a free trip with me to California, but he was married with kids—need I say more?

In 1978, I called my brother from somewhere on the road, and in the middle of our usual conversation I popped the question again. He was now divorced and his kids were grown up.

"Can you juggle your schedule around to free yourself for, say, the next two weeks?"

"I think so, why?"

"How about going to London with me?"

"Well, I'll have to make a few calls to take care of some things but I'll call you back in the next couple days and let you know."

"Okay, talk to you soon."

Ten minutes later the phone rang.

"Hello."

"Yes, Mr. Brenner, your brother is calling."

"Fine, operator, put him through."

"Hello, Dave?"

"Yeah."

"Of course we'll go! After I hung up and told Sherry [his girl friend] about your offer she asked me how I could take it so calmly and put the decision off for a few days. I was in shock!

God, The Brothers' Trip at last!"

And what a trip it was! Long awaited, yes, but when it came, we did it right. Moby Dick came into New York the morning before we were to leave so we had a Manhattan day and night to kick off the trip right. The next day we were drinking champagne and eating caviar aboard the Concorde (both of us would have preferred tuna and milkshakes, but what the hell). I had hired a Rolls-Royce limo for our two-week tour of London and the English countryside, and we had a wonderful two-bedroom suite at the quaint Berkley Hotel, complete with croissants and coffee in the morning. The trip was everything both of us had dreamed it would be. We walked, talked, laughed, ate, drank, ran, toured, rode, saw, touched, tasted, shared. It was perfect!

We gambled, too. One night, dressed in the one good suit each of us brought—doing it all in jeans and old shirts most of the time (and, never to be left behind nor forgotten, my high-top canvas sneakers)—we Rolls-Royced it to one of the private casinos where we had dinner. I'm not really a big gambler even in Las Vegas and Atlantic City, but we wanted to have the experience of playing in London, so I sat down at a twenty-one table among the high-rolling Arabs. Matter of fact, Moby Dick and I were the only non-Arabs in the whole casino (except for the employees). Anyway, within fifteen minutes I had made a small killing at the table. I got up and cashed in my chips. I suggested to my brother that we do something specific with the money, so we'd always remember the night we won in a London gambling club. The idea came to me as we entered our hotel. I asked the concierge to book us two round-trip tickets to Dublin, Ireland, on the first flight out in the morning and the last flight back at night.

It was such a very special twelve hours! That's all the time we spent in Dublin and the countryside surrounding it, but in that short time my brother and I came to similar conclusions—we absolutely loved and adored the Irish people and their gorgeous country. All I can say is, "Go there!"

On our last night back in London, Moby Dick and I took a long walk, as we Brenner males love to do. We ended up going through Hyde Park until it closed and then we hit the streets again. A small crowd was gathered in front of a restaurant, and we could see large movie lights and cameras and a lot of people scurrying about. We both love British films so we walked over. Standing in the spotlights were two beautiful English models in long, flowing evening gowns. They were on either side of an extremely handsome man wearing a tuxedo. He looked familiar. Oh, my God, Omar Sharif! I had just whispered to my brother who he was, knowing he was as big a fan of his as I, when Omar spotted me. We had appeared together on several television talk shows. A wonderful gentleman.

"David! David!" he yelled, smiling and running toward me. We hugged and I introduced him to my brother. He explained that he was doing a commercial and then asked us to join him for dinner. We explained that we had already eaten. He then asked us to join him for a night at the casinos or for a few drinks. We wanted to spend time with him, but we hadn't slept much the night before and still had to pack and get up early to catch the Concorde back to the States. We explained that we couldn't, said our farewells and left. On the way back to our hotel a few blocks away, Moby Dick started laughing out loud as he often does.

"Okay, Moby, what is it this time?"

"I've just had such a funny image pop into my mind. I see myself telling Sherry and some female friends of ours about how Omar Sharif, the heartthrob of millions of women throughout the world, kept asking us to have dinner, or drinks, or go to the casino with him and how we kept turning him down. No woman is ever going to believe it!"

And my brother was right—no woman ever believed the story. But ladies, I swear, it's the truth. If you still don't believe me, when you see Omar Sharif, ask him. Who am I kidding—what woman upon meeting Omar Sharif would think only of asking him whether he actually met my brother and me in London? If any woman told me that she did that, I'd never believe her. Never! Neither would my brother. Neither would Omar.


## THE FAN

WALKING TOWARD MY FRIENDS and me was one of New York's screaming loonies. At the top of their lungs they yell their complaints about one thing or another, ranging from the unfair policies of the present mayoral administration to the infiltration of Martians in their apartment building, both of which could be valid complaints in that city of cities.

This time the loonie was a woman in her late fifties and she was screaming about some "goddamn" injustice of some kind. She was so loud, she was partially unintelligible. I have found that if you yell something back to them, it usually snaps them into a quieter unreality and they'll mumble away. As the woman was alongside us, I yelled, "You tell 'em, lady!"

The woman stopped yelling, looked at me for a moment or two and then screamed, "Fuck you, Brenner! I listen to enough of your shit on television!"

She then turned and yelled her way through the crowd that was laughing along with us. I just never stopped to think that even the insane, partially or fully, watch TV and could be fans. Since then, I've shown more respect for New York's screaming loonies.

## YOUR FAVORITE JOKE

THIS SEEMS TO BE the joke most people ask me to tell. This is the dumbest thing anyone ever said to me. Actually, it happened to me twice within a week and a half. It is a true story. It took place in New York, although it could've been anywhere in the world. I was sitting on a subway and I was sitting on a newspaper. A man walked up to me and said, "Are you reading that paper?" Now, what are you going to say, that you're nearsighted? I didn't say anything. I just stared at him. The next time it happened, I was ready. I said, "Yes!" stood up, turned the page and sat down again!

## AUTOGRAPHS

WHY WOULD ANYONE WANT someone else's name on a piece of paper? I've never been able to figure out that one. But, if it makes someone happy to have it, what's the big deal? So what if you're in a hurry, or in the middle of an important conversation, or in pain, or not in the mood, or whatever. It really is a very small price to pay for all the wonders and joys show business brings into one's life. So, sign your name and be pleasant. You're making someone happy.

I've only refused to sign one autograph and that was when I had my arms full of carry-on baggage and had one minute to catch the last plane to San Francisco. Even then I had the couple I had turned down call me when they returned to San Francisco and subsequently treated them to my show. Another time, a young lady who had had a couple too many told me, amid several four-letter words, to hurry up signing my autograph because she wanted to leave the disco, so I just folded the paper napkin she had handed me to sign and put it into her drink.

There have been many unusual events surrounding the signing of autographs. Oftentimes, people will say "write anything," so I do just that—I wrote "anything" and sign my name. One woman told me she couldn't go home from Las Vegas without my autograph or her daughter would kill her. Then she added that her daughter actually didn't care whose autograph she got, so I signed "Wayne Newton."

One time, a little joke backfired. I was playing blackjack with Frank Daddabbo, a Las Vegas pit boss who's a friend of mine. We were just passing the time and hoping to win a few million dollars. A young couple came up to me, saying they were big fans and would I please write my John Hancock on their piece of paper. I wrote "John Hancock." As they left I told Frank to watch their reaction when they saw what I wrote. I figured they would laugh and I'd call them back and give them a real autograph, but instead they looked at it and kept going.

I felt terrible and left the table, but I couldn't find them. I asked Frank to help me look for them and the two of us searched everywhere, including the men's and ladies' rooms. No sign of them. We went back to playing cards. I felt terrible. About an hour later, I saw the couple walking across the lobby, heading for the elevators. I grabbed a pad of paper and a pen belonging to the dealer and ran over to them.

"Boy, am I glad to see you! I looked all over for you! Sorry about before. It was just a joke. Here."

I wrote my name and handed it to them. They each looked at it and then the man said, "What the hell is this?"

"It's my autograph."

"Who are you?"

It was a different couple. Not big TV fans either. I came back to the table where Frank was doubled up with laughter.

"Okay, Frank, you had your laugh. What do you say we play cards?"

"Anything you say, John Hancock!"

This happened about four years ago. You'd think Frank could stop laughing about it by now, but he hasn't.

You wouldn't believe some of the "things" I've been asked to autograph. Besides the *usual:* dollar bills, personal checks (I always sign on the "Pay To" line), phone bills, envelopes, greeting cards, body casts, various articles of clothing, neck braces, a Bible, wet cement, paper bags and various scraps of paper, dry and wet. I've been requested to put my name on some weird things:

—On a rolled "joint," so a father could give his six-month-old son a toke off it on his sixteenth birthday.

—On a beautiful, white, patent leather pocketbook, so a seventy-year-old lady could "show it off to all my card-playing friends."

—A hooker's ass in Las Vegas and I'm not going to tell you whose name was already on her other cheek when she flashed it in the hotel lobby.

—A request by some very loud woman in front of children to sign her "left teat," was answered by my saying, as I looked at the place to be signed, "You'd better settle for just my initials, lady."

—A young lady's thigh so she could make her boyfriend jealous. Denied. Who needs some madman coming after me? I signed her arm instead.

—The wall of a restaurant that had no other names on it. Why not?

The strangest request of all took place in lower Manhattan's Little Italy during the street Feast of San Gennaro, one of my favorite New York events. The best Italian cooking is on sale in one booth after another. Mulberry Street is alive with earthy excitement as only Italians can deliver. If I'm in New York during feast time, I always go!

One year when I went, my friend Wynn and I were inching our way through the crowd in the street. I had just bought a canelloni and was just about to take my first bite when I was recognized. Twice before over the years I had to have the police rescue me at the feast because of the loving fans who almost crushed a few booths and me. A crowd started gathering around asking for autographs. I gave Wynn my canelloni to hold. Two cops who saw the commotion moved in and were acting as buffers for me. New York cops are the best! I was signing all the pieces of paper being passed to me for about ten minutes. It was close to becoming out of hand but still okay. From the back of the crowd I heard this hoarse voice, right out of the movie *The Godfather.*

"Hey, Brenner, how about signing my leg?"

The crowd laughed and I answered, "Sure, just pass it up." I continued signing autographs, when, out of the corner of my eye, I saw an artificial leg, complete with a short white sock and a shoe on it, being passed hand-over-hand above the heads of the people. They handed it to me and I signed it and it was passed back over the crowd. I had this image of some guy on the outside of the crowd hopping on one leg waiting for his autograph. As the leg reached the outside of the circle the hoarse voice called out again.

"Thanks a lot, Dave!"

"You're welcome," I replied. "Now send up your dick!"

Sometimes I forget to censor my thoughts. Well, if you know Italian people, you know they all laughed warmly, including my one-legged *paisano.*

The only place I've learned to draw the line about signing autographs is when I'm eating in a restaurant. About two years ago, I just got tired of eating cold potatoes with cold gravy, so I nicely ask the people to either leave the paper and pen and I'll sign when I finish my food, or I ask them to return when they see I have finished. So far most people have understood and I'm enjoying my food a lot more.

I think most people are considerate, but there are some who really don't care where you are or what you're doing. They are going to get your autograph! One such person was a lady who approached me as I was getting a physical checkup at the Sunrise Hospital in Las Vegas.

I was lying on my back on an examining table, a dye being fed into my vein intravenously when the door crashed open and a woman ran up to me, waving a paper in my face.

"Give me your autograph."

"Lady, are you out of your mind?"

"I'll be glad to wait outside."

"You didn't hear me. I said, are you out of your mind?"

"Right outside the door."

She left, not understanding one word I said. I rang for the nurse. They managed to slip me out of another door in the room. As we crossed the far end of the hall, I looked up to see what looked like a scene out of an avant-garde foreign film—people on crutches were swinging along with paper in hand, there were people in wheelchairs with legs in traction and casts holding marking pens, bandaged heads, arms in casts, the walking wounded being led on by the woman who had burst in on me, screaming that I was somewhere in the hospital, acting as the Pied Piper of autograph seekers. I had to laugh. Before someone came crawling out of the operating room holding his new pacemaker, I decided to stop and sign the autographs. People are weird . . . and wonderful.

Now I'll tell you about my nightmare. I'm in a public men's room, sitting on the toilet, when the stall door flies open and a woman is standing over me.

"I saw you come in. Give me your autograph!"

"Lady, could you wait until I finish?"

"No. I've got a roast on a low flame. It'll burn."

"Okay, give me paper and a pen."

"You don't carry your own?"

"No. I don't collect autographs."

"Here, use this paper. Roll it out, double up the sheets. Here, use my lipstick, but don't break it."

"Okay, there."

"David Bren? What's this an *n* or a *u*?"

"It's *n*, double *n*, Brenner."

"David Brenner? You're David Brenner? I thought you were Garfunkel. Here, wipe."

"Hey, lady, the least you could've done was close the stall door!"

"Say, aren't you David Brenner? Could I have . . ."


## FANS I'LL NEVER FORGET—NEVER!

I GOT A CALL at the motel where I was staying during an engagement in Rochester, New York. A twelve-year-old girl with a congenital heart defect was a big fan of mine and wanted to meet me in person. I said I'd be glad to go over to her house, but the doctor told me that the girl insisted that she come to see me. I voiced my concern about her making the trip. The doctor said the accomplishment of the trip would be as good as any medicine he could ever recommend, and that they would build temporary ramps wherever needed for her wheelchair. I asked if the excitement might be too much. He said she was "very, very sick" and this was "very, very important" to her. I understood and agreed.

I've never been so nervous waiting for someone to come see me as I was waiting for that little girl. I saw the special van pull up and the back door open. On an automatic lift, the girl in the wheelchair was lowered to the pavement. They wheeled her up the ramp constructed on the first-floor stairs. There was a knock on the door. I opened it and looked at that precious little girl, dressed in her Sunday best, holding a little bouquet of flowers, hair neatly combed and fixed with a blue bow, a wide and happy smile on her face. God, she was wonderful!

I looked at my watch and said with fake sternness, "You're ten and a half minutes late!"

She laughed heartily. We talked, laughed a lot, and took pictures together until she tired. She looked so sad as they wheeled her to the door. I kissed her cheek and whispered in her ear. She left laughing. What I said was, "Next time you'd better be on time!" Yes, she laughed, even though she knew there could never be a next time. What a wonderful little girl.

He was handsome as only Italian boys of seventeen can be handsome. We were in my dressing room after my second and last show at the Westbury Music Fair on Long Island. He apologized for the thinning out of his hair, which had been very thick before the cobalt radiation treatments began. He had a maximum of six months to live. When he got the news, he asked for three things—to visit Europe, where he was going with his grandparents in a couple of days; to see me perform and meet me; and to see Cher perform and to meet her. Cher was opening the following night and we had worked together back in the Sonny & Cher days, so I wrote a letter of introduction so he could get backstage to see her. He thanked me and we talked some more. He told me that he hoped he hadn't depressed me. I told him he hadn't at all, even though actually I was feeling so badly inside. We spoke mostly about all the things any seventeen-year-old fan and I would talk about—what Johnny Carson was really like, how I got started, why I chose comedy, what I was like as a kid, what stars I had met, how I write jokes, what I do in my spare time, how he likes school, what sports he likes, how many girl friends he has, what he wants to see in Europe. We talked about almost everything, except what he wanted to be when he grew up. He apologized for taking so much of my time. I told him he didn't take any time at all. We shook hands. I didn't know what to say, so I just told him to have a great time in Europe and thanked him for stopping in to see me.

One night, after I came offstage in some town somewhere, I looked at the calendar on the mirror in my dressing room and said to my manager:

"Six months. That beautiful boy is dead."

I've thought about him a lot.


## MY FEATHERED FAMILY

IN 1978, FRANK PALUMBO, owner of America's oldest continuously operating nightclub, located in South Philadelphia, honored me by presenting two toucan birds to the Philadelphia Zoo, naming one David and the other Brenner. On June 23, 1982, the first toucan birth in captivity took place. Given the chance to name him I said he would be called Kingy, and, as I told the press—"I am very proud and hope they bring him up Jewish." I also promised to foot the bill when Kingy is sixteen to get him a nose job.


## COMING HOME

PART OF THE 1976 bicentennial celebration in Philadelphia were free summer weekend concerts held outside the Art Museum on the Benjamin Franklin Parkway. I was asked to perform one of the dates and agreed. I talked to a friend of mine, a fellow comedian, who was hot at the time, about the gig, since he had already played it. He told me it was great and that twenty-two thousand fans had come to see him, which was the record attendance for the event. I had hoped to outdraw him, not because I was "hotter" or a bigger attraction, but because it was my hometown. I hoped to top the record by, say, three thousand—twenty-five thousand people.

The day of the concert my road manager and I arrived at the Philadelphia International Airport and were picked up by a limo. As we headed toward our hotel in Center City I noticed the streets were kind of desolate.

"What's going on today, driver? No one's around."

"Labor Day weekend."

God, I hadn't looked at the calendar when we accepted the date! Labor Day weekend? No one stays in Philly! Everyone is down the shore, Atlantic City, Wildwood, Ocean City, Cape May. It's the end of the summer. The town is dead! What a mistake! Now I began hoping that I wouldn't be too embarrassed. Forget the attendance record. Just give me a decent number, say twenty thousand, eighteen thousand. Fifteen thousand would be fine, too. What a mistake!

We checked into the hotel. I stood looking out the window of my room. In a half hour I counted seven people walking by on the street below and I think I counted one man twice. Only seven persons in the main section of a major city in a half hour? I figured I was ruined!

The limo arrived to take us to the concert. We drove up the parkway, coming in the back way to avoid the crowd (what crowd?). From the limo, they rushed me into an RV van used as a dressing room. The chief of police security introduced himself to me. I asked the dangerous question.

"How many are out there?"

"Well, we stopped counting an hour ago and a lot have come in since then. Our last estimate was forty-six."

"Forty-six?" I cried out. "Forty-six people?"

The chief laughed.

"Forty-six thousand people! You set the record! Congratulations, Dave."

They were there all right, all of them, as far as the eye could see in all directions. They covered the steps leading up to the museum and right on back to the entrance doors, down the grass sidings alongside the museum to the river (many out of sight of the stage), across the parkway to the apartment houses one block away and even as far behind the stage as one city block—forty-six thousand screaming, applauding fans!

After doing an act for an hour and a half, I ended my show differently than I usually do—not with a big laugh.

"As I have been performing up here a thought flashed through my mind a few times. When I was a kid I used to swim in the water of the fountain that is under this stage. We'd take off our clothes and jump in, in our underwear, and splash around until the cops chased us. Then about fifteen minutes later, they'd let us swim around again before chasing us again. Like poor kids still do, I guess. This is a wonderful way to come back home. You've given me the most memorable day of my career. Thank you, Philadelphia. I love you!"

I always will!

## A MAN'S CASTLE

EVER SINCE I GOT the New York City bug as a little kid, I used to dream and talk about someday owning a town house in the heart of Manhattan. I would help design and decorate every room of it. I would fix every inch of it to my liking, not for anyone else to admire, but for me to enjoy. I used to stand on the street corner and tell my friends all about my dream town house and they would laugh, as I described it, because no one we knew would ever be able to afford something like that. It was bizarre to even think about it. But my street corner pals did like to hear about it and would just make one comment—"fuckin' Brenner." In other words, me and my crazy ideas.

I started checking into town houses as soon as I moved to Manhattan, even though I couldn't even afford the front doorknob. I went on open house walking tours and had realtors show me town houses. I also read architectural books and magazines. It was informative and fun.

When my comedy career happened, I started to seriously look at town houses. One day I got a call about a co-op apartment at One East End Avenue, overlooking the East River, with east, south and west views. I told the realtor that I wasn't interested in apartments, but she told me it was a duplex and an absolutely once-in-a-lifetime buy. Something unique. I went to see it. She was right. Seven bedrooms, seven baths, a huge country-style kitchen, a formal dining room, living room with bay windows, a winding staircase going up to the second floor backed by a two-story glass window overlooking the river, marble fireplaces galore, a private elevator inside the apartment as well as a private elevator from the lobby up to the apartment. Absolutely sensational! A town house within an apartment building—my childhood dream come true. The price was very reasonable, too.

I had been involved in the New York real estate market long enough to know some of the pitfalls, including the hidden ones, so I asked the big question.

"Is this building restricted against Jews or entertainers?"

"No."

"Well, make one hundred percent certain. If it's not, call me and I'll take the apartment."

The One East End cooperative board chairman was contacted, told about my interest in the apartment and my concern about restrictions. He guaranteed that no such policy existed in that building. My business manager sent in a check for the deposit. I got letters of recommendation from three of this nation's leading White Anglo-Saxon Protestants and made an appointment to appear before the building's co-op board, at which time they'd ask certain questions, financial and personal, to determine whether to allow me into their building. Not to my liking, but I wanted the apartment and had nothing to hide or worry about. I hadn't even had a parking ticket in my life, and I don't entertain more than two or three people at a time. Even those are rare occasions. I don't throw parties, nor do I go to them. I am a quiet, private person in my home. I had no consternation about the interview, and was getting very excited at the prospect of buying the apartment.

The Co-op Board changed the date of the meeting, making it necessary for me to cancel an appearance on the "Tonight Show," something I had never done, not even when burning up with a high fever. In addition, in order to make the new meeting date and time, I had to fly all night via Dallas. But it was going to be worth it!

When I got to my apartment, I called my answering service for messages. There was one to call my realtor right away. I called.

"What's up?"

"I don't know how to tell you this, David."

"Just tell me, plain and simple."

"The chairman of the One East End Avenue Co-op Board

called this morning and said that in no way would they ever allow an entertainer to move into their building. I'm sorry."

I was stunned. I couldn't believe it.

"Wait a minute. They knew I was an entertainer from the beginning, didn't they? I mean, you did do what I asked you to. You did ask about the restrictions."

"Yes, I did and was reassured by the very man who called this morning that there weren't any."

"Then why did he cancel the interview and why did he wait until the last minute to do it? He knew I had to cancel a show and fly all night to get here."

"I don't know."

"Something's not right here. Did you tell him I'm not crazy, that I don't entertain, that I'm a loner?"

"Yes. David, your letters of recommendation were as fine as any letters could be."

"Yeah, and my check was as good, too. Something stinks here. Either someone poisoned my waterhole, and I would have no idea who and for what reason, or there's more to this than my being an entertainer. I want you to find out how many Jews are living in that building. I'm not going to take this like a scared rabbit! I'm either going to beat this or make them damn sorry they ever did this to me!"

"David, you can't fight City Hall!"

"You're wrong—you can't *beat* City Hall, but you sure as hell can *fight* it and I'm going to fight as hard as I can! I didn't take that kind of prejudice when I was a kid and I'm sure as hell not going to take it now! Get that information for me as soon as you can. I've got some thinking to do."

There was only one Jewish person living in the building, as far as we could tell—a woman who was married to a non-Jew. Most of the time, in buildings or organizations that are restricted, they will have a token minority group member so no one can bring charges of discrimination against them. It's so smart, you'd think that a Jew had thought of it first.

The law also only protects against housing discrimination in respect to race, religion, creed and sex. It does not protect anyone from discrimination regarding occupation, age, financial standing, or whether or not one is a parent.

I didn't have a legal leg to stand on, but I did have two legs that were strong enough to climb their way out of a slum. I also had something else going for me—access to mass media.

First I sent a letter to every tenant living in One East End Avenue, including doormen, maintenance personnel, the mailman and superintendent, telling what happened and my intention of battling the decision. I also sent copies of my letter to every network news department, local TV and radio news departments, the mayor, the governor of New York, all state representatives, every magazine publisher, the UPI and Associated Press, every major newspaper, the President of the United States and to members of my immediate family, so they could see that I had learned well what they had taught me. Actually, I had been taught not only in word but in deed.

When I was a little boy, living on Sansom Street in West Philadelphia, only one block from where the black ghetto began, our neighbor and family friend, Mrs. Kramer, came to our house. She invited my father and mother to come to a meeting being held one night later in the week to discuss what could be done to keep out the black family that was moving in on our street, right next door to us, as a matter of fact. She mentioned the possibility of everyone chipping in to buy back the house. My father listened patiently to Mrs. Kramer, puffing on his cigar and nodding his head in understanding of what she was saying. When she finished, he took the cigar out of his mouth, looked at me, then at my mother, then at Mrs. Kramer.

"Mrs. Kramer, do you remember the story you told us about what happened when you moved into your house down the street and were upstairs lying in bed pregnant with your son, David?"

"You mean about them shooting bullets through my bedroom window?"

"Why did they shoot rifle bullets through your window?"

"I told you—because we were Jewish. Who could forget?"

"I couldn't, Mrs. Kramer, but it is obvious that *you* have. The last person who should be prejudiced in this whole world, Mrs. Kramer, is a Jew. Who knows and feels the horror of prejudice more than we? Six and a half million of us were slaughtered because of it only a few years ago, and now you want to run from another people, not because of their religious beliefs but because their skin is a different color? Mrs. Kramer, I want you to go to that meeting Wednesday night and I want you to tell everyone there that Lou Brenner will not be there and from now on no one who is at that meeting is my friend. No one who goes there is allowed to ever talk to me or to anyone in my family ever again! This includes you, Mrs. Kramer! Now, please leave my house!"

They held the meeting and my father never talked to our old friends and neighbors again. None of us did. The black family moved in next door to us, then another family, then another, until we and old Mrs. Morrisson were the only white people left on the block and, soon after that, in the entire neighborhood. We lived in that house another ten years until it was too much housework for my mother and my parents moved to a small apartment. But I stayed in the neighborhood four more years. We never had a problem with any of our new neighbors either. Maybe it was because the people living there figured that there would be only two reasons for us to be living with them—either we weren't prejudiced or we were crazy. Actually, we were both!

Now back to One East End Avenue. I did all I could to call attention to the unfair treatment I was receiving. I went on TV, standing in front of the building and telling how, according to the law, they could keep me from moving in because I was an entertainer, which meant that such other persons as President and Mrs. Reagan, Kate Smith—Miss Apple Pie and Stars and Stripes herself—couldn't move in, but, because the law states that housing discrimination is not allowed in the areas of race, religion, creed and sex—a black, Buddhist, Haitian transvestite could move in—unless, of course, he or she earned his or her living by playing the flute or juggling.

I talked about it on many other TV shows, had hundreds of newspaper articles and interviews done about it, wrote a column in New York magazine, but nothing changed as far as my being able to move in. Hopefully, something changed in the minds of some people.

I sent a notice to all the tenants that I *wouldn't* move into their building and that I didn't want any of them to ever watch me on TV because they were not deserving of receiving laughter from me.

I was not allowed to sleep at One East End Avenue but I was able to sleep at night and face myself in the morning. I won!

Where do I live now? Well, I am living in my dream town house in Manhattan, and anyone—regardless of race, creed, religion, sex and occupation—is allowed in, with one exception—anyone who resides at One East End Avenue!

Oh, a little postscript. When my house was completed, every

inch of which I helped to plan and design, along with the creative minds of Edigal Associates of New York City, I moved in and invited as my houseguests Beb, Morty the Bird and Stan the Dancer. I gave them a Cook's Tour of the house, and as we stood on the roof, having drinks, looking out at the buildings of Manhattan, Stan the Dancer laughed softly and said to Beb and the Bird—"Fuckin' Brenner." Today, among my few really prized possessions in my town house are a bench from Philadelphia's Fairmount Park and a chewing gum machine from my old el stop at Sixtieth and Market Streets—guess who got them for me and guess how they got them.

# THE MOUNTAIN

NO LIFE AND NO life-style is without problems. Don't get me wrong. I'd much rather have the problems I have in my life now than the ones I had when I was poor. When I was poor, I suffered. Now, I only hurt.

A couple of years ago, I was in various stages of trying to rectify my professional and personal problems. The pressure was getting to me, so I decided to just "get away from it all" for a couple weeks. Away from work, decisions—everything, including women. Now, that's really pushing "getting away." I called my dear childhood friend Beb, inviting him to go with me to St. Maarten Island in the Dutch West Indies. I had spent a couple days there on a sailing trip a few years back and remembered it as a jewel in the sea.

I rented a beach house at La Samana, supposedly the finest hotel in the Caribbean. It was perfect. Two bedrooms with baths, a kitchen, a good-sized living room and, best of all, double doors that opened out right onto the beach. In the morning I'd brush my teeth, drink a glass of fresh orange juice, run across the beach and dive into the aqua-colored Caribbean. The cobwebs were clearing out of my head, thanks to the company of my great pal and to that special island.

I don't want to go into a whole long description of the island and what's so great about it, sounding like a tourist bureau, so I'll just tell you that of all the islands I've either stayed on or sailed to, and that extends from as far north as Puerto Rico and as far south as Trinidad, the half-French and half-Dutch island of St. Maarten is my favorite. No contest! I've been there a total of about twenty weeks since my first time and my good feelings only get better with each trip. Now, back to the vacation with Beb.

Realizing how therapeutic the island was for me, I commented to Beb and some people who lived on the island with whom we were having drinks, how maybe someday I'd like to have a get-away-from-it-all house there. Someone mentioned hearing about a house for sale, and that it could be arranged for me to see it, if I were interested. The next day we went to see it. It was a nice house, but not really my style. However, it was located in one of the most scenic parts of the island.

As we were leaving the homeowner said that he either wanted to sell his house and build on a piece of land he owned close by, or sell the land and keep the house. He pointed out his land—a mountain, not the Rockies, but a mountain! I asked if we could see it from the land he had leveled off for building the house. He said fine, and his realtor friend led us up the mountain path.

Standing on the homesite, you can see a couple of the neighboring islands, the rooftops of a handful of houses in the valley below, the mile-long, white sand beach, the blue, clear, aqua green water. I could also see the patio I would be standing on, extending out over the mountain directly outside of the living room of the two-story, white Moroccan-style house, and the swimming pool next to the large rock. Yes, you can see into the future. I did. Without turning to look at the real estate agent, who was standing a few feet behind me, I said, "Tell the gentleman to keep his house—he just sold his land."

Beb, who had stood next to me on the front porch of all my decrepit row houses, who had stood by my side all those years on the street corner, who was now standing next to me in Paradise, his eyes transfixed by the view, said in a soft voice, only for my ears, "You just bought a whole fuckin' mountain, Brenner!" Yes, I did, but not for only me. Someday I'm going to build the house on top of it and give copies of the front door keys to the special people in my life so they can share my luck.

I called the property "Lone Eagle Rock" until the day my mother and father returned from a cruise I had sent them on. I had arranged for someone to meet them at the dock in St. Maarten and drive them to see my land. When they called me to tell me about their trip, the first thing my father said to me was,

"Well, we saw Kingy's Mountain!" And that'll be its name—
"Kingy's Mountain." As we say in my family, whenever anything
luxuriously special happens, "It's a long way from Sixtieth
Street!" Yes, it is—thank God!

*"I'm shooting for the highest star up there, mom, because, if I miss, the
worse that'll happen is I'll fall onto the moon, but if I aim only for the
moon and miss, I'm liable to land right back here in the neighborhood."*

David Brenner
Age thirteen

# EPILOGUE

WHILE I WAS IN my twenties, I was told the following story. There was a middle-aged couple who had two children, one fully grown and the other nearly grown. Times were bad. The couple was very poor. They lived day to day, hand to mouth. The woman accidently became pregnant. She loved children, but how could she have one now? Everything about it was wrong. She and her husband were unable to make a decision about what to do.

The woman's best girl friend suggested that she should have the baby because when the other children reached adulthood and moved out of the house, the baby would keep the couple young.

After much deliberation, hours of soul-searching, frank and open discussions, advice from those closest to them, the couple decided not to have the child. The woman did everything she could to lose the embryo but nothing worked. Finally she went to her doctor and told him what she had been doing. He examined her.

"Medically this should not be alive, but it lives! It has the strongest life drive I've ever seen! It's not for me to tell you what to do, but, whatever this is, perhaps it has an important purpose in life! Maybe you should let it live!"

The woman did. Seven months later, I was born. When my mother told me this story I felt the pain of her decision and felt an even stronger life drive than ever. I just knew I was going to someday fulfill the doctor's prophesy. As the whole family says when they look at me now—"some mistake!"

Years and years later, another woman had to make a similar decision. She was single and pregnant. She, too, decided to have the child and on February 17, 1982, at 11:58 A.M. in Lenox Hill

297

Hospital in Manhattan, a little boy was born. His name is Cole Jay Brenner—my son.

He was conceived with love and is loved today by his mother and father. He always will be. I hope he loves and respects us in return, as much as I love and respect my parents. I also hope that his life will be as exciting and rewarding as mine has been. And this book, these stories of my life—my experiences, my pain, my laughter, my beliefs, my feelings—this is the legacy I leave him. To Cole Jay Brenner, from David Norris Brenner. From one "accident" to another—with a lot of love.

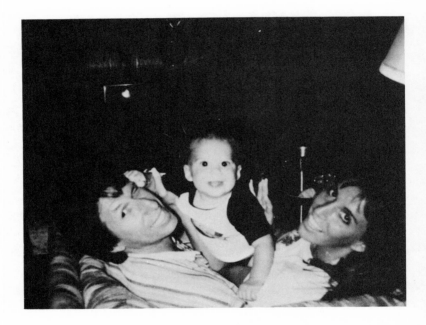